ARKANSAS HIKING TRAILS

A GUIDE TO 78 SELECTED TRAILS IN "THE NATURAL STATE"

BY

TIM ERNST

The photograph on the cover is of Kings River Falls,
an Arkansas Natural Area.
It was taken on a spring afternoon by the author.
The hiker is Lora Linn.
See page 62 for trail description.

TIM ERNST PUBLISHING
Jasper, Arkansas
Order direct from Tim: **www.TimErnst.com**

Made in the USA

Other publications by Tim Ernst:
Arkansas Waterfalls guidebook
Arkansas Nature Lover's guidebook
Ozark Highlands Trail guidebook
Buffalo River Hiking Trails guidebook
Arkansas Dayhikes For Kids guidebook
Ouachita Trail guidebook
Arkansas Greatest Hits picture book (2020)
Arkansas Splendor picture book (2019)
Arkansas Beauty picture book (2017)
Arkansas In My Own Backyard picture book (2016)
A Rare Quality Of Light picture book (2015)
Arkansas Nightscapes picture book (2014)
Buffalo River Beauty picture book (2013)
Arkansas Portfolio I, II, & III picture books (1994, 2004, 2011)
Arkansas Autumn picture book (2010)
Arkansas Wildlife picture book (2009)
Arkansas Landscape I & II picture books (2008, 2012)
Arkansas Waterfalls picture book (2007)
Buffalo River Dreams picture book (2006)
Arkansas Wilderness picture book (2002)
Arkansas Spring picture book (2000)
Buffalo River Wilderness picture book (1998)
Wilderness Reflections picture book (1996)
The Search For Haley
The Cloudland Journal ~ Book One

... I know a place, where no one ever goes.
There's peace and quiet, beauty and repose.
It's hidden in a valley, beside a mountain stream.
And lying there beside the stream, I find that I can dream.
Only of things, of beauty to the eye.
Snow–capped mountains, towering in the sky...

This book is dedicated to the pursuit of those places described in the above lyrics from a song I learned in kindergarten. I have sought out such places ever since, and discovered a multitude of them in my home state of Arkansas (no snow–capped mountains yet though!). You will find many of them described within the pages of this book. Take care of these special places as you visit, to insure that young people for many generations to come will have such natural treasures to seek out.

TABLE OF CONTENTS

FOREWORD..6
INTRODUCTION...8
   Backpacking...10
   Bugs...15
   Dayhikes...9
   Equipment..18
   Fires...12
   Food...21
   Glossary of Terms...22
   Hiking Pace..13
   Hunting and Fishing..14
   Lost in the Woods...22
   Low Impact Use...11
   Maps and Mileages...10
   Seasons...15
   Thank Yous..23
   Water...12
   Weather, a Month–by–Month Guide.............................16
   Weather Forecasting...16
   Wildlife, including Snakes and Bears..............................13

TRAIL MAPS AND DESCRIPTIONS

(●/allowed, */allowed on part of trail only)

Trail	Page	Camping	Bicycles	Dogs	Horses
Alum Cove Loop—1.1 miles	63			●	
Artist Point Trail—(closed due to vandalism)	47			●	
Athens–Big Fork Trail—9.1 miles one way	169	●		●	
Bear Creek Loop—1.0 mile	112			●	
Bell Slough Wildlife Loop—2.3 miles	133			●	
Big Creek Loop—2.6 miles	106			●	
Black Fork Mountain Trail—11.6 miles round trip	137	●		●	
Bona Dea System Loops—3.5 miles outside loop	158			●	
Bridge Rock Loop—.6 mile	129			●	
Brushy Creek Loop—6.9 miles	141	●		●	
Buckeye Mountain Trail—9.1 miles round trip	176	●		●	
Buffalo River Trail—S. Boxley to Ponca—11.0 miles one way	71	●			
Buffalo River Trail-Ponca to Pruitt—25.5 miles one way	73	●			
Buffalo River Trail-Woolum to Hwy. 65—15.0 miles one way	83	●			
Burns Park Scout Loop—8.3 miles	115			●	
Butterfield Loop—14.7 miles	41	●	*	●	*
Caddo Bend Loop—3.9 miles	153			●	
Caney Creek Trail—9.6 miles one way	173	●		●	●
Cecil Cove Loop—7.4 miles	66	●			●
Cedar Falls Trail—2.0 miles round trip	119			●	
Charlton Trail—4.2 miles one way	175	●	●	●	
Cove Lake Loop—3.5 miles	125		●	●	
Crack In Rock Loop—1.5 miles	45			●	
Crystal Mountain Scenic Area Loop—.5 mile	160			●	
Crystal Recreation Area Loop—.7 mile	161			●	
Dogwood Nature Trail—3.0 miles round trip	95			●	
Eagle Rock Loop—26.8 miles	163	●		●	*
Earthquake Ridge Loop—2.1 miles	135	●	●	●	
Friendship Interpretive Loop—.9 mile	159			●	
Glory Hole—1.9 miles round trip	60	●		●	
Hawksbill Crag Trail—3.0 miles round trip	59			●	

Trail	Page	Camping	Bicycles	Dogs	Horses
Hemmed–In Hollow Trail—5.0 miles round trip	76	*			
Hideout Hollow Trail—2.0 miles round trip	80	•			
Hole In The Ground Mountain Trail—7.3 miles round trip	130	•		•	
Hunts Loop—4.3 miles	146	•	*	•	
Indian Rockhouse Loop—3.0 miles	89				
Kings River Falls Trail—1.7 miles round trip	62				•
Kings River Overlook Trail—1.0 mile round trip	27				•
Koen Interpretive Loop—.5 mile	69				•
Lake Catherine Loop—6.3 miles	181				•
Lake Norfork Trail—5.2 miles one way	99				•
Lake Leatherwood/Beacham Loop—3.7 miles	29			•	•
Lake Sylvia Loop—4.1 miles	149				•
Lake Wedington Trail—15.4 miles round trip	25	•		•	•
Little Blakely Loops—18.6 miles total	155	•		•	•
Little Missouri Trail—15.7 miles one way	165	•			•
Lost Bridge Loop—5.0 miles	33	•			•
Lost Valley Trail—2.3 miles round trip	79				
Lovers' Leap Loop—1.1 miles	134				•
Mill Creek Loop—2.2 miles round trip	64				
Mt. Magazine Trail—14.2 miles one way	127	•	*		•
Mt. Nebo System Loops—1.0, 3.4, and 4.0 mile loops	123	•	*		•
Pea Ridge Loop—8.7 miles	30				•
Pedestal Rocks/King's Bluff Loops—1.9 and 2.6 mile loops	56				•
Pigeon Roost Loops—4.2 and 8.4 mile loops	39	•			•
Pinnacle Mountain Summit Loop—2.6 miles	116				•
Redding/Spy Rock Loop—8.8 miles	54	•			•
Rim Rock Loop—1.0 mile	28				•
Robinson Point Trail—3.3 miles round trip	96				•
Round Top Mountain Loop—3.6 miles	49				•
Rush Mountain Loop—3.6 miles	93				
Serendipity Interpretive Loop—1.0 mile	139				•
Seven Hollows Loop—4.2 miles	120				•
Shaddox Hollow Loop—1.5 miles	36				•
Shores Lake/White Rock Loop—13.4 miles	51	•			•
Sugar Loaf Mountain Loop—2.0 miles	105				•
Sunset Loop—8.0 miles	151				
Sylamore Creek Trail—13.7 miles one way	101	•			•
Tall Peak Trail—6.4 miles round trip	178	•			•
Tanyard Creek Loop —1.9 miles	44				•
Tyler Bend Trails System—.9 to 4.0 miles	86				
Village Creek Loop—6.3 miles	110				•
War Eagle Trail—2.0 miles round trip	35				•
Waterfowl Way Trail—1.5 miles	183				•
White Cliffs Loop—1.5 miles	171				•
White Oak Lake Loop—3.0 miles	184				•
White Rock Rim Loop—2.1 miles	52	•	*		•
Womble Trail—39.5 miles one way	143	•	*		•
Woolly Hollow Loop—3.5 miles	108				•

AGENCY LIST ... 186
TRAILHEAD GPS COORDINATES ... 188
GUIDEBOOKS ... 190
ABOUT THE AUTHOR ... 191
LEGEND / LOCATOR MAP ... 192

FOREWORD

Greetings:

During our travels throughout the United States, Hillary and I have seen many wonderful places. However, the scenic countryside of Arkansas is as beautiful as any place in this nation.

Arkansas' parks, forests, streams, and trails offer spectacular beauty and solitude for families wanting to take an afternoon walk in the woods, or for those who are looking for an extended outdoor challenge. Arkansas Hiking Trails is another outstanding example of the unique skills with which Tim Ernst illustrates the experience of Arkansas' trails, and many of the state's best kept secrets. Tim has a gift of painting a picture with words. His guides not only describe each trail, they relate that experience. Through his volunteer efforts, Tim has built more miles of trail than most people have walked.

I invite you to pick one of the many trails described in this guide, and explore Arkansas on your own.

Sincerely,

Bill Clinton of Arkansas
Attorney General, Governor, President

INTRODUCTION

Welcome to this edition of **ARKANSAS HIKING TRAILS!** It is basically the same as previous printings, with several new trails added, and others updated. And if you bought this book, *thanks* for donating to the construction and maintenance of our trail systems—I contribute some of my time to trail work for each guidebook purchased. The book that you have in your hands is the best resource available for hiking trails in Arkansas. With it you will find wonderful places and things to do all over the state.

The first thing that you need to do is to read all of this introduction. Once you've waded through it, you'll be ready to pick your favorite trail and head to the woods. The book is designed to be easy to navigate through. There is a quick reference list on the back cover that has all of the hikes described in this book—it shows their length, the page number where you can find the description and map, a number that is keyed to a location map just inside the back cover, and a check–off square so that you can keep track of how many trails you've hiked (transfer from first edition).

This book was written *by* a hiker, *for* hikers, in a first–person format. I am not a writer. I'm a hiker. The descriptions in this book were edited down from tapes that I made while hiking the trails. My goal was to put something in your hands that was as close as I could get to a real person standing there giving you information. In the process, the "flavor" of my speech was retained—sorry about that. I spend the majority of my time *in* the woods, not learning correct grammar.

Although I try to point out as many special scenic spots (SSS's) as I can, I don't pretend to tell you about every wonderful place to visit. In fact, I'm sure that there are ten times more SSS's along the way than the ones I tell you about. You'll just have to discover all the rest on your own. Please excuse my liberal use of superlatives to describe the landscape—you'd use that many too if you'd hiked all of these trails!

The trails are not "rated" as to difficulty. The main reason is that what may be an easy trail for one of you, could be a real challenge to another. And a difficult trail for one may be a piece of cake for everyone else. Many of the trails are so well used that they are beat–down, wide paths that are easy to follow. Others are blazed with paint or marked in other ways so that you'll find your way. There are several areas here and there that may be difficult to follow, especially during the summertime, when everything gets so grown up. Try to use some common sense, and look for the *trail tread* or route through the woods, not necessarily for blazes. Also look for clues like cut branches, rocks lined up in a row, and other signs of man that show the way. If you follow along with my description, and stay alert, you shouldn't have any problems.

There is a map and narrative description included for each trail. I don't take my information from what others have said or written, or guess about such things as mileage. I hiked every trail in this book within the last couple of years, pushing a measuring wheel and carrying a tape recorder all the while. The information presented here is as accurate as I know how to produce. Of course, it was impossible for me to include everything about every trail. At the end of each descriptive section there is an "Agency List #"—this is where you can write/call to get further information—the list is on page 186. Often the agencies have a separate brochure or booklet about the trail that is available, and they are always happy to answer your questions and help out if needed.

The Ozark Highlands Trail is no longer in this guide–just too much info to include here. There is a separate 136-page guidebook that details the Ozark

Highlands Trail. There are also books on the Ouachita Trail and a guide to 30 or more trails in the Buffalo National River area. See page 190 for ordering information.

To find a trail in this book, if you know the name, simply look it up in the table of contents, or on the quick reference page on the back cover. Some of the trails may not be listed where you think they are—if not, try looking under the name of the *Park* instead. Like for instance, the Rim Trail at Mt. Nebo State Park is listed under "Mt. Nebo System" instead of "Rim Trail." But most of the trails are listed by their own names. If you are just looking for a trail in a certain area, then refer to the locator map on the last page—all of the hikes are listed by number there—find the one(s) in that area and look up that number from the list on the back cover.

The trail descriptions are generally grouped throughout this book in geographical order as much as possible. If you are reading about a trail in a certain area, check the other trails next to it in the text, and you may discover another hike to do on the same trip. Because of the way the maps and pages laid out, I did have to scatter some of them around, though. Before you hike one of the trails, be sure to read the entire description of it, just in case you need to know something that I don't tell ya 'till the end!

We have nearly 3 million acres of National Forest land in Arkansas, over 150,000 acres of designated Wilderness (13 areas), 52 "Natural Areas" managed by the Arkansas Natural Heritage Commission, 48 State Parks, five areas managed by the National Park Service, and scores of lake areas managed by the Corps of Engineers.

Not all trails on these lands are contained in this guidebook—we've got over 240 trails that are considered "hiking" trails—most of them short. The 78 hikes described here include all of the longer trails, as well as a good sampling of the other trails from around the state. There are actually more than 78 trails in this book—96 or 97 I think. Many of the "hikes" are actually more than one trail combined. For instance, the Lake Catherine Loop. It contains three different trails. I just combined them to form a longer hike. In many cases I did this so that you could continue on and make a loop back to the beginning. There are eight trails included in this edition for the first time, plus several others that have either new trail segments described or expanded text.

There is a great deal of information in this introduction that deals with other stuff, like the weather, bugs, camping, water, low impact use, etc., that I hoped you would find useful. Plus a special section on equipment. Of course all the reading in the world won't help if you don't get out and kick up a little dust, so I hope that you are able to use this book and do some hiking!!!

DAYHIKES

Every trail in this book is great for dayhiking. Many of them are short interpretive nature trails that require only an hour or two to hike. Others are longer loops, requiring most of the day. But even the lengthy trails make good dayhikes—simply choose an access point that interests you, hike in one direction or the other, and turn around and hike back. Lots of folks tell me that they only want to hike loops, 'cause they don't want to "see the same stuff again" on the way back. Trust me, it will feel like an *entirely different* trail on the way back from a "one way" hike—you will be looking at everything from a different angle, and will see a lot of new things. The sunshine coming from the other side of everything makes the forest a whole new place. So don't hesitate to hike any trail as long as you want in one direction, then turn around and hike back. The key is to only go in one direction for no more than *half* of your total time—leave enough time to get back to your vehicle!

BACKPACKING

Many of our trails are long enough that you can spend two or more days on them. In fact it takes two weeks or longer to hike the Ouachita or Ozark Highlands trails. Camping is allowed on most of the longer trails, but not on most of the shorter ones. I've tried to indicate this in the descriptions. Generally speaking, trails located on the National Forests and in Buffalo National River are open to camping along the trail route. Camping is not permitted on most state park or Corps of Engineers trails, although there are several notable exceptions (like the Butterfield, Pigeon Roost and Lost Bridge trails). If you are uncertain about it, be sure to check with the listed agency before camping. There are usually campgrounds at or near the trailheads on most of the trails. Many of these trails were developed to accommodate campground users.

Permits are usually not required for camping, except on the Butterfield Trail at Devil's Den State Park, and the Pigeon Roost Trail at Beaver Lake State Park, which *do* require a reservation for one of the campsites. Most state parks may also charge an entrance/parking fee—check at office for current information about fees and permits. And the only regulations that apply out on the trail are just common sense things—no new fire rings, put out your fire, *Pack It In—Pack It Out,* get at least 200 feet away from trails and water sources, be courteous to fellow hikers, hunters and other trail users, and leave the place at least as nice as you found it (a good thing to do everywhere in life!).

If you are looking for a new trail to backpack, run down the list on the back cover and look for the longer trails—you may discover that perfect trail that you never even knew existed! We are getting more and more longer trails every year, and they seem to be being built through some pretty nice areas.

MAPS AND MILEAGES

Most of the maps in this book were created on computers by master map maker Ken Eastin (I drew a couple). Some of them were drawn from existing maps, others were drawn from scratch. We feel that the information on them is pretty accurate—let me know anytime that you find out otherwise. There are no contours on the maps—for many folks that just clutters things up. If you feel the need to have a quad map with you, the name of each quad is listed in the descriptions section for the trail. They are available at most outdoor stores, or direct from the Arkansas Geological Commission—see page 189. Very few of the trails are shown on the USGS quads, though.

Many of the trails have separate booklets or brochures that the Agency puts out—check with them for availability (an address list of all the Agencies, keyed to the number at the end of each trail description, is on page 186). There are also a couple of other outlets that carry a variety of maps and guidebooks—Ozark Society Books and the Ozark Interpretive Association—see page 189.

And of course I have a number of other trail guides available that I wrote—see page 190 for complete information about them and how to place an order. I will continue to update my books as time goes on, and write new ones as needed. If you have any suggestions or comments, positive or especially negative, please contact me—my address is on page 2. Several of your suggestions have been utilized in this edition.

Most of the mileages that I quote in this book are my own—generated by a measuring wheel that I pushed in front of me. It has proven to be the most accurate device that I know of. I point out a lot of specific spots along the trail, and try to tie them to mileage. Several of the longer trails have mile markers put up every mile—this is a great help. I must tell you about one of these, though. It seems that something was wrong with their wheel when they laid out these markers, 'cause every one of them is about 1/10 of a mile short—you'll love hiking this trail, 'cause you'll really feel like you are getting somewhere! I have two different methods to double check my wheel as I hike, so I'm pretty confident of my mileages. By the way, when there are mileage markers put up on a trail, I will usually default to them in the descriptions, even if they are wrong (like the above example), so as not to confuse the issue.

LOW IMPACT USE

As more and more of us use our trails, we need to be especially careful that we don't impact the special areas that we visit. It's easy to destroy a fragile spot, but it's just as easy to tread lightly and keep from messing up the things that we came out to see in the first place. All it takes is a little common sense. If we all do our part, this "Natural State" of ours will stay that way so that generations to follow will be able to enjoy the raw scenic beauty that we do.

Stay on the trail. Our trails were designed to carry you from one point to another in the most efficient (and/or scenic) way. When folks cut switchbacks, erosion begins, and soon the trail is messed up and there is an ugly scar. It is not rude to ask someone that you see doing this to kindly get back on the trail.

Hike in small groups. It's fun to go out with a large gang, but that doesn't always work too well in the backcountry—it destroys the character and solitude of the place. Not to mention increasing the possibility of damage to the trail and surrounding areas. We always limit our group size to 10 or less when we're going to be camping. Fewer is generally better. Besides, you'll have more campsite selection if you only have one or two tents to set up! Have your parties at home—come to the woods to enjoy nature, not Billboard's top ten. Speaking of noise, be considerate of others—they just might be out on the trail to get away from all the hustle and bustle of city life. Enjoy the peaceful solitude, and let others do the same.

Camp in established sites when possible. Overnight stays have more impact on the land than probably anything else we do while hiking. If everyone camped in a new location every night, the damage would be much more wide spread. By concentrating this damage to several sites, the area will stay more primitive. If you must set up in a new spot, choose a site at least 200 *feet away from the trail* and any water source, and preferably out of sight (and please, *please* don't build a new fire ring). I hate to hike down a nice trail and see tents scattered along the way. Don't you?

Protect our water. Clean water adds so much to the outdoor experience, not to mention our quality of life in general. Here is a simple guideline to remember when in the backcountry—don't put *anything* into the water. Period! I know, I know, you use "biodegradable soap." What if the guy just upstream is using it too, and takes a bath in the creek that you're getting your kool aid water out of? You'll have suds in your punch! Oh yea, it will be biodegradable punch, but suds just the same. Yuk! Think about downstream—we all live there. Use biodegradable soap if you have to, but use it *away* from the stream. Or better yet, don't use soap of any kind.

Keep bathroom duties out of sight. This seems rather obvious, but not everyone seems to understand. You need to get completely *out of sight* of the trail and any water supply to do your business. Dig a small hole, fill it in and cover it up when you're done. Why do people still leave their mess next to the trail?

Cook with a stove. We haven't reached a firewood shortage yet here in Arkansas, but if we all built big fires every day we would have. Do all of your cooking with one of the lightweight stoves available—they're quicker and a whole lot cleaner anyway. Campfires are OK, but keep them small, *don't* build a fire ring, and only use dead branches that are on the ground and that you can break with you hands—if you have to saw it, it's too darn big! (The reason for this is that large wood seldom ever burns up completely, and what you have left over is an ugly black stick.)

Leave No Trace. This should be your goal on any trip on a trail—when you leave there should be no sign of your ever having been there. It really seems silly to even mention this, but because there are still a few stupid people in the woods, I will. *Pack It In, Pack It Out*. Don't litter! Don't carve up trees. Don't cut or destroy *any* living thing. Leave it as you found it. In fact, leave it cleaner than you found it—carry a trash bag for not only your own stuff, but for other litter that you see along the way, too.

FIRES

Open fires are allowed on many of the backpacking trails, and permits are not required. But as just discussed, limit your use of campfires. Here are a few points to remember. New fire rings are not allowed. If you aren't camping in an area that already has a fire ring, then please don't build one. It isn't really necessary (cook on your stove), and the blackened rocks will be an ugly scar for a long time.

To build a low–impact fire, first clear away all of the leaves and other duff, down to bear dirt. Build a small fire in the middle of the cleared–out area. Use dead branches that are on the ground, *not* broken from tree trunks. I usually build a "pile fire"—add alternate layers of leaves and small twigs. As the leaves burn, the twigs will too. Gradually add bigger twigs 'till they will burn each other. It's not too pretty, and does get a little smoky, but it's the fastest and easiest way that I know to build a small fire.

When you are finished, and this is the most important step of all, make sure that your fire is *completely out*. Drown it, stir it, drown it, and stir it again. You've all seen those Smoky the Bear commercials. He isn't kidding. It's a shame to burn down a wonderful forest. And guess what, if you accidently start a forest fire, *you* may have to pay to get it put out! You should be able to lay your hand on the fire and not feel **any** heat. Once you're convinced that it's dead out, cover the area with leaves and twigs so that you can't tell you've built a fire there.

WATER

Most of the time you will cross water many, many times during a hike in Arkansas. The more developed trails will have nice bridges across the larger streams, but most of the primitive trails won't have any. March through June is the wet season here, and you may have to wade a few creeks now and then during that period. Just be careful and take it easy. I have found that the best and lightest footwear to wear when wading is a wool sock. Not only does it save your feet from rock cuts, but you get to wash your socks at the same time! If you hike during the late summer and early fall, plan to carry more water, as the streams do tend to dry up.

The water quality is excellent, and is generally clean and free of pollution. But that doesn't mean that it won't make you sick. There are lots of tiny critters swimming around in the water that may not match what your system is used to. It is best to be sure and treat all the water that you drink out on the trail. You can use tablets, iodine crystals, water filters (all available at your local outdoor store), or simply boil your water. For short hikes, I usually carry "Pola Pure" iodine crystals. On longer hikes, I carry a "First Need" filter. If you don't like the taste of tables or iodine, then use a filter, or lots of lemonade!

HIKING PACE

The question that I get asked most often is "how far can I hike in a day?" That is a good question, and no one knows the answer to that except *you*. How far or how fast you hike is determined by many different factors, the least of which is the trail. Our trails are usually built to standards which enable most folks to hike them with no problem. If the hill gets a little too steep, just slow down, and enjoy the view!

Generally speaking, if you are an average hiker, including rest stops and lunch, you can probably average about a mile an hour when you are carrying a backpack. Most people who don't **backpack** much, *and there is a big difference between backpacking and just hiking with no weight on your back,* can hike six to ten miles a day without too much trouble. Although it's been my experience that for most people less miles and more time to look around is best.

If you are in good shape, hike a lot, and aren't interested in spending a great deal of time messing around, sure you can hike fifteen or more miles a day. When I go out and get serious I average about three miles an hour, and typically cover twenty plus miles a day. But, of course, it hurts.

For dayhikers, one mile an hour or less is about right. If the area is especially scenic, and/or you plan to have lunch, then think about spending a couple of hours per mile or so. I've gone into places and spent all day just checking out the first mile.

A word of caution. When it is cold out you tend to start hiking with too many clothes on, and soon break out in a sweat. *This can kill you*, and you may not even realize what is happening! Of course I'm talking about hypothermia. I'm not going to tell you all about it or how to treat it—you should read up on it, though, before you go into the woods. I will say this—use the "layering method" when you hike, i.e. remove clothing as you get warm, and always hike so that you don't work up a sweat (slow down your pace if you have to). In fact, I always start off feeling slightly chilled in colder weather, knowing that my motor (and the hill ahead!) will heat things up soon enough.

WILDLIFE, INCLUDING SNAKES AND BEARS

There is an abundance of wildlife along the trails in Arkansas, both large and small. I have seen everything from colorful lizards and hummingbirds, to bald eagles, deer, bears, and even elk (in the Buffalo River area). Most of these critters will flee at the first sign (or noise) of a hiker, so you probably won't see many while you are hiking. But when you stop and take time out, that is another story.

Yes, there are bears. Black bears have been stocked by the Arkansas Game and Fish Commission for many years. They are not the huge grizzlies that you hear and see so much of on TV, though. They are pretty small, actually about the same size as you and me. And, they aren't really much of a problem. We have only had one incident of physical harm to a hiker that I'm aware of. I have been hiking in the woods in Arkansas for 30 years, and I have only seen a couple of bears in all that time.

Even though bears have not been much of a problem in the past, that doesn't mean that you can ignore them. They are strong, and under the wrong circumstances, can be quite dangerous. I only hear reports of bear sightings once in a while. Although it's probably not a necessity to "bear bag" your food when you camp, it's a good idea. ***Do not keep food in your tent with you.*** Be a clean and neat camper, and you shouldn't have any problems. Most of them will take off just as fast as they can, if they see or scent you. Any loud noise will usually send a curious one off into the woods in a hurry. If you see a bear, and it is obvious that he has seen you, shout at the top of your lungs. If that doesn't work, good luck.

And yes, there are snakes. Lots of snakes. Copperheads. Rattlesnakes. And cottonmouths. And they do bite. But snake bites are rare, and are usually the result of someone playing with one. Bees kill more people nationwide than snakes do, so it's not a real serious problem. But they are there. Watch out for them. Look at them. But for goodness sakes, don't play with them. A snake will not seek you out and bite you. If you reach down and pick one up, or step on one, sure it will bite you. What else can it do? Watch your step, mind your own business, and you shouldn't have any problems.

If you do happen to get bit, the best thing that you can do is relax, you aren't going to die. And get to a doctor as soon as you can. Most people don't know how to use a snakebite kit, so they aren't much good. I do recommend that you carry a device called *"The Extractor"* — it does work (on bee stings too!). The main thing, is to just try and stay out of their way.

I'm not much of a bird person, but I can tell you that there are lots and lots of birds out there. My favorite ones are the eagles, of course. We have bald eagles and even a few golden eagles. They come down from the north and spend the winter here. And we are just now beginning to have a few of them stay here and nest. Seeing one of these wonderful guys will make you stop whatever you are doing, and stare, breathless, at this incredible living thing. Many of the trails around the larger lakes are great places to do some eagle–watching during the wintertime.

HUNTING AND FISHING

Arkansas has an abundance of game animals, and the lakes and rivers support many species of sport fish. The large numbers of hunters and fisherman are responsible for a lot of the wildlife being here in such large numbers. You see, their hunting and fishing licenses support the aggressive stocking programs of both game and non–game species throughout the state. Licenses are required of all resident and nonresident sportsman over the age of 16. For information, contact: Arkansas Game & Fish Commission • 2 Natural Resources Drive • Little Rock, AR   72205 • 501–223–6300.

There are few conflicts between hunters and hikers. A lot of folks are afraid to hike during the hunting season. There is a hunting season of one sort or another going on from September through the middle of June. Why would you want to stay home during all of the best hiking seasons? If you are concerned about it, though, stay with the State Park trails during the peak of the hunting seasons in November. Hunting is not allowed in the Parks. Unlike most National Parks, hunting *is* allowed at Buffalo River.

We do have some great fishing in the streams and lakes of Arkansas. However, unlike what I'm used to in my summer–stomping grounds in the Wind River Mountains of Wyoming (where nearly every fly cast gets a strike), you can't rely on fish as a food source while hiking Arkansas trails. You can have some fun with ultra light equipment

14

fighting bluegill and smallmouth bass on the streams. The last two world record brown trout were caught in Arkansas, but we don't have any good trout–stream trails yet (you can catch some good ones along the Little Missouri Trail in the wintertime though).

BUGS

We have all kinds of bugs in Arkansas. Mosquitoes start to come out near the end of April and May. Ticks too. And chiggers like to show up during the summer. Just about the time that they are all getting burned up by the dry weather and heat, horseflies and gnats come out and really bug you!

There is no surefire way to keep them all from bothering you. A good 100% DEET repellant will help. Avon Skin So Soft works great for some people, not at all for others. In addition to repellants, a couple of other things will help. First, don't smell good. Take a shower before you go into the woods, but don't *add* any sweet scents to your body. And campfire smoke really knocks down the bugs. It smells a lot better than perfume anyway. (You might say that campfire smoke is trail perfume!)

In August and September, sometimes the spider webs across the trails just drive you nuts. A headnet will usually do the trick, but then you don't get as much protein that way. The net will keep you from accidentally eating those fat rascals! This is a good time of the year to hike with a tall friend—let them lead.

By late October most of the bugs should be gone 'till spring, although I have seen ticks out all winter before. And speaking of ticks, they have been getting a lot of press lately, and I think that many folks are just plain afraid to go into the woods any-more. If you find a tick on you, just reach down and pull it off. No big deal. However, since Lyme disease is becoming more prevalent, if you suspect a problem, not only go to a doctor, but *tell* him that you've been in the woods and to consider ticks as a culprit (it's easily treatable if caught in time).

SEASONS

Spring. An excellent time to hike. It's very magical here in March and April as everything comes to life. There's usually lots of water too, creating literally thousands of waterfalls all around the state. Of course we've got lots of wildflowers, but the trees flower wildly as well. Especially the dogwoods, redbuds and serviceberry.

Summer. It gets pretty hot and muggy towards July and August. Everyone heads to the lakes. Which leaves many of the trails deserted. Several of them do visit lakes, but there are a couple that follow streams deep into the wilderness, and are par-ticularly inviting. Did someone mention skinny dipping in the warm moonlight? One of my favorite things is getting caught out in a summer thunderstorm.

Fall. Each season has a certain smell to it, but none so nice as the scent of a crisp October day in the woods. Forget about all the blaze of color. Forget the deep blue sky. Forget the craft fairs. Fall just *feels* so good! Pick any trail, and you'll find a winner.

Winter. This is the longest hiking season here. Some years we have long stretches of 60–70 degree days, with brilliant sunshine. Many of the trails that run through endless tunnels of heavy forests the rest of the year, are now open to the world—with no leaves on the trees you can see deep into the hills and hollows, and out across the countryside. There are no bugs or snakes, and seldom other hikers. Of course it can get down right nasty too!

WEATHER FORECASTING

Are you kidding—you can't forecast the weather!!! Actually, here is my fool-proof method: When you get up in the morning, step outside of your tent. If you get wet (from up above), then it's raining. If the sun is in your eyes, you slept too late, and it's probably not raining. If the sun is in your eyes and you still get wet from up above, then you had better call everyone else to get up and out too 'cause there should be a rainbow somewhere!

A general rule to plan for here, or anywhere else for that matter, is to plan for rain. If it does rain, you'll be prepared and dry. If it doesn't, then you'll be so glad it didn't rain that you'll forget all about having to pack all of that extra weight. I always pack rain gear in the wintertime, just because it can double as protection from an unexpected cold front too.

WEATHER

The weather in Arkansas is just like everywhere else—difficult to predict and constantly changing. Here is a breakdown by month of the type of weather that you are likely to see while hiking. There are certainly no absolutes, 'cause it is just as likely to be 70 degrees on Christmas Day as it is to be 0. But here are some averages.

January. This is a great month to hike. Lots of nice, clear views, and probably some ice formations too. It is one of the coldest months. Daytime highs in the 30's and 40's, with some days in the 50's and even 60's. Nighttime lows may be in the teens and twenties, but often down to zero, and once in a while below zero for a short period. It may snow some, but not too much, and it probably won't stay around for long. Rain is likely too. But the real killer is an ice storm. They don't happen too often. When they do, the forest is just incredible!

February. Expect weather just like January. Possibly a little colder. Witch hazel bushes will pop open on sunny afternoons along the streams, and the fragrance will soothe the beast in you. I wish that they made a perfume that smelled like this—I'd marry her (my search continues).

March. Things are beginning to warm up, and get a little wetter. Daytime highs in the 50's and 60's, sometimes up into the 70's. Nighttime lows are milder, in the 30's and 40's, with a cold snap down into the 20's once in a while. Some snow, but not much. There are often long, soaking rains. Wildflowers begin to pop out. Serviceberry, wild plum and redbud trees come out and show their colors too.

April. One of the best months of the year. Daytime temps reach into the 70's and even some 80's. The mild nights are in the 40's and 50's, with still a cold snap once in a great while. Sometimes a heavy, wet snow, but this is rare. There can be some great spring thunderstorms. It's a wet month, and all of the waterfalls usually are running at full tilt. Wildflowers are everywhere. And the dogwoods pop out in full bloom, and they are the most common understory tree so it is quite a sight! They will linger around some into May. The rest of the trees begin to green up too. And, as a photographer I notice this, the new growth is just a brilliant kind of green that you don't see any other time.

May. Another great month, and it is the wettest month of the year. It may rain for days on end. The daytime temps reach into the upper 80's, and the nights seldom get below 60. Wild azaleas are in full bloom now. And there are still lots of wildflowers around. And waterfalls, and more waterfalls. And plenty of sunshine. The trees are all leafed out now.

June. Still good hiking weather. Less rain, and warmer temperatures. The days may reach 90, and it will drop into the 70's at night. This is the last really good month to hike for a while. The bugs start to come out, and the humidity goes up a little.

July. This is an "ify" month. It could be cool and wet, but most of the time it is pretty dry and beginning to get hot, up into the 90's, with nights still down into the 70's, or even 60's. When it does rain, it usually does so with lots of power. It's hard to beat spending the afternoon sitting out a summer thunderstorm under a bluff. *But beware*— Arkansas is the fourth leading lightning killer in the country. And I've always heard that an overhang acts like a gap in a spark plug—the lightning jumps this gap and fries who ever is sitting under the bluff! It's also a wonderful experience to hike in the warm rain. Put on your tennis shoes and try it sometime.

August. This is a good month to go to the beach or lake. Not a good time to be out hiking, unless you do one of the lake trails, or one like Caney Creek or Little Missouri that stays next to a river all the time. Daytime highs can reach 100, with humidity readings to match. Sometimes it doesn't get below 80 at night. And there are lots of ticks, chiggers and other assorted bugs just waiting for you. And lots of spider webs strung across the trail. So if you do go hiking, remember to take that tall friend with you and let them lead (or wear a headnet).

September. This is also a good month to stay home. It is often a worse month than August. Everything is pretty much the same except that horseflies come out, and they are really a pain! Towards the end of the month, it does begin to cool off a bit. That's a good sign that better hiking is just around the corner, so you had better dust off that equipment, and maybe get into shape. Try doing some early morning hikes. You'll be surprised at who else you'll find out there on the trails with you.

October. This is the other best month of the year. The first part of it is usually still quite warm, dry and buggy. But towards the middle the nights get cooler, down into the 50's, 40's and even 30's, and then it frosts. Yet the days are in the 70's and some 80's. By the end of the month it's crisp, clear days and nights, and in the Ozarks the forest transforms from the dull green that you have gotten used to since May, into one of the most incredible displays of color anywhere. It can be just as pretty as New England or Colorado. And out on the trails the last week of the month is always best. The bugs are pretty much gone too. Great hiking weather. The best colors down in the Ouachitas don't usually happen 'till early November.

November. Early in the month is still kind of like October, and the best colors are happening down in the Ouachitas. Still some warm days and fall colors up in the Ozarks. But it can change quickly. The leaves die and fall off the trees. This turns everything the same color of brown, but also opens up lots of views that have been hidden since April. The days get cooler, down into the 40's and even 30's, with some nice warm days in the 60's. The nights fall into the 20's and 30's more often, and once in a while there will be a cold snap. Rain is more frequent, and once in a great while, some snow. This is the month when hunters are most active.

December. A good month to hike. The days are usually in the 30's and 40's, but are often in the 50's and above. The nights get cold, and can drop down to zero once in a while. Snow is more likely, but not too much. And it can rain a lot. This is a typical flood month, though it is usually pretty dry, with some rain now and then and, once in a while, some ice. The ice begins to accumulate on some of the bluffs. A campfire, a mug of hot chocolate and a warm friend feel great!

17

EQUIPMENT

If you do a lot of hiking, you probably already know what to take with you. For those of you new to the sport, here is a bare–bones list of gear that you should probably take with you. Begin with the first list, then add on as needed. You can always take other stuff that you think you might want, but just don't go overboard—remember, you'll be carrying all of it. One good way to keep track of all this stuff is to make up a list of everything that you take on your hike. When you return, take a look at the stuff you thought was useless, and maybe remove it from the list. Use the same list to add items that you wish you had taken. Do this every time that you go hiking. Eventually, your list will be just the items that you really need.

If you are just going to hike a very short trail, and be out for an hour or two, you can pretty much get by with a set of comfortable clothes that you are wearing, plus:

- ❑ Map or guidebook (always have with you!)
- ❑ Fanny pack or daypack
- ❑ Small first aid kit
- ❑ Waterproof matches and/or bic lighter
- ❑ Water, a liter
- ❑ Pocket knife (folding Swiss–Army type)
- ❑ Comfortable footwear—tennis shoes are OK
- ❑ Small trash bag for the "collectibles" that others left behind
- ❑ Warm clothes, if winter
- ❑ Sunscreen, if summer
- ❑ Rain jacket, if it looks like rain
- ❑ Insect repellant, if it looks like bugs
- ❑ A snack
- ❑ Optional stuff like a camera, hiking stick, binoculars, sketch pad, whistle

For more of an extended dayhike, one that may last most of the day, add the following items to your daypack:

- ❑ Lunch, plus another snack
- ❑ More water
- ❑ Lightweight boots instead of tennis shoes
- ❑ Small flashlight, the kind that takes AA batteries
- ❑ Whistle
- ❑ Extra film
- ❑ Rain gear, if winter, no matter what the sky looks like
- ❑ Hat
- ❑ Light jacket or sweater, if chilly
- ❑ Warm jacket, if cold
- ❑ Plastic trowel for toilet duties
- ❑ Toilet paper
- ❑ ID books for flowers, birds etc.

For an overnight stay in the woods, you'll need to carry all of your gear on your back. The general rule is **keep it simple**, i.e. *light*. If you hike with someone else, you can save a lot of weight by sharing group equipment (tent, stove etc.). You should have all of the items on the other lists plus:

- ❏ Backpack instead of daypack
- ❏ Sturdy boots, broken in (lightweight boots are OK if you've worn them before)
- ❏ Sleeping bag
- ❏ Sleeping pad
- ❏ Stocking cap
- ❏ Tent, w/ground cloth
- ❏ Small cook stove
- ❏ Cook pot
- ❏ Cooking/eating utensils
- ❏ Cup (insulated plastic mug works great)
- ❏ Two small trash bags
- ❏ Rain cover for backpack
- ❏ Rope, 25'
- ❏ Water filter/tablets/iodine crystals
- ❏ Polypropylene or similar underwear, if the weather is cool
- ❏ More food, including snacks and drink mixes
- ❏ Personal stuff like toothbrush, small towel, etc.
- ❏ Spare batteries for flashlight
- ❏ Zip lock bags, assorted sizes
- ❏ Aspirin, or equivalent
- ❏ Spare socks
- ❏ Change of clothes
- ❏ Tennis shoes for around camp
- ❏ Sewing kit
- ❏ Stuff sacks for organizing stuff
- ❏ A large stuff sack to "bear bag" your food if needed, plus extra rope

For an extended trip on one of our longer trails, you need to really pare down your weight, and add the following gear:

- ❏ Extra fuel for stove
- ❏ Food for the trip, plus an extra meal or two
- ❏ Clothing for all types of weather expected that time of year
- ❏ Gloves
- ❏ Emergency money
- ❏ Gaiters
- ❏ More aspirin, plus a private masseuse if you have the room
- ❏ An itinerary left with someone responsible

People always want to know what kind of gear I use. Since I work and generally live out on the trails much of the year, my stuff has to be pretty good. Of course, equipment is purely a personal choice—and there are lots of great products out these days. But here are a few thoughts on some of the major equipment that I carry into the woods, and rely on to work day in and day out.

But first let me say something about buying equipment. I feel that it pays to shop at your local outdoor store, if possible, and buy name brand gear. If you use your stuff much, you'll come out ahead in the long run. Besides, most likely your local outdoor store supports the trail activities in your area, and you should shop there. My local "candy store" is the *Pack Rat Outdoor Center* here in Fayetteville. It seems like I spend more time in there than I do at home when I'm in town. I'd be lost without them. There is one mail–order store that is worth supporting too, and that's *Recreational Equipment Incorporated* (REI). They give a great deal of support to trails at the national level, as well as to local groups, like the Ozark Highlands Trail Association.

Boots. I've worn lots and lots of boots and have had many blisters to prove it. Don't get a pair of boots that are too heavy, or your feet will suffer. There are a lot of lightweight nylon/leather combos out these days—they are good for dayhiking and short backpack trips. The weight you intend to carry on your back, and the rougher the terrain you plan to hike, the heaver your boots should be. The most important thing about boots, is to get a pair that is comfortable and that *fits, and break them in*!

Tents. I own and use several different tents—one is very small and light for my quick solo trips in fair weather; another one is roomy enough for my wife and camera gear; and a third one that is pretty heavy but will withstand gale-force winds. My main advise here is this: If you are only going to be a fair–weather camper, then a Wal–Mart variety will be just fine. But if you plan to do some serious backpacking, and want your tent to last a long time, spend a few bucks and get a name brand. The two most important factors to me are that the tent must be freestanding, and have a vestibule with lots of room to stash gear outside of the tent.

Daypack. Everyone has a daypack/bookpack these days that will carry lots of stuff and these will probably work just fine for your shorter dayhikes. If you plant to be out all day and/or carry a lot of gear then spend some time at your local outdoor store and find one that is comfortable and well made.

Backpack. I have both an external frame pack and an internal frame pack. The external is great when the temps are high so my sweaty back can keep cool; but I use an internal pack at all other times—they just seem to fit better and feel more comfortable under heavy loads. Two things about selecting a backpack—one is to be sure that it fits right when fully loaded. If the outdoor store that you are buying it from won't let you load it up with 40 pounds of gear, then help you fit it, walk out of the store and go somewhere else. And two, remember that no matter how large a pack you buy, you will always bring along enough junk to fill it up—don't get a pack that's too big, or you won't be able to pick it up!

Sleeping bag. I've used two high-quality goose down bags for more than 25 years, and have never had any problems taking care of them. One is a lightweight "summer" bag that has kept me warm down to 20 degrees, while the other is a monster down bag that I've used in twenty below zero weather. Down is the best, but there are some great imitation down bags out these days that seem to be a pretty good deal, although

I doubt that they can stand up to years and years of constant use like down does. All sleeping bags are "rated" for their minimum temperatures. Take this figure with a grain of salt—not only is everyone different, many environmental factors come into play when determining just how warm a bag will keep you on any given night. A pad, tent, midnight candy bar, stocking cap, and tentmate will all keep you warmer.

Sleeping pad. I'm getting to be a wimp in my old age I guess, so I finally broke down and bought a Therm–a–Rest *Ultralight* pad a few years ago. It's got one of those covers that make into a chair, and it's the first thing that is loaded into my backpack before a trip. Before it, I used one of the "blue foam" type pads for many years. They are cheap, light weight and pretty effective.

Stove. Nothing beats my MSR *WhisperLite*. It just keeps on going and going, like that stupid bunny on TV. And it heats in a hurry. A good, basic stove (this is the stove that I loan out) is the Coleman *Peak I*—it's pretty simple to operate, and a good performer. If you are only going to camp during warm weather, and not do too much cooking, one of those cheap "gaz" cannister stoves work fine. But for colder use, or at high altitude, get a stove with a pump.

Water filter. For short trips, I use iodine crystals. But for longer trips I use the *Sawyer-Mini* filter. It's simple, effective, and light weight. There are a number of excellent filters on the market of late—made by PUR, Katadyn and MSR, but they are a bit heavy and pricey.

FOOD

Boy, this is a tough subject for me to talk about, 'cause I have very little taste— I'll eat almost anything. But you don't have to. Back in the early 1970's when I first got into backpacking, the only choice was pretty tasteless freeze–dried meals. These days, not only are there lots of regular store–bought goods that are perfect for backpacking, but the freeze–dried stuff is much better!

You can pretty much eat just like you do at home while in the woods, with a little repackaging and substituting here and there. The key is to keep the meals simple, and of course as light as possible. There are lots of prepackaged rice and noodle side dishes, for example, and of course Ramen noodle packets, that make a pretty good meal when you throw in some fresh veggies, and maybe a small can of tuna or chicken.

For your breads, carry bagels, pita pockets and flour tortillas instead of regular bread, 'cause they won't crush. There are a zillion kinds of gorp and trail mixes around, even one called "Ozark Highland Trail Mix." These often make up a large portion of my daily ration. You can find them these days that are loaded with all kinds of exotic nuts, dried fruits and seeds. And they are pretty darn good. I also consume large quantities of granola bars from the grocery store. And popular items now are all the energy bars available. They are quite expensive, but worth it for a really tough hike. (Here is a tip that works—nibble throughout the day instead of eating a big lunch. You will have more energy, and your tummy will thank you for it.)

I know of five or six different brands of freeze–dried foods available now. All of them are good, and some are special vegetarian style. My two favorites are good old *Mountain House* and *Backpacker's Pantry*. I use the kinds that don't require any cooking, and can be made and eaten right out of the bag. I don't recommend freeze–dried ice cream, but I do highly recommend most of the other freeze–dried desserts.

I also cook such things as marinated shrimp kabobs and a "Hurricane Creek

21

Omelet," but those are a little more trouble to whip up than freeze–dried beef stew, so only special guests get to chomp on them. But the point is that you *can* dine in the wilderness, with a little extra planning and preparation time. Or you can just eat right out of the bag like I do most of the time!

If you are going to be doing a lot of cooking, you should get one of those zip up bags that can carry twenty or thirty different things in individual sections, and use it as your kitchen pantry. There are a number of good cookbooks out now that will give you all kinds of ideas—check with your local outdoor stores for current titles.

GLOSSARY OF TERMS

Here are a few words that I use over and over again in this guide that you may not be familiar with.

Bench. This is part of a hill, a section that is usually level and runs along the hill for a while. If there was a giant around he could sit on it, like a bench.

FR#. This is the name of a forest road, and will be followed by a number, like FR# 1003. These are roads built and maintained by the U.S. Forest Service, and are usually dirt or gravel.

Leaf–off. This is the season after all the leaves on the trees fall off, and before they grow new ones in the Spring. There are always a lot more views out through the trees during leaf–off.

Leaf–on. The opposite of leaf–off.

Road trace. These are old roads that have not been used for a while, and are usually grown up with trees and other vegetation, and/or covered over with deep duff. They often make great trails 'cause they are wide enough to allow two hikers to walk side–by–side and carry on a conversation.

Saddle. This is a low spot in a ridge. Trails like to pass through them 'cause it's easier than climbing all the way to the top!

SSS. This means *"Special Scenic Spot."* There are a lot of places along the trails that may or may not be well known, but are just neat little areas that I find very attractive. The better trails have more SSS's!

LOST IN THE WOODS

I have always hiked alone most of the time, and have more or less decided that if anything serious ever happened to me, well, then I would either make it home or I would end my life in one of the most beautiful places in the world. When there are other people involved, then you have to start thinking about what to do and how to get help if something goes wrong.

It's always a good idea to have either this guide or a topo map of the area with you when you are on a trail. If you do have a problem and have to get to help in a hurry, you will be able to tell where you are and find a road that will get you to help. And you should always, *always* sign in at every trail register that you pass.

If you get lost, there are two things that you can do. If you feel pretty confident in your ability then you should just try and figure it out, and then make an attempt to get un–lost. Sometimes this may involve following a stream a couple of miles to a forest road and then walking a few more miles around to a known spot or help.

If you are really lost and have no hope of finding your way, then lets hope that there are other hikers, hunters or someone else in that particular section of woods. The best thing to do is get comfortable, make yourself at home, and start a fire. Eventually someone will come along looking for you. The main thing is to not panic. *Panic kills*. So you end up spending a day or two in the woods that you hadn't counted on. It just might be the best thing that has happened to you in a while. Remember, stay calm. You'll be all right. And stay put.

THANK YOUS

There were a large number of folks from all over the state that helped me a great deal with one aspect or another in the production of the various editions of this book. It was great to see so many people eager to help out. I could not have completed my task without them.

Thanks a million, in no particular order, to: John Vinson, Becky Faldon, the Reverend Arnold Hearn, Randy Carter, Don Monk, Jessie James, Thomas Brashears, Cindy Sanderlin, Bryan Kellar, Jim Rawlins, Tom Ferguson, Cary Frost, Erna Hassebrock, Lyle Erbisch, David Samuel, Gary Monk, David Saugey, Ken Eastin, Ivan Chambers, O.D Hopper, Doug Wilson, Keiko Peterson, Darrell Schwilling, Terry Eastin, Jon Hiser, Lisa Hlass, Tom Ledbetter, Becky Cahoone, John Beneke, Marny Apel, Carl "Wildman" Ownbey, Jim McDaniel, Amanada Hurd, Dennis Heter ("Hete,"), Mark Clippinger, Mary McCutchan, Lora Linn, Bob Talbert, Neil Curry, Bill Paxton, John Apel, Angela Coleman, John Watkins, Steve Wright, Greg Heinze, Joy Serrano–Wilks, Roy Senyard, John Archer, Dewey Watson, Jennie Freidhof, Gary Hawkins, Joe Wallace, Jamie Schwartz, Carl Garner, Scott Springer, C.D. Lassiter, James Wilborn, Harry Harnish, Vicki Trimble, David Carter, Richard Mills, Douglas Keller, Robert Raines, Jeff Pawelczak, Earl Adams, Scott and Carolyn Crook and their great staff of the Pack Rat Outdoor Center in Fayetteville, the helpful folks at the Arkansas Geological Commission in Little Rock. Also thanks to my text editors Beth Motherwell, my mom, and my lovely bride Pamela. Jim Liles for his extra efforts, and Ken Smith of Bill Clinton's staff so many moons ago. Many thanks to all of the folks at the various government agencies—they always had the time and patience to stop what they were doing and answer my questions.

And, of course, I must give special thanks to former president Bill Clinton himself, who said some very kind things in the foreword to this book. He may have retired, but his words still ring true. Arkansas is a wonderful state to live in, with clear, unpolluted mountain streams, fresh air, friendly people, and of course lots of hiking trails. We were proud to have had one of our own sitting in the White House for eight years. Thanks, Mr. President, for all that you did for Arkansas, and the country.

It has been a great pleasure working on this book over the years. The project has taken me to many special places that I'd never been to before, and gave me the opportunity to meet and work with the most talented people in the trail business in this state. My goal the whole time was to give you a useful document that would help you get out to experience and enjoy Arkansas. I hope that I've succeeded, and you will be able to use this guidebook again and again, discovering your own hidden treasures. Please let me know if you have any suggestions for future editions of this book. Thanks for reading, and for taking care of Arkansas, *The Natural State*.

See ya in the woods...

Tim J. Ernst

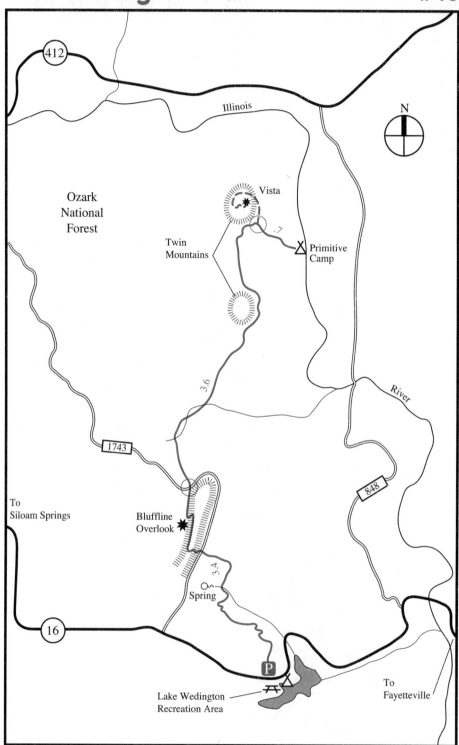

Lake Wedington Trail—15.4 miles round trip

This backpacking trail is located in a small but important section of the Ozark National Forest just west of Fayetteville. It visits a spectacular bluff area, runs through lots of typical Ozark forest, and ends at the banks of the Illinois River. There is no real access at that end, so you have to backtrack to return to the trailhead. Camping is permitted along the trail—but make sure that you get at least 200 feet, and out of sight of the trail. To get to the trailhead at Lake Wedington (wonderful spot—swim beach, campgrounds, fishing and great cabins), take Hwy. 16 west out of Fayetteville to the recreation area—the trailhead is located on the right, next to the highway, across from the campground. Wheeler, Rhea, Robinson & Gallatin quads.

The trail begins at the signboard, off to the left, and heads up into the pine forest. It is marked with white plastic diamonds. It drops down into and across a small drainage, then heads up the other side. It levels off and crosses a ridge, then drops down into another small hollow again. Once on top again the trail joins an old road trace and runs along level to mile 1.0. The trail dips just a bit, and right beyond, at a giant oak tree, it leaves the road trace TO THE RIGHT. (You may hear a lot of gunfire once in a while—there is a shooting range nearby—it is safe.)

It runs across the ridge, then down, across and up the other side of another small hollow. It goes through a couple more of these hollows. They are generally pretty lush, with lots of ferns, mosses and wildflowers. The trail skirts around the right side of an open area, then intersects with a jeep road at 1.5—TURN RIGHT and continue down the road (Be sure to watch for this turn on the way back!). There is a spring on the left at the bottom of the hill.

There are some blue blazes along the road as it heads up a hill, then levels out. Soon after passing a lesser trace that is on the right, the trail leaves the road TO THE LEFT at 1.8—watch for the blue painted rocks. It winds around through a pine forest, past 2.0. It goes on and off of a couple of traces, which are all marked. The trail begins to head uphill some, and comes out to and crosses FR#1743 at 2.3.

In the woods the trail heads uphill and turns to the right at the base of a nice bluff, following it—all of the trail from here on along the base is an SSS. At 2.7 the trail turns back to the left and up through the bluffline—a really neat spot! Up on top is a narrow ridge—the trail turns to the right and follows down this ridgetop. There are lots of wildflowers all around. It's very level, but rocky. The trail passes a couple of nice openings with views, a turtle, and mile 3.0. Just beyond, it swings over to a wonderful SSS view, that is right on top of another, larger bluff. This is a terrific sunset spot.

From the viewpoint, the trail turns to the right and continues along the bluff. You can look down and see chunks that have split away from the bluff—some have "bridge" rocks over to them. At 3.2 the trail drops down through a split in the bluff—an SSS. It continues along the base of the bluff, and there are several spots where the trail goes between the chunks and the bluff—SSS's. The trail comes to a bluff shelter, then turns to the left and heads down the hill. It crosses the same forest road again at 3.4.

It runs out into the woods and winds around on a four–wheeler trail, eventually crossing under a powerline at 4.0. It drops down the hill, levels out and crosses a creek. The vegetation is rather thick and lush in here. The trail stays next to the creek, crossing it twice more. At 4.6 our trail veers away from the four–wheeler trail that we've been following to swing over and look at an SSS waterfall (small one), then rejoins it. Soon after, the trail heads to the left, away from the stream, and up a steep hillside. Once on top it levels off and runs down the ridge. It rises just a tad, past mile 5.0, then levels off and crosses a road at 5.5, and again soon after.

There is an open meadow area off to the left that we skirt around, then head up hill a little, and soon level off. There are a number of different colored blazes that we're following through here. It eases down just a little, past mile 6.0, as the trail makes its way around the base of the first peak of Twin Mountain. Eventually the trail swings back to the right and down a little, across a level bench, then intersects with an old road at 6.2—TURN RIGHT and continue on the road.

The road is mostly level, and marked sparsely—be on the lookout for blazes where other traces intersect. At 6.8 the trail veers TO THE RIGHT, and enters an SSS area with some large hardwoods. It swings on around to the left, then joins another four–wheeler trail—continue TO THE RIGHT. During leaf–off you would have some pretty nice views out to the right. Soon the trail forks—TURN LEFT following the blazes and head uphill. It quickly levels off, and comes to an intersection at 7.0. Straight ahead is the spur trail that heads up to the second peak of Twin Mountain. The main trail TURNS RIGHT and continues on to the river.

SPUR TO TWIN MOUNTAIN. From the intersection the trail heads out level and swings left, up the hill. It comes underneath a bluffline, then follows it along from a distance, on around to the left. It finally makes a steep run up through a break in the bluff. Once on top, the trail heads back to the left, and over to a large fire pit. There is an SSS view here, and it is a great place to watch the sunrise. It's a good spot to camp too, as long as you brought plenty of water! It's almost a half mile up to here from the main trail.

BACK AT THE MAIN TRAIL, it heads downhill and joins an old roadbed, then continues along a narrow ridgetop. It gets a little steep at times, as it makes its way down. At 7.7 the trail hits the lush bottomland and levels off. The Illinois River is right out in front. There is a maze of ATV trails in here, and if you were here when they weren't, it would be an OK place to camp. To get back to the trailhead, return the same way that you came in.

Agency List #3

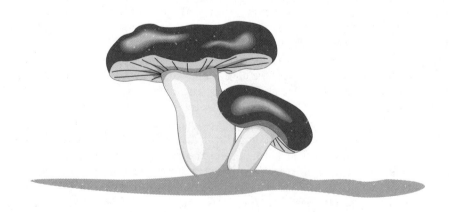

Kings River Overlook Nature Trail #26

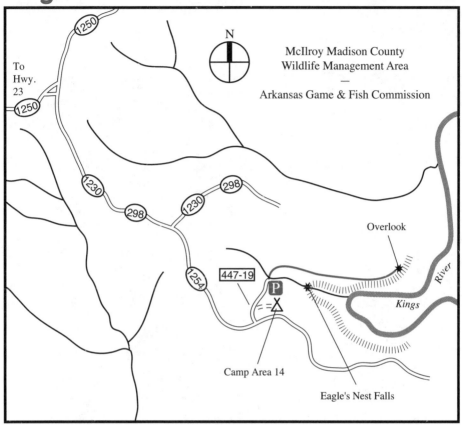

Kings River Overlook Nature Trail—1.0 mile round trip

This is a short, easy hike on an old jeep road to a spectacular overlook of the Kings River in the McIlroy Madison County Wildlife Management Area. It is located between Huntsville and Eureka Springs off of Hwy. 23. From Forum go north 3.7 miles on Hwy. 23 and TURN RIGHT onto CR#1250 at the Management Area Sign (gravel); or from Eureka Springs head south on Hwy. 23 and go 4.2 miles *past* the Hwy. 12 intersection and TURN LEFT onto CR#1250. Go .1 mile and then follow signs to the trailhead. [From the highway go 3.1 miles and TURN RIGHT onto CR#1230/298. Go 1.0 miles and CONTINUE STRAIGHT onto CR#1254–Private Road (CR#1230 turns to the left there). Go another .7 miles and TURN LEFT onto management area road #447–19. Continue down the hill— *go past* Camp Area #14 for .3 to the big sign and gate and PARK on the right.]

From the parking area hike past the gate and sign on and old jeep road and go across a small stream. The road/trail curves to the right and remains mostly level. Continue on this route until you come to the very end of the road at .5, and then just off to your right will be the terrific overlook of the Kings River. *DANGER:* The overlook is at the edge of a tall bluff and there are no barriers—hold onto your kids all the time!

Eagle's Nest Falls is located below the trail about 1/3 of the way in. There may be a beaten path to it but it is not marked (see map above). This is a high bluff area too.

Arkansas Game & Fish Commission, Eureka Springs office, 866–253–2506

Lake Leatherwood/Beacham Trail #52

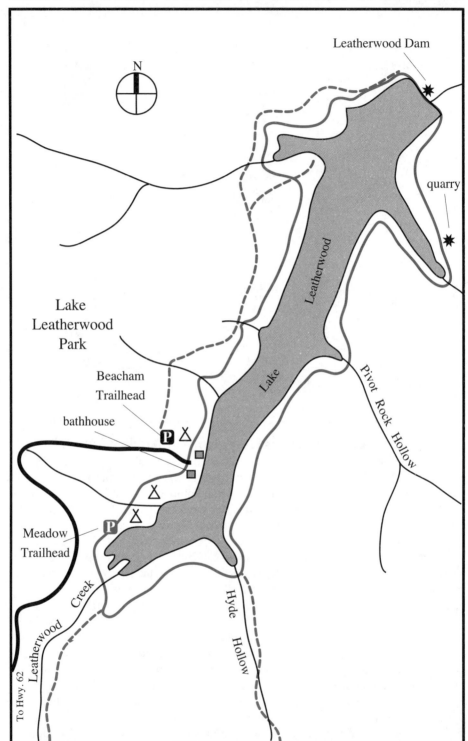

Leatherwood Dam

quarry

N

Lake
Leatherwood
Park

Beacham
Trailhead

bathhouse

Leatherwood

Lake

Pivot Rock Hollow

Meadow
Trailhead

Leatherwood Creek

To Hwy. 62

Hyde Hollow

Lake Leatherwood/Beacham Trail—3.7 miles

This trail is located at the edge of Eureka Springs and loops around a neat mountain lake, and over the dam that is made of cut limestone rocks. There are numerous trails in this park, most of them open to mountain bikes, but this loop that combines the Beacham and Fuller Trails is the best for hiking. To reach the park, go north on Hwy. 62 from Eureka Springs, past Thorncrown Chapel, and turn right at the bottom of the hill just past the turnoff to the ball fields. The paved road ends at the park. We will begin our hike from the Meadow Trailhead, which you get to by turning right and following the road down into the lower campgrounds.

The trail begins in the bottomland next to the lake, and heads around the upper part of the lake, over a couple of bridges that cross Leatherwood Creek. Be on the lookout for a turn to THE LEFT soon after you cross the big bridge (the other trail continues straight ahead and ends up at the ball fields).

The trail climbs up the hill to the left, then soon levels off. There are some good views out across the lake during leafoff, and lots of wildflowers all over the place in the springtime. The trail curves back to the right, then drops on down the hill and crosses Hyde Hollow at .6, then TURNS LEFT and heads back towards the lake (the trail to the right at the creek goes up the hollow and connects with other trails). You can look across and see the dock and swimming areas from this side of the lake.

Back up the hill we go again, but level trail is ahead. Just as the trail crosses under a powerline, it drops on down the hill and comes right alongside the lake at the 1.0 mile point. The trail soon turns away from the lake to the right and drops down to and across Pivot Rock Hollow at 1.2, then curves back TO THE LEFT and heads back out towards the lake again.

It passes through the first of several wet and delicate cedar glades, and runs along but just above the shoreline. Almost all of this is level and very easy hiking. The trail veers away from the lake once again, and follows another hollow back to the right, coming down and crossing the creek at 1.8. Just beyond this creek crossing the trail enters a rocky area of forest, then comes out onto a flat rock area—this is the rock quarry that was used to build the dam—TURN LEFT and follow along the level rock bed.

At the far end of the quarry you will enter forest once again and head uphill just a little bit and to the right, then will TURN LEFT and level out past the 2.0 mile point (next to a big cactus plant!). This will take you over to the end of the dam at 2.1.

The view of the lake from the dam is very nice. And if you are careful, you can look around and see the limestone rocks below you—these were cut from the quarry that we just hiked through. At the time it was constructed in the 1930's, this was the largest cut limestone dam in the world. Certainly all of this is an SSS!

At the far end of the dam TURN LEFT and follow a road for a little ways, then TURN LEFT and leave the road on plain trail at 2.3. The Beacham Trail actually stays on the road all the way back to the Beacham Trailhead, but we are going to take the Fuller Trail back, which runs along the lake shore much of the way and is more scenic.

There are a couple of trail intersections along the way, but you will want to remain straight and continue to generally follow the lake shore, although sometimes the trail is back in the woods and away from the lake. There are also many volunteer trails right down next to the lake. The trail comes out just behind the boat dock next to campsite #18. This spot is where I first laid eyes on my bride Pamela, and where we returned on the first day of spring to get married—I really like this trail!

Eureka Springs Parks & Recreation Dept.—870–253–2866; boat dock—870–253–8624

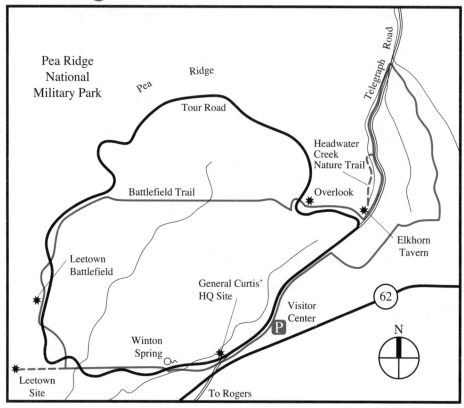

Pea Ridge Loop—8.7 miles

What a pleasant surprise! I thought this would be a dull trail, nothing but history, but I was wrong. This loop trail is historical sure, but also interesting and scenic. It is pretty easy to hike, as it follows many old roads through open fields. There are lots of deer around. The trail is located at Pea Ridge National Military Park (National Park Service). There is a Visitor Center there, complete with interpretive programs, exhibits and a book shop. Pick up a free copy of their tour map, which includes this trail, and explains many of the numbered tour stops that I'll mention. This is the largest Civil War Park west of the Mississippi River. To get there, take exit 67 off of Hwy. 71 at Rogers, head east on Hwy. 62, 10 miles to the Park. There is an entrance fee of $2 per adult, and the Park is open from 8am 'till 5pm. Park at the Visitor Center, go inside and look around, pay your fee and get your tour map. Pea Ridge quad.

The trail begins at the Visitor Center. Come out the front door and TURN RIGHT, then follow the Tour Road. Our trail follows the driving tour of the Park here and there, and crosses it many times. Watch for the hiker signs that mark the way. The trail takes off down Telegraph Road (paved), past a picnic area (lots of big trees!), and on to our first cannon at .4 (also stop #1 on the park map). It eases downhill a little, then levels off. At .7 we come to a neat little clear–water spring—Winton Spring. This is tour stop #2, and an SSS. Soon after the trail leaves the road TO THE RIGHT, and heads into the woods up a small hill—watch for the hiker sign.

It levels off quickly, and is a wide, mowed path that parallels the tour road. At 1.0 the trail comes back onto the road for just a couple of hundred feet, then leaves the road again TO THE RIGHT. We ease on down a hill and cross the road at 1.3. Just beyond there is a small bridge across Lee creek, and then we head uphill a little. As the route levels off there is an intersection which is tour stop #3 at 1.5—TURN RIGHT and continue on a lesser trail. (The wider route continues straight ahead on to the Leetown Site). This takes you to the tour road and a parking area—go across the road into the woods. It swings around through some large oaks, and eventually comes back out to the tour road at 1.8. This is stop #4. There are a couple more cannons here, which is the Leetown Battlefield site. TURN RIGHT and hike down the road a little ways, then turn off of the road TO THE LEFT at 2.0. It's all pretty level through here.

At 2.4 we cross the tour road once again, then head up a slight hill to the right. It swings back to the left, and meanders on the level through a cedar thicket. At 2.5 we rejoin the road—TURN RIGHT and continue along the road, past stop #5. It stays on the road (past an old horse trail), 'till at 2.7 it leaves the road TO THE RIGHT on an old roadbed. It swings back quickly, and straightens out as it heads through more cedars, past mile 3.0. At 3.1 there is a sign that talks about the "Ford Road," which we are on. Just beyond the trail dips down to and across a small, dry drainage (Lee Creek again), and past a big twin sycamore tree. At 3.5 we come out to the edge of a giant field—this is the main field in the park, and stretches all the way back to the Visitor Center. Continue straight across this field, past several large, stately trees that live out all by themselves. There are a couple of cannons way off in the distance to the right. You also get a good view of Pea Ridge, which is the hill on the left.

At 3.9 we intersect with another road (not the tour road). TURN RIGHT (actually straight ahead) and continue along the road. (The Ford Cemetery is back to the left.) A little ways beyond the trail leaves this road TO THE LEFT, and heads out into the woods. It winds around a little, heading uphill some, and CROSSES the tour road at 4.2. After a short, steep run the trail comes out at 4.2 at stop #7, which is a neat pavilion and wonderful overlook. There are some terrific bluffs in this area too, making it a double SSS! The trail continues along the top of the bluff, then at 4.5 it heads down through a split in the bluff, another SSS. It heads down the hill to a trail intersection—go STRAIGHT AHEAD. A little ways beyond the trail makes it to Elkhorn Tavern, stop #8. Wind around the Tavern to the left, and follow the Telegraph Road to the left (Huntsville Road takes off in front of the tavern). The Headwaters Creek Nature Trail heads out from behind the tavern—this is an alternate route—if you take it you will come out on the main trail (booklet available for .50 at Visitor Center).

The main trail continues along the old road—the nature trail rejoins from the left at 5.0. It swings back and forth, past lots of large trees. At 5.5 there is an open area (Tanyard site)—TURN RIGHT here and go alongside a small stream. At 5.7 TURN RIGHT again and head *up* the hill. There are lots of nice trees in this area. It levels off somewhat by 6.0, then runs along on top of a broad ridge. At 6.8 we hit the Huntsville Road—TURN RIGHT and walk down the road. At 7.0 is the Clemens homesite. Just past it, TURN LEFT off of the road, and continue along the edge of a big field. It leaves the field area, swings around through the forest some (a few big trees!), then at 8.0 we hit the Telegraph Road (paved) once again—TURN LEFT. Just beyond is stop #10 and 4 cannons. We are on this road all the way back to the Visitor Center (stop #11 & more cannons at 8.3), which completes the loop at 8.7 miles.

Agency List #19

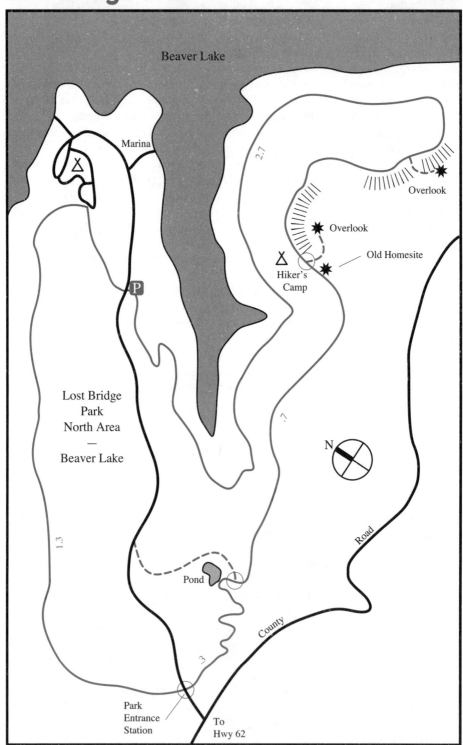

Beaver Lake

Marina

2.7

Overlook

Overlook

Old Homesite

Hiker's
Camp

P

Lost Bridge
Park
North Area
—
Beaver Lake

.7

N

1.3

Road

Pond

County

.3

Park
Entrance
Station

To
Hwy 62

Lost Bridge Loop—5.0 miles

This loop trail is one of the shorter backpacking trails in the state, and it has some great views of Beaver Lake, several bluffs, and visits a historical homestead site. It is located in Lost Bridge Park, between Rogers and Gateway. To get there, take Hwy. 62 east out of Rogers to Garfield, turn south on Hwy. 127 and go 7 miles to the park (veer left on Hwy. 127 S to the north park). Head towards the boat dock. Just before you get there, park on the right at the sign for the trail. There are several campgrounds in this park, and a large marina. The area is a very popular boating and scuba diving area. Garfield quad.

The trail is marked with paint blazes. It meanders out through the woods and a couple of boulder fields, does some up–and–downing, as it heads up around the cove. There is a minor SSS at one point where it passes through some neat rock formations, which are actually next to the entrance road. It switchbacks down to the left, then the right, and runs along the lake at .3. It wraps around the cove to the left, staying basically level for a while, then heads up the hill at a pretty good clip, then levels off again to the left. At .8 there is a nice little bluff overhang SSS.

From the bluff the trail begins to drop down the hill back towards the lake, then levels off as it continues along the lake shore, through mile 1.0. The trail winds its way through a nice open woods, mostly on the level. You can look across the cove and see the marina. This area is usually full of boats tied up to buoys. By 1.5 the trail has come out to the end of the cove, and there are some great views of the rest of the lake. Indian Creek Park is also visible to the north across the lake.

The trail swings to the right, around a small point. It remains level, and just back into the woods. If it's summertime, and you are carrying a heavy pack, the lake looks mighty inviting! It goes around another small point, then at 1.9 swings away from the lake to the right and heads uphill. On the way up, it passes by several large trees, and mile 2.0. It soon levels off as it turns to the right, just under a small bluff. It runs level for a while, then dips, then heads back uphill through a couple of graceful turns. It comes underneath a bluffline, a minor SSS, and at 2.4 comes to an intersection. The main trail goes STRAIGHT AHEAD. But for a nice overlook of the lake area, take the left fork, up through a split in the bluff, and climb up on top of the bluff to the left. The SSS view is best during leaf–off. There is a sign–map of the area at the overlook.

Back on the main trail, it continues along the base of the bluff. At one point, a large chunk of the bluff has dropped off and landed on the trail—proof that the Ozarks are still active! Leaving the bluff area, the trail heads out through more open woods. It drops slightly down through a slab boulder field, then rises up and rejoins the bluffline. Here it comes to a large SSS bluff overhang at 2.6, and is typical of the shelters used by Indians of the area.

At the end of the bluff, there is another trail that branches up and to the left—this goes on top of the bluff and over to another SSS overlook area. The main trail continues on STRAIGHT AHEAD and drops on down the hill to the old homesite area at 2.7. Here is the chimney at the cabin site of the Schrader family. It is one of the best that you'll see in the woods. This whole area is a historical SSS. A sign tells the story of the history of the family and the area. They lived and worked here in the early 1900's.

At this point also there is a trail that heads back to the right, and goes to the camp area and a spring. The spring is actually just a bit below the Indian shelter that we saw earlier. The camp area is a primitive one, really quite limited, and you may have to look around some to find a spot to put up a tent—there aren't many level spots! It is located just a couple hundred feet down this spur trail, and off to the left.

From the homesite area, the trail continues on as fairly level trail. It goes through some thick woods, past mile 3.0, then eases up the hill to the bluffline again, which is now broken up somewhat. It levels off, eventually leaves the bluff area, and heads to a trail intersection at 3.4. There is an SSS waterfall during wet periods located just down the right–hand fork. This fork is a shortcut back to the parking lot—it's just over a half mile, which would make your total loop 4 miles.

The main trail TURNS LEFT and heads up to a pond, which is usually rich with life. After going along the edge, it leaves the pond and turns sharply left to begin a steep climb up the hill. It switchbacks on up, passing through a broken bluffline at one point, then levels off. At 3.7 it comes out to and crosses the road near the park entrance station. It begins to drop downhill some as it goes across a steep hillside. The trail lands in a drainage, then turns to the right and follows right down the middle of this gravel ravine.

Just before this ravine gets real steep, the trail leaves it to the right, runs out on the level to another bluff overhang. Here it makes a sharp turn to the left and straight down the hill. It soon levels off and passes through mile 4.0. The trail remains level for a while, past some low broken bluffs. At 4.4 it comes to an SSS area of neat "block" boulders. From there it continues to wind on around this level bench. Eventually you begin to see identification signs (names for Scout campsites). Soon after, at 4.9, the trail comes into the end of the campground area at the pavilion. Go across a footbridge and the access road, then follow an old roadbed that continues straight ahead and on the level. It was not signed when I was here, so be alert. If you are confused, just head down through the campground and you'll eventually find your way back!

The trail goes along the roadbed for just a couple of hundred yards, then TURNS LEFT off of the road. It heads on down the hill, down a set of steps, and comes out at the trailhead parking area right at 5.0 miles. There is another, very short nature trail—the Fish Trap Trail—that is located in the south area of the park that you might want to inquire about and hike.

Agency List #20

War Eagle Trail   #72

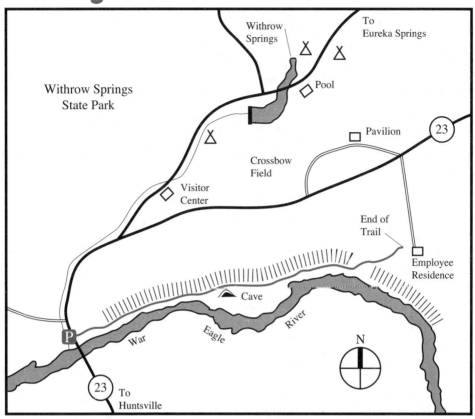

War Eagle Trail—2.0 miles round trip

   This short, easy trail runs alongside beautiful War Eagle River, and visits a cave (bring your flashlight) and towering bluff in the Withrow Springs State Park. This is a nice park with swimming pool, campground, hookups and canoe rentals. To get there, take Hwy. 23 north out of Huntsville 5 miles to the Park entrance (about 20 miles south of Eureka Springs). Pull off and park on the left near the big entrance sign. The trail begins just across the highway. Forum quad.

   It runs level across a steep, lush, bluffy hillside, just above the War Eagle River. It soon comes to War Eagle Cave, which has a walk–in entrance that will take you slightly down to a creek in the back of it! An SSS of course. The trail continues on past the cave to the right, and comes to a slick bluff area, where there are cables strung to help you out. This area is not recommended for little kids. Not too long after, the trail heads up a hill and away from the river. It's a pretty steep climb part way, but the view from up there is worth it—an SSS view for sure. A little further up there is a sign proclaiming the trail's end—turn around and return via the same route. Your hike will be just under 2 miles total.

   You may want to hike the other two trails in the park during your visit—the Forest Trail and the Dogwood Trail, or canoe the War Eagle River (in season).

   Agency List #37

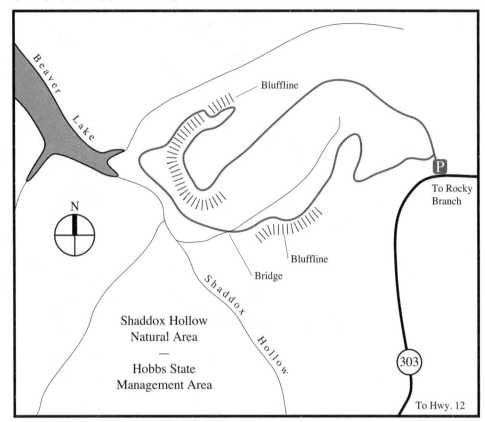

Shaddox Hollow Loop—1.5 miles

This is a short, popular loop that visits Shaddox Hollow Natural Area, which is jointly managed by the Natural Heritage Commission and Arkansas State Parks. It is part of the Hobbs State Management Area, and is located along the shores of Beaver Lake in NW Arkansas near Rocky Branch. Besides lots of bluffs and streamsides, this area contains a wide variety of fauna and flora, and is frequented by school science classes and used as a training aid. The scenery is pretty darn nice too! The trail was built as a tribute to Virginia Allred, a longtime resident of the area and well–known conservationist. War Eagle quad.

To get to the trail, take Hwy. 12 east out of Rogers, past Beaver Lake, turn north on Hwy. 303 (this is the turn off to Rocky Branch) and go about one mile—the parking lot is on the left. There is lots of room to park. The trail begins at the carved wood sign, down a set of steps. We'll hike this trail in a counterclockwise direction, so TURN RIGHT at the sign. The trail takes off fairly level and swings around the head of a hollow to the left. It heads down the middle of a ridgetop. There is an SSS of sorts, as the trail passes the remains of an old Ford car. All along here there is a thick cover of huckleberry, which is actually wild blueberry. They ripen in early summer.

It continues along the ridgetop, remaining level. During leaf–off there are some pretty nice views through here. As the trail gets on out to the end of the ridge, it swings to the left, then to the right as it drops on down the hill at .5 mile. There is an SSS view out over Beaver Lake here. (This is the turn around point if you don't want to do the whole trail—once you head down the hill, you'll have to climb back out, so you may want to go back the easy way.) It curves back to the right as it continues to drop. You'll notice that much of the tread and the hillside look like gravel—a natural pile! As the trail comes up on a small ravine, it switchbacks to the left and continues on down the hill.

There is an interesting "hole" just off to the left—this is a sink hole, which is actually a place where water comes gushing into some cave system deep below. An SSS. Just beyond, the trail makes its way down a set of steps through the bluffline at .7, then levels out and runs along the base—all of this area is an SSS. You can get up close to the bluff and see lots of neat stuff. If you look close, you'll see places where critters live! The trail swings around the bluff to the left, then leaves the bluff area TO THE RIGHT, and heads down hill.

As it curves back to the left there is a spur trail that goes off to the right to the shore of the lake. The main trail goes over and comes alongside a wonderful little stream, and follows it upsteam. This area along the stream is another SSS. There is a short footbridge over a side drainage, and the trail continues on the level near the stream. Here and there you'll pass a few large trees. And of course in the springtime, there are lots and lots of wildflowers along the way. Eventually the trail swings back to the left and comes to a larger bridge at .9—I must say that these timbers, which were hauled in from the lake, are *heavy!* (I built this trail and bridges, with the help of lots of volunteers, back in 1988.) When the water is running this is a great spot to sit and dangle your feet off.

Past the bridge the trail works its way uphill just a tad and into a real neat little ravine, coming to an SSS overhanging bluff. It's the largest bluff along the trail. The tread gets kind of narrow just beyond, as it goes across the steep hillside. All through this section you can look down on the creek. Eventually the hillside levels out just a bit, and the trail turns to the right, goes up another small drainage a few feet, and crosses a stream just below a waterfall. It begins to head uphill some, as it goes across the nose of a ridge.

The hillside gets pretty steep again as the trail swings to the right into a small ravine and an SSS. This is a neat little stream crossing—everything is covered with moss, and there is a waterfall upstream. From here the trail heads uphill again, and swings wide around the edge of a hillside, and turns up to the right. It gets a little steep at times. The trail curves back to the right across the hillside, then back to the left. It's not quite as steep through here. A little more uphill, then the trail ends back at the parking lot.

NOTE that deer hunting is allowed in this park and this hiking trail may be closed during the season—check with the state park office for the latest information.

Agency List # 25

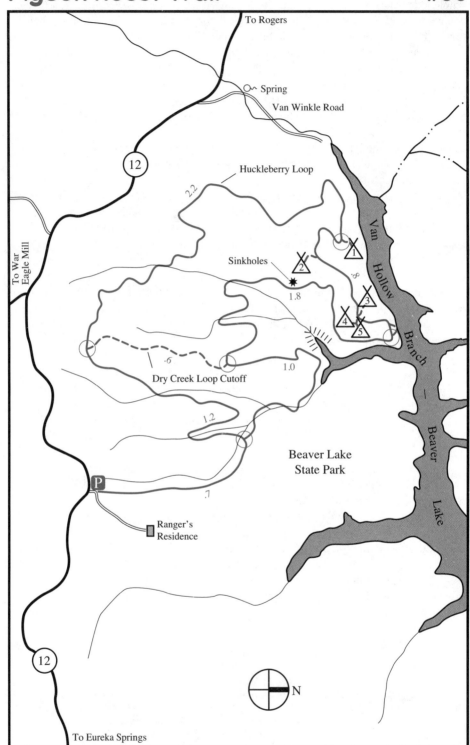

To Rogers

Spring

Van Winkle Road

12

Huckleberry Loop

2.2

Sinkholes

1

.8

2

Van Hollow Branch

1.8

3

4

5

.6

Dry Creek Loop Cutoff

1.0

To War Eagle Mill

1.2

Beaver Lake State Park

P

.7

Ranger's Residence

Beaver Lake

12

N

To Eureka Springs

Pigeon Roost Trail—4.2 & 8.4 mile loops

This trail is located at Beaver Lake State Park, which is part of the Hobbs State Management Area. There are actually two loops on this trail, and they make up a figure eight sort of pattern. We're going to hike the longer loop, which also takes in almost all of the shorter loop. Overnight camping is allowed on the longer loop—there are 5 small primitive sites available. Check with the Ranger for a campsite reservation form (there may also be a parking fee required). NOTE that deer hunting is allowed in this park and this hiking trail may be closed during the season—check with the state park office for the latest information. War Eagle quad.

To get to the trailhead, take Hwy. 12 east out of Rogers, go over Beaver Lake, and continue on past the turnoff to Rocky Branch, then about a mile past the turnoff to War Eagle Mill turn left into the gravel parking area—there is also a road here that runs on down through a gate to the Park Ranger's house. The trail begins at the far end of the parking area, and is marked with white paint. It heads off on an old road trace (this may someday be the main road to a Visitor Center). It remains on this road 'till .4, where it leaves the road TO THE LEFT. The trail heads down the hill to an intersection at .7—TURN LEFT here and follow the trail up a ravine. It turns back to the right, climbs up and over the ridge to the left, then down into another drainage, passing an SSS spot (and the only real waterfall on the trail) at 1.5.

It crosses the creek and heads up a hill. At 1.9 the trail crosses a road—go STRAIGHT AHEAD (the shorter loop turns right and follows the road). From here the trail winds around along the hillside, dips down to and across a streambed (usually dry), then heads up to and across another road crossing. It swings back to the left, then to the right around the head of a hollow. It eventually heads back to the right and joins an old roadbed that runs along the top of a ridge—be sure to follow the white blazes.

Eventually the trail comes around to an SSS viewpoint that overlooks the lake. It cuts back to the right, and soon comes to a spur trail (blue blazed) that goes down to the first of 5 campsites at 4.1. Most of these sites are very small—only room for a couple of backpacker tents. The second campsite spur is around the hill at 4.4, and the spur to the third, fourth and fifth sites is at 4.7. Beyond these sites the trail drops on down to the lake shore, then swings back up the hill, heading up into Pigeon Roost Hollow. It winds around on top some, then heads back downhill, past a giant pine tree, then goes to a most unique SSS area at 5.5—a series of deep sinkholes, which funnel water into a cave system below.

The trail continues on down the hill, heads into another dry drainage, climbs up a hill, down into another ravine, then up another ridge. At 6.7 it hits a road—TURN LEFT and walk down the road (the shorter loop comes in from the right here). The trail eventually continues off of the end of it, swings over and drops on down the hillside. At 7.2 there is a wonderful SSS right on the lake, at Pigeon Roost Hollow. I've seen lots of bald eagles roosting in the dead trees here during the winter months. If you're real lucky, you can watch one fish!

The trail leaves the lake area and follows a stream to the right, crossing it several times, and eventually comes to a trail intersection at 7.7—this completes the big loop. TURN LEFT and follow the trail back up the hillside to the trailhead, for a total distance of 8.4 miles.

Agency List # 25

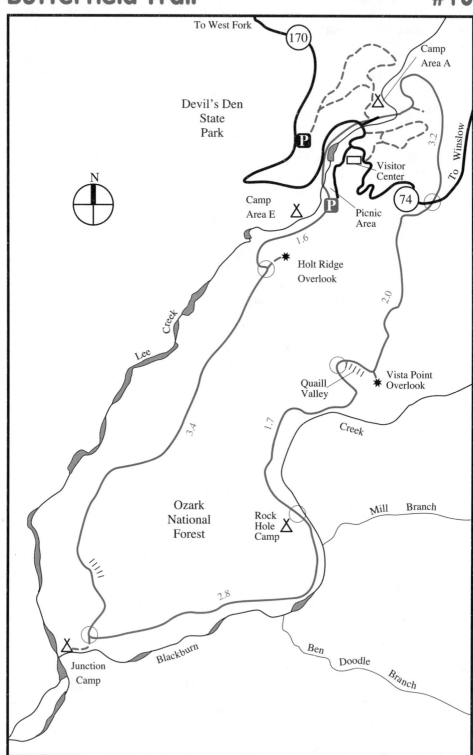

To West Fork

170

Devil's Den
State
Park

Camp
Area A

3.2

To Winslow

P

Visitor
Center

N

Camp
Area E

P

Picnic
Area

74

1.6

Holt Ridge
Overlook

2.0

Lee Creek

3.4

Quaill
Valley

Vista Point
Overlook

1.7

Creek

Ozark
National
Forest

Rock
Hole
Camp

Mill   Branch

2.8

Junction
Camp

Blackburn

Ben   Doodle   Branch

Butterfield Loop Trail—14.7 miles

This is the longest of several trails at Devil's Den State Park. Camping is permitted at two primitive campsites along the way. Probably more backpackers have "cut their teeth" on this trail than any other in the state. Part of this loop follows picturesque Blackburn and Lee Creeks. Great views of both valleys are had from the ridgetop. There are numerous geological formations to explore, including the wonderful Quaill Valley area, and there are lots of vistas and other SSS's along the way. The trail was named after the historical Butterfield Overland Stage Route that operated from Missouri to California in the late 1850's. Although none of the trail actually follows the route, it passes near it.

To get to Devil's Den, either take Exit 53 on I-540 and follow Hwy. 170 for 17 miles, or take Exit 45 on I-540 and take Hwy. 74 for 7 miles. There are some great cabins here, lots of camping, a swimming pool, small lake for paddle–boating around, and a strong naturalist program at the park. The trailhead is located in the day use area, just downstream from the dam. You do need to stop by the Visitor Center first and pick up a free permit if you are going to camp.

You may encounter some mountain bikes or horses along the trail—several stretches of the trail are open to them, and at times is heavily used by them. And once in a while they elect to break the law and do the whole trail. Sometimes the "horse mud" gets pretty deep! Just grin and bear it, I guess. In Camp Area A the trail crosses Lee Creek (no bridge there), and since the creek can get up and running during high water conditions, you may want to bypass this crossing (and the first 3.0 miles of the trail), and begin your hike on Hwy. 74 (it crosses the highway at the park entrance sign). Check with the nice folks at the office for a possible ride. Strickler, Rudy N.E. and Winslow quads.

The trail is marked with blue blazes in both directions. White carsonite posts serve as mile markers. The trail begins at the trailhead at the far end of the picnic area. Go across Lee Creek on the suspension bridge and head upstream. The first mile takes you through the park around the back side of the lake, across the highway and into Camp Area A. It crosses Lee Creek again (this time, no bridge), then continues up a little and to the left, and levels off. For the next one half mile the trail coincides with the Lee Creek Trail and Fossil Flats Mountain Bike Trail. Keep going STRAIGHT at the junction with the walk-in campsite spur. After another quarter mile the trail veers off to the RIGHT and heads up the hill on an old road trace.

This road winds around up the hillside, steeply at times, past mile 2.0. It runs level once in a while. During leaf–off there are some great views through the trees of the Lee Creek Valley. As the road trace approaches the highway at 2.9, the trail leaves it TO THE RIGHT and continues on the level as plain trail. It does some up–and-downing below the highway, past mile 3.0. It comes out to Hwy. 74 at a parking area.

Go across the highway and pick up the Holt Road, which is wide, and often muddy. The trail leaves this road TO THE LEFT at 3.4. It also leaves the state park here, and enters the Ozark National Forest (where we will be to mile 13.0). It heads uphill just a little, cris–crosses an old, rocky pioneer road, then tops out and levels off. It heads downhill some, and joins a larger road trace that comes in from the left at 3.8. It's a nice, gentle downhill grade here. The mile post at 4.0 is placed a little further than normal, but we'll call it even, since there is a short mile later on. Just beyond is a leaf–off SSS view down into the Blackburn Valley.

The road trace continues downhill, switchbacks to the left, and crosses another road. It gets pretty steep and rocky at times. At 4.6 we intersect with a horse trail and TURN RIGHT on it, which is also an old road trace (the main road continues straight ahead, on out to Vista Point, and SSS overlook). Our trail heads down a rocky slab, across a tiny creek, then uphill some. There are some great SSS views just off of the trail on the left, from on top of a bluff. You will see some "horseshoe" blazes along the trail for a little while, and there is some horse mud, which is what you get when there is mud, but no water to make it — think about it!

The road levels a bit, then heads steeply down the hill to, and across a creek at 4.9. Just beyond, the trail splits, and the horse trail takes off to the right and uphill (yea!), and the hiking trail goes TO THE LEFT, and actually heads down the creek, crossing it a second time. This begins the most scenic spot around — Quaill Valley. Yes, it qualifies as an SSS! It appears that the earth has just split open. There is a long bluffline, actually two of them, facing each other. The trail heads up the hill and around the bluffs, then levels off and passes mile 5.0. There is more of Quaill Valley to come. (It is named after park employee Jack Quaill, not the bird!)

The trail swings to the left, next to the sandstone bluff. A spur trail heads back to the left, and runs between the two bluffs that are facing each other. Needless to say, you should stop and spend some time exploring this area. A unique spot. (The Wildman wrestled a huge timber rattlesnake here — just thought I would mention that!) The main trail continues on at the base of the bluff for just a short distance, then heads away from the bluff and drops down the hill.

At 5.4 the trail comes to an old road trace and TURNS RIGHT onto it. Soon after, there are a number of roads that all come together — continue STRAIGHT through this mess, and watch for blazes. The trail crosses the stream that comes down from Quail Valley, then heads up the hill, and levels off, past mile 6.0.

It continues along a broken bench of sorts, doing some up–and–downing, crossing several small streams. There are a few good leaf–off views along the way. The trail itself is very rocky, so watch your step. It swings down to the left and intersects with a four–wheeler trail at 6.5 — TURN RIGHT and follow this old road bed.

It runs alongside Blackburn Creek, then comes to the Rock Hole Primitive Campsite area at 6.9, which is right on the creek (and the road). Just beyond, right before the road trace crosses the creek, the trail leaves it TO THE RIGHT, and continues as plain trail, past mile 7.0.

The trail visits the creek again for a moment, then heads *up* the hill and levels off on the next bench. It is *very* rocky at times! Keep in mind that while hiking this whole stretch of trail, that there are lots of great swimming holes right over there on Blackburn Creek. If it is warm, a dip is required! Also along this stretch, there is a bluffline just above the trail that will follow us for a while. Perhaps worth a look see.

The trail swings to the right, away from the creek at 7.8, and climbs up onto another bench, then levels out again, past mile 8.0. It drops down to the next bench, then back up again, then repeats.

The trail continues its up–and–downing across broken benches, across a small stream or two, to mile 9.0. This was a very short mile, so we are now even! From there it heads up the hill, then levels off, then heads up some more. It is now heading on over towards the Lee Creek drainage, and that bluffline just above is still with us. At 9.7 we hit a road trace, and also the yellow–blazed spur trail that leads steeply down the hill to the left to Junction Camp.

Back up at the spur intersection, the main trail TURNS RIGHT, joins the old road, and heads *up* the hill. A short, tough climb with a backpack. Just as it levels off, the trail leaves the road TO THE LEFT, and continues on the level as plain, but rocky, trail. You are now heading up the Lee Creek Valley, which will lead us all the way back to the state park.

The trail goes through an SSS rock garden area, then past mile 10.0. It enters another SSS rock garden area just beyond, then heads up the hill to the right, up to a small bluff at 10.2, where it literally goes right up the face of the bluff. It is rocky, but an SSS! There is a spring that pours out from the middle of the bluff. Pretty nice.

From there the trail heads uphill at a less grade, then intersects with a mountain bike trail—TURN LEFT and follow it. It soon levels off and begins a long, leisurely hike past stately old oak trees. Just after mile 11.0, there is an SSS view of the Lee Creek Valley. The hillside drops off steeply below. There are some giant grape vines around too, clinging to the tall trees.

The trail continues on the level, past more leaf–off views and big trees, to mile 12.0. Just beyond, at 12.2, the trail turns to the left and heads down the hill. It turns to the right and follows an old road trace for just a little bit, then leaves it TO THE LEFT, on the level, as plain trail—be sure to follow the blazes. It switchbacks on down the hill some more, then levels out. At 12.4 it intersects with the horse trail again—TURN RIGHT and follow it. There are more great views along here, level trail, and horse mud. It heads up to the right to the next bench, then levels off again. Just before mile 13.0, the trail leaves the Ozark National Forest and reenters the state park.

At 13.1 we intersect with a road trace, and a well–used horse trail. You can follow it to the right, on over to the Holt Ridge Overlook—an SSS view that looks out over the state park. The hiking trail TURNS LEFT onto the road, and heads *down* the hill, bypassing some even steeper trail that used to be part of the route. This re-routed section adds a little bit to the length, but since you are going downhill, you won't mind!

At the bottom of the hill a horse trail comes in from the left (and coincides with our trail almost all the way back to the trailhead). This begins a nice SSS run along Lee Creek. There is another horse trail that joins in from the left a little ways beyond (it comes from the horse camp across the creek)—stay on the old road trace, which heads uphill just a little to the right. Once in a while this area gets a lot of horse use, and you may have to wade through a little horse mud, especially when everything is wet!

The trail stays near the creek, passes mile 14.0, and does a lot of up–and–down-ing. There is a fork in the trail ahead, just past the park maintenance shop—take the LEFT FORK and follow it on over to the trailhead and the end of your hike at 14.7. Be sure to visit the Devil's Den Trail while you are in the park, which is one of the most scenic short trails in the state.

Agency List #26

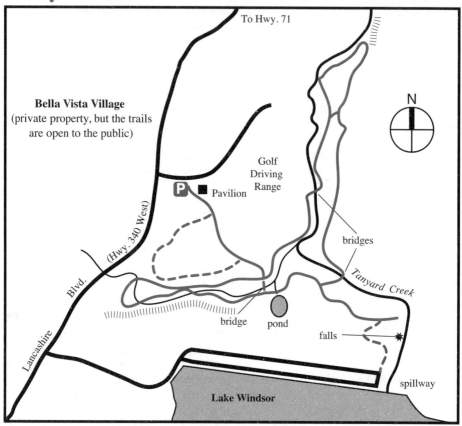

Tanyard Creek Nature Trail—1.9 miles

This is a wonderful trail right in the middle of Bella Vista. It was built and is maintained by volunteers, who have also posted at least 100 little signs along the way that tell all sorts of interesting details about things you will see. You can make a quick 30-minute hike to the waterfall and back, or spend half a day on this easy trail reading all of the signs. It is a "dog friendly" trail, and they even have a special dog-watering station.

To get to the trailhead from the middle of Bella Vista, head north on Hwy. 71 and take the Hwy. 340/Town Center exit, then TURN LEFT. Go just about a mile on Hwy. 340/Lancashire Blvd. and TURN LEFT —it is signed as "Tanyard Creek Recreation." Then TURN RIGHT into the parking lot. There is a pavilion there, and toilets.

The trail begins next to the pavilion—TURN RIGHT and follow the paved trail out across an open field. Continue straight ahead past a couple of intersections until you pass under a powerline, then go just a little bit farther and past the end of the pavement. At the edge of the woods you will come to a large sign that details the trail system— TURN RIGHT just before the sign and follow the little trail upstream.

It will pass a bridge to the left—continue STRAIGHT AHEAD and to the right, then will go over an arched bridge, and curve around to the left and come to the base of a small limestone bluff and a historical site at .4, all of it being an SSS (be sure to spend some time and read all of the little signs). Follow the trail downstream along the bluff (crossing back over the little stream) until you meet up with the trail again—TURN RIGHT and cross over the creek on a bridge. The trail remains on the far side of the creek now, past neat rock formations, and comes to another trail intersection. There is a big bridge across the creek to the left that goes back to the big trail sign at .6—continue STRAIGHT AHEAD at this intersection unless you are already pooped out.

There will be a small pond on your right, and soon the trail comes to another intersection—TURN RIGHT and head up the hill. This will take you to the overlook of Tanyard Creek Falls at .8, a beautiful SSS waterfall that is definitely worth the side trip! (There is also another side trail that goes up to the top of the dam and spillway, but we are not going to take it.) Once you have finished admiring the waterfall, turn around and go back to the intersection at the bottom of the hill, and TURN RIGHT there.

The trail heads on over to the main Tanyard Creek and crosses it on a large bridge. There is a nice SSS view upstream of some cascades. (You can also turn right just after the bridge and go upstream to a bench that has an even better view.) TURN LEFT after the bridge and head downstream. The trail joins an old roadbed here, and heads uphill just a little bit, then drops on down the other side to a point where it leaves the old roadbed at 1.1—TURN LEFT here.

The next trail intersection is a short cut, but it is easy hiking ahead so continue STRAIGHT AHEAD. The trail will eventually come to the base of a small bluff and the main creek, then curve back to the left. It is an easy stroll next to the creek. At 1.4 the short-cut trail comes in from the left—continue STRAIGHT AHEAD.

A little ways beyond the home place the trail comes to and goes across a suspension bridge, then TURNS LEFT and continues upstream. It eventually winds back up to the large trail sign at 1.7 where you first entered the woods, completing your loop. TURN RIGHT and follow the paved trail back to the trailhead for a total hike of 1.9 miles.

Crack In Rock Trail—1.5 miles (see map next page)

Here is another trail just outside of a town that is a hidden gem. There are waterfalls, a stream, moss-covered boulders, and a bluff with a nice crevasse or "crack" in it. This is one of three trails in the park near the dam site of the Lee Creek Reservoir, located near Van Buren. This is the most scenic of the trails (aka Split Rock Trail).

To get to the trailhead take Hwy. 59 north from Van Buren (exit #5 on I-40) 1.1 miles and TURN LEFT onto Old Uniontown Road. Follow this road 1.5 miles and TURN LEFT on Pine Hollow Drive. Take this road 1.9 miles and TURN LEFT onto Gelly Road (at the Assembly of God Church) and go .7 mile to the parking area and park on the left just across from the restrooms. This is the Reservoir Recreation Area.

The Crack In Rock Trail begins next to the restrooms, and for the first .3 mile is also the Homestead Trail. It heads out through thick forest, mostly on the level, and soon comes to an unmarked intersection—GO STRAIGHT there. (The trail to the left goes up to an old homesite & grave up on top of a hill, while the trail to the right goes over to the powerline and then down the hill to intersect with our trail later on.)

A short distance later there is a fork in the trail at .2, and there is an old cemetery on the left side of the trail. You want to take the RIGHT FORK that heads downhill. Soon this trail comes out under a powerline and intersects with a trail coming down from the right (this goes back up the hill to the very first intersection)—TURN LEFT /STRAIGHT AHEAD and continue down the hill and under the powerline.

At .3 there is another trail intersection, which is just before you cross Mill

Crack In Rock Trail

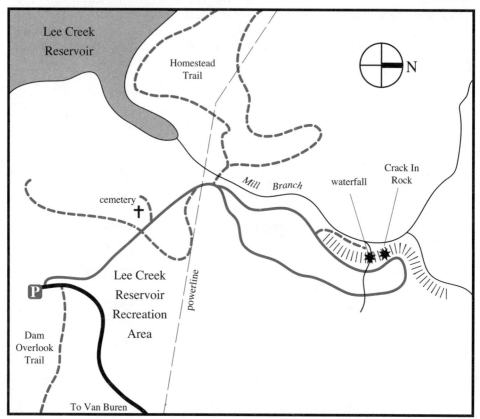

(continued from previous page) Branch. The Homestead Trail continues across the creek (total length about 3.3 miles), but we want to TURN RIGHT and take the Crack In Rock Loop. Both ends of the loop are here, and we will take the LEFT FORK, which follows the creek upstream.

There is a nice green pool in the creek at .4, an SSS, and then as the trail eases up the hill a little bit there is a fork in the trail at .5. Actually there is just an unofficial trail that goes to the left, drops back down to the creek and follows along the base of a neat bluff to the bottom of a waterfall—all of this is a wonderful SSS, especially when there is lots of water. Back at the fork, the main trail continues up the hill, above this bluff, until it crosses the little creek that feeds the waterfall at .7. The trail wraps around the top of this falls and a cascade just above it, and you can get a good look at the falls just ahead. Less than 100 feet past the falls is where the bluff has actually split open, forming a deep crevasse known as "Crack In Rock." A great SSS, but *be careful* here!

The trail continues along the top of the bluff and works its way to the right up into a side drainage (nice off-trail SSS), then begins to double back through the forest, crossing through a fence that we saw before. The trail intersects an old road at .9, TURNS RIGHT and follows the road downhill, past the 1.0 mile point. It soon becomes just trail again, and ends up back at the intersection with the Homestead Trail at 1.2—TURN LEFT and follow the trail back to the trailhead for a total hike of 1.5 miles.

Property Manager, City of Ft. Smith • 3900 Kelley Hwy. • Ft. Smith, AR 77904 • 479–784–2231

Artist Point Trail—CLOSED TO THE PUBLIC

This trail has been closed by the land owners due to vandalism and is no longer open to the public. *Please be respectful* of all the surroundings as you hike and always practice a good LEAVE NO TRACE ethic:

LEAVE nothing but footprints.
TAKE nothing but pictures.
KILL nothing but time.

THANK YOU!

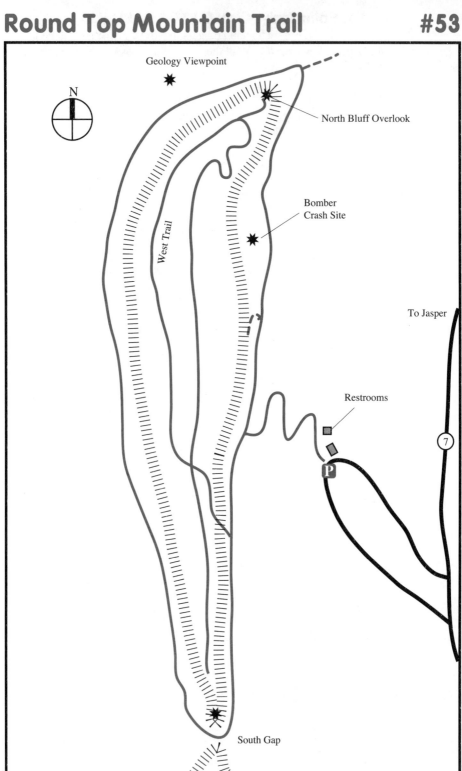

Geology Viewpoint

N

North Bluff Overlook

West Trail

Bomber
Crash Site

To Jasper

Restrooms

7

P

South Gap

Round Top Mountain Loop—3.6 miles

No doubt this is one of the most scenic trails in Arkansas, and also there is some rare history to go with it—some fragmented remains of a WWII bomber that crashed in 1948 can be viewed along the trail. The first part of the trail is all uphill, but it soon levels out and visits a terrific bluffline with great views, and has tons of wild-flower beds all over the place. To get to the trailhead, take Hwy. 7 south out of Jasper up the hill a couple of miles and turn right at the trail sign, then park at the end of the drive near the small building. The property is owned and maintained by volunteers from the Newton County Resource Council.

The trail starts out by climbing the steep hillside in four winding switchbacks—there are benches at every switchback! In fact, there are more than 30 benches located all along the route. At .2 there is a trail intersection—TURN RIGHT to visit the entire trail. It is all level now as the trail goes along a flat bench that is located just below the massive sandstone bluff that is up to your left—ALL of this area from here on is an SSS. Not only is the bluff beautiful, but you'll find thousands of wildflowers here in March and April. At .4 there is a small trail that goes to the left up to the base of the bluff, and to a little tunnel cave. The main trail continues along the bench and comes to the crash site at .5. There is an old rock wall and a bronze plaque that lists the date and names of the crew. You may find bits and pieces of the B-25 bomber that smashed into the hillside—like the wildflow-ers, these are all *protected*. Remain quiet at this site, and remember the sacrifice that our military folks make in order for us to live free in this country.

The trail continues along near the base of the bluff, past another little trail that drops down the hill to the right to a lookout point—if you are going to the top, the view is much better from up there. The main trail curves around the nose of the bluffline to the left, and comes to the Geology Viewpoint at .7, a special SSS area with giant moss-covered blocks of sandstone and a terrific view.

The trail remains level as it curves around to the left and to the back side of the mountain, past the 1.0 mile point. There are some views out towards the Little Buffalo Valley, and scores of wildflower fields on the forest floor. By 1.5 the trail has bumped up to a break in the bluffline known as South Gap, another great SSS! Once through the gap the trail turns to the left and remains close to the base of the bluff, going past a Na-tive American campsite area, and through a split in the bluffline, all of it an SSS.

There is a trail intersection at 1.7—TURN LEFT and go up a flight of stairs that will lead you to the top of the mountain. There is another intersection ahead—TURN RIGHT to head up to the main overlook (we will return to this spot via the West Trail). The trail eases up the hill some, following the top of the ridge, past milepoint 2.0, then tops out at the high point on the mountain. From there the trail begins to ease on down the hill to the right, and drops on down to another intersection—TURN RIGHT, then follow the trail on down to where it ends at the North Bluff Overlook at 2.3, a terrific SSS with a 200 degree view!

Now, take the trail back up to the last intersection and GO STRAIGHT, which will take you around the back side of the mountain on the West Trail. It is level and there are some great views. It will intersect with the main trail at 2.9—TURN RIGHT and take the short spur out to the top of South Gap, another great SSS, then return to the same intersection and TURN RIGHT and go back down the long flight of steps. TURN LEFT at the bottom of the steps, which will take you back to the last intersection at 3.4—TURN RIGHT and follow the switchbacks to the trailhead, a total hike of 3.6 miles.

Newton County Resource Council, 870–446–5898

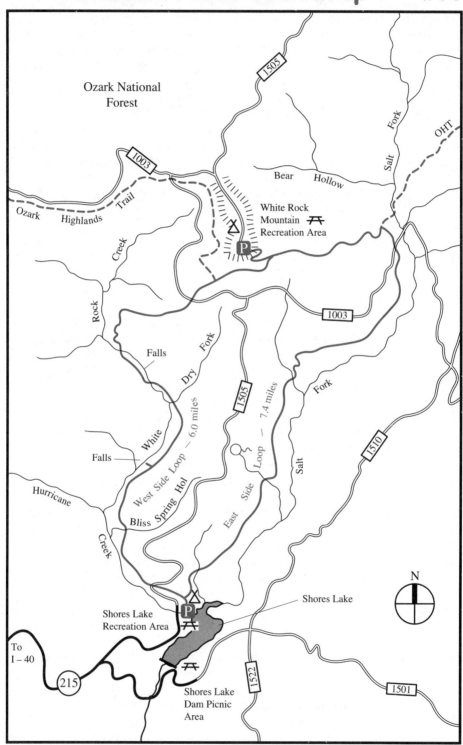

Shores Lake/White Rock Loop—13.4 miles

Shores Lake and White Rock are two of the most popular recreation areas in the Ozark National Forest, located northeast of Ft. Smith. This loop trail runs from Shores Lake past several nice waterfalls, up to the spectacular White Rock Mountain, then returns to the lake down through the Salt Fork drainage. This is the perfect weekend hike, especially if you are lucky enough to get a cabin at White Rock. Or you can dayhike either side of the loop, if you run a shuttle. The trail gains over 1700 feet in elevation during several good climbs. Bidville quad.

To get to the trailhead, take exit #24 off of I–40 (Mulberry exit), go north on Hwy. 215 to Fern, continue 3 miles and turn left at the sign onto FR#1505 (paved, also County Road 75), go to almost the end of the pavement and turn right into the campground and follow the signs to the trailhead. The trail is marked with blue blazes.

The trail begins at the signboard and heads out through the rocky forest, then splits—TURN LEFT on the *West Loop* (we'll return on the *East Loop* from the right). It runs past lots of big pines, crosses FR#1505, and continues through a rock garden area. It crosses Bliss Spring Hollow at 1.0, an SSS, then runs along the hillside and follows a couple of jeep roads down in the bottom. It passes a spur trail that heads down the hill to a waterfall on the creek—continue STRAIGHT AHEAD. The trail comes off the hillside, crosses Dry Creek, runs on another jeep road for a short distance, then crosses White Rock Creek at 2.7. Just beyond is a terrific SSS waterfall.

Soon the trail crosses the creek again, and begins a long, steep climb. It finally levels off at 4.1, and runs over to and across FR#1003 at 4.5. It follows an old roadbed up the hill to an intersection with the Ozark Highlands Trail (17.7 miles to the left to Lake Ft. Smith)—TURN RIGHT here (white blazes). Follow the OHT to another intersection at 5.6—TURN LEFT onto blue–blazed trail. This spur takes you on up to White Rock Mountain (see p. 52) at 6.0, a terrific place to spend the night, and one of the best sunset views in the state! The whole place is an SSS. Rent a cabin or the lodge and really enjoy your stay. The reservation number is 501–369–4128.

Now lets head back down the trail to Shores Lake. Head down the same spur trail that you came up on, and TURN LEFT at the OHT intersection (white blazes again)—we'll keep the mileage total running to include this spur—so this will be 6.4. The trail heads steeply down the hill, past some nice big trees, winding down off of the hillside. It runs on a jeep road part of the way. At 8.0 (just beyond OHT mile marker #20), TURN RIGHT off of the OHT and head off level—this is the EAST LOOP. This runs on over to a spur trail at 8.7 (it goes up a rocky hillside to the right to an SSS waterfall)—continue STRAIGHT here and cross FR#1003 just beyond.

This next section of trail is especially nice during leaf–off, 'cause the views are wonderful. It runs along mostly level, but dropping just a little. It drops on down to and across a creek at 10.5, then heads up to another SSS waterfall, and then joins a jeep road—TURN LEFT and run along the road a half mile to 11.2, then TURN LEFT off of the road. The trail runs along a steep hillside—lots of SSS views, then runs level for a while. It heads up the hill past a wonderful SSS area of boulders and huge trees, then drops on down the hillside and back to the intersection with the West Loop at 13.3. TURN LEFT here and return to the trailhead, for a total loop of 13.4 miles.

For a more complete description of this hike, as well as maps and descriptions of all the trails that connect with the Ozark Highlands Trail, be sure to get a copy of my *Ozark Highlands Trail Guide.*.

Agency List #3

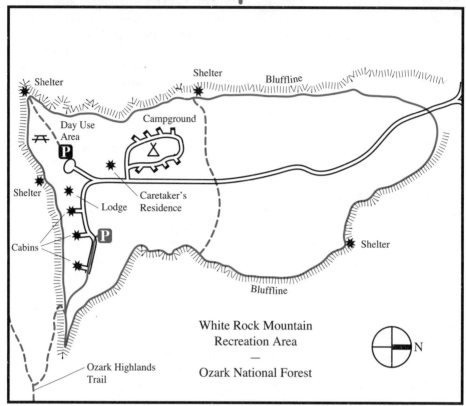

White Rock Rim Loop—2.1 miles

This is easily one of the most scenic hikes in Arkansas—*all* of it a definite SSS!!! The trail follows along the top of the bluffline up on White Rock Mountain. Along the trail you will find a great spot to watch the sunrise, and what I consider the best sunset in the entire state. The views are spectacular all year. This is a great getaway spot too—there are three cabins available for rent, as well as a "lodge" that sleeps up to 28, and a campground (call 479–369–4128 for reservations). Although this is a real easy trail to hike, nearly level all the way, you should not take small children with you—the risk of a fatal fall is just too great. To optimize the views, the trail runs close to the edge of the tall bluff most of the way. It's not a good idea to hike after dark (in fact much of the trail is closed after sunset), or while intoxicated—there have been a number of deaths related to these factors in the past few years. Bidville quad.

There are many ways to get to White Rock (at least nine that I know of), and all of them involve dirt road. RV's are not recommended. Here is the way with the *least* amount of dirt roads: Take exit #24 off of Interstate 40, go north on Hwy. 215 to Fern, continue about 3 miles to FR#1505 (paved, road names keep changing)—turn left here at the sign and go just over one mile to Shores Lake (the pavement ends here). Continue past the lake area on dirt road to FR#1003—turn left here, then right at the next intersection (FR#1505), then bear right at the next intersection (past the carved entrance rock), and follow the road on up the hill and into the White Rock Recreation Area. Past the campground the road forks—turn left and go past the Lodge and cabins and park at the trailhead for the Ozark Highlands Trail, which is marked with a *red* "P" on the map.

Head down this same road, following blue blazes, past the last cabin—the trail takes off at the end of the road. As it runs on out towards the end of the point, a trail comes in from the right—this is where we'll finish this loop—continue STRAIGHT AHEAD to the second intersection. The Ozark Highlands Trail takes off to the right here (one of the best long–distance trails in the country), but we want to once again continue STRAIGHT AHEAD. The trail from this point on is not marked or blazed, but it is easy to follow. Soon beyond, the trail comes to the end of the point and swings sharply back to the left—this point is a good spot to watch the sun rise during leaf–off.

As the trail heads on around on top of the bluff, you get some great views down onto the bluff itself—lots of lichen and moss and even a few ferns growing on the rock. By the way, this is a sandstone bluff. The drainage out in front of you is the Salt Fork Creek valley. The trail continues to hug the bluff, going past several large hardwood trees. At .4 the trail passes by a wonderful rock well cover. There are a number of open views through here. In fact, you can look out across Salt Fork to the first mountain beyond, which is Potato Knob Mountain, and see six or seven ridges past that. Needless to say, all of this is an SSS! Please remember to watch your step as you soak up everything.

At .8 there is a lesser cutoff trail that heads up the hill to the left—this is a short trail that goes up to the entrance road near the campground, and on over to the Rim Trail on the other side. At .9 the trail comes to one of the four rock pavilions along the trail—another fine example of CCC work. This is another great spot to watch the sunrise. Just beyond this shelter, you'll see a lot of rocks both above and below the trail that are covered with a thick carpet of moss—a special SSS area.

The trail swings away from the bluff to the left some at 1.0, then comes out onto the forest road that leads up to White Rock at 1.1. TURN LEFT and head up this road for just a hundred feet or so, then turn off of the road TO THE RIGHT, back on trail again. There was no sign here, so be alert for the trail. It continues along pretty level, passes under a power line, and then joins the top of the bluff on this west side at 1.2. You'll have a great view to the west from this point on for a while—a super SSS all the way! The trail eventually heads up a flight of steps and actually goes right through the second pavilion at 1.3. The cutoff trail that we passed on the other side joins us here—it goes up to the entrance road and down to the Rim Trail on the other side. Just past this spot there are a couple of other trails to the left that go up to the campground.

One of the best views is along here looking to the south at the rest of the bluffline out in front of you—and the third pavilion that is perched out on it in the distance. Everywhere is a great sunset view too. And a spectacular spot to view the colors in late October. The trail makes its way on over to that third pavilion at 1.7—the wide trail there that heads up the hill to the left goes into the picnic area (and toilets) and day use parking. This is perhaps the most scenic, and popular, spot on the mountain. No need to explain why. Our trail wraps around the point, swinging back to the left, and heads to the fourth and final pavilion at 1.8. This last stretch of trail runs just below the lodge and cabins, and there is at least one trail that goes up to each one of them.

As the trail makes its way to the east below the cabins, there are still some nice views to the south. After passing the last cabin, the trail swings left and intersects with the beginning of our loop at 2.0—TURN LEFT and head back up to the trailhead. The complete loop is 2.1 miles total.

Agency List # 3

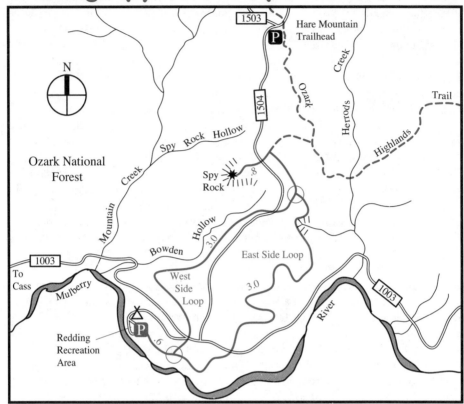

Redding/Spy Rock Loop—8.8 miles

This is one of four loop trails that connect with the Ozark Highlands Trail (OHT). It passes several nice waterfalls, and has a spur that goes on out to a wonderful view area called Spy Rock. Many folks use this trail to access the OHT. It's also a good dayhike—spend the day on the trail, eating lunch at Spy Rock. Redding Campground is a popular area with floaters, since it is right on the Mulberry River. There are 27 campsites here, plus flush toilets and showers (in season), and water.

To get to Redding, which is located on the Ozark National Forest, go just north of the community of Cass on Hwy. 23 (the Pig Trail), turn east onto FR#1003 (County Road 83—dirt), go about 3 miles and turn right onto the Redding Campground access road (big sign there), take the road on into the campground and you'll find a parking area on the right, next to the river. Cass quad.

The trail begins in the campground at the parking area that is shared with the river folks. It winds through the campground, past the bathhouse, and across the road into the woods. It is marked with blue blazes. The trail takes off TO THE RIGHT down a wide corridor that is actually the sewer line. It eventually leaves this wide corridor TO THE RIGHT and continues through a stand of pine trees. These were planted in 1962. If you look around a bit you can see the rows that the trees were planted in. In fact the trail goes right down some of these rows.

It winds around in the bottom, crosses an old roadbed, then comes to an intersection at .6. The left fork becomes the West Loop. The trail that goes straight ahead is the *East Loop*. We will go up the West Loop, on out to Spy Rock, and come back down the East Loop, so TURN LEFT here.

The West Loop runs alongside the stand of pines and comes out and crosses FR#1003 right at the entrance to Redding Campground at .8. It begins to climb up the hill into the woods. It winds around, past mile marker 1.0, then swings up and across a ridge. It turns right and continues climbing gradually, past mile 2.0. It eventually swings back to the left, and runs just below FR#1504.

In this area there is a pine tree marked with two blue blazes in the shape of a cross. Just down the hill from this spot is a large dug/blasted out hole with an old cable around it. *Caution*: If you have a dog or kids with you make sure that they stay well away from the edge—a fall in could be fatal. I won't go into the complete story about this hole, but here is the short version. It was dug (like many others in the area) by locals that were (still are) looking for a pot of gold that the Spanish buried some-where around when the area was first explored. "Spy Rock" got its name from this same era—a lookout was stationed there while the others buried the gold! I've never heard if anyone has ever found anything.

As the trail makes it way around the hill to the right you can look out to the north and see a rock outcrop at the end of a small ridge. This is Spy Rock. There is a spur trail on this route that runs out the top of that ridge to the nice view there. We continue around the hill, fairly level, past mile 3.0, then across FR#1504 at 3.2. The trail climbs up and over a hill, crosses an old road, and intersects with the East Loop at 3.6. (If you turn right here, it's 3.6 miles back to the campground via the East Loop—7.2 miles total loop.)

We're going to TURN LEFT here and head towards Spy Rock and the main OHT. The trail towards Spy Rock heads off down into the woods. It eventually eases up the hill just a little, then comes to a trail intersection at 4.0. TURN LEFT to go to Spy Rock. (If you turned right, you would head on over, down the hill just a little, and inter-sect with the main OHT after a little more than a half mile.) The trail crosses FR#1504, then runs on out the top of the ridge to Spy Rock at 4.4, and a terrific SSS view down into the Mulberry River Valley.

Now lets hike back to the East–West Loop intersection—I'm keeping a running mileage total that includes the trip out to Spy Rock and back, so back to this intersec-tion would be 5.2 total so far for the hike. We'll take the East Loop back. The East Loop makes its way on around the hill, down past an SSS view during leaf–off and passing a nice SSS waterfall at 5.7. There is a lot of neat stuff growing at the base of this falls—if you can only figure out how to get down and have a look at it! (The trail eventually passes mile marker #3, which is the mileage to Redding). It drops down and skirts around a regeneration area—be alert to where the trail is going. There are some SSS views along here during leaf–off.

It begins to drop down the hill, past another SSS waterfall at 6.7, (mile marker #2 is just beyond), and continues to work its way down the hill. It eventually crosses FR#1003 at 7.7. Just beyond, TURN LEFT onto a jeep road for a hundred feet, then TURN RIGHT, through an open campsite area and down into the woods. It winds up in the bottoms close to the Mulberry River, and eventually makes its way back to the intersection with the West Loop at 8.2. GO STRAIGHT AHEAD here, and follow the trail back to Redding. The total loop is 8.8 miles.

Agency List #6

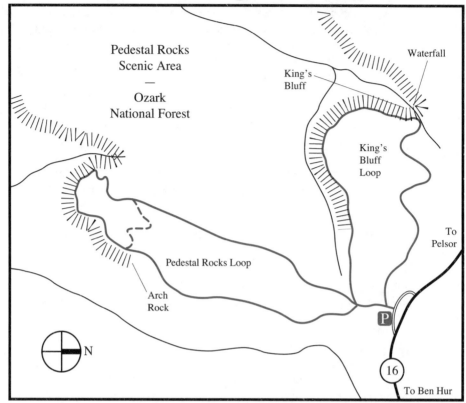

Pedestal Rocks
Scenic Area
—
Ozark
National Forest

King's
Bluff

Waterfall

King's
Bluff
Loop

Pedestal Rocks Loop

Arch
Rock

To
Pelsor

P

N

16

To Ben Hur

Pedestal Rocks/Kings Bluff Loops—4.3 miles total

There are actually two loops here, and both of them visit some spectacular and unique sandstone bluff formations, and have terrific SSS views. You will be awed by Kings Bluff, and the waterfall there. And won't believe how the wind and water have shaped Pedestal Rocks. All of this is located in the Pedestal Rocks Scenic Area, located near Ben Hur, just off of Hwy. 16 in the Ozark National Forest .

To get to the trailhead, turn off of Scenic 7 National Scenic Byway at the community of Pelsor (be sure to stop in Hankins Store there—it's an SSS!), which is north of Russellville and south of Jasper, onto Hwy. 16 east. Go about 6 miles and look for the sign on the right to the trailhead. If you make it to Ben Hur, you've gone too far—go back 2.5 miles.

***A word of caution. These trails hug the edge of high bluffs much of their route—this is *not* a place for small children, or intoxicated hikers! Railings have been added in certain areas, but you should be extremely careful everywhere.**

Both trails begin at the parking lot, cross a native stone bridge, and head over to a signboard—this is where they split. I will describe them separately, but you could always combine them for a longer hike, and more scenery! Either trail is wonderful. Sand Gap quad.

PEDESTAL ROCKS LOOP—2.6 miles total. From the parking lot, head into the woods across the rock bridge to the fork in the trail and go STRAIGHT AHEAD

(Kings Bluff trail goes to the right). It runs on around a small hill and down to a road intersection—TURN LEFT and head down the road. Soon it intersects with the end of the Kings Bluff Trail (comes in from the right)—the road goes straight ahead (we'll return from there), but you want to TURN LEFT off of the road and into the woods.

The trail continues along and drops just a little on another road trace—TURN RIGHT off of the road as it gets steep, and head across the hillside. It eventually drops down to and joins the road again, then runs fairly level, past a neat SSS waterfall on the left at .5, and continues to work on around the ridge. It stays on the road trace for a while, passing a couple of smaller falls and low bluffs. Soon you come to the first of many SSS's at .8, and "arch rock" on the left—it's big enough to drive a truck under!

This begins the main bluff area, and the trail from now on for a while follows along the top of the bluffline—it's simply spectacular. The rock formations. The view. Take your time and be careful. At .9 there is a lesser trail that heads up the hill to the right—it connects back to the road. We continue STRAIGHT AHEAD, through a wonderland of sandstone. There are several "pedestals," and lots of other neat stuff. You are looking down into the Illinois Bayou drainage.

The trail continues on the bluffline around the ridge to the right, past a set of steps that lead under the bluffs, and finally to the "main" pedestal at 1.4. Just beyond the trail begins to switchback gradually up the hill, back across the hillside. It finally levels out and intersects with a road trace at 1.7—TURN RIGHT and follow the road (just beyond, the cutoff trail that goes down to the "arch rock" takes off to the right). The hike back is a nice stroll, and ends at the trailhead at 2.6.

KINGS BLUFF LOOP—1.9 miles total. From the trailhead, go across the rock bridge to where the trail splits and TURN RIGHT. The trail takes off on an old road trace. It swings to the right some, uphill just a little, then levels off and begins to descend. There are lots of large trees through here, and open woods. BEAR LEFT AT .3, and then TURN RIGHT soon after as the trail leaves the road trace and heads down the hill. It swings back to the left, into a small drainage, then switchbacks to the right, swinging on down the hillside. Another left turn, then back to the right, and finally at .9 it comes to a creek and swings to the left, and comes out on the top of Kings Bluff—a spectacular SSS area!

This is one remarkable spot. The view out in front is wonderful. And the creek spills over the edge as one of the tallest waterfalls in this part of the Ozarks—nearly 100 feet. *Be careful all through this area,* and stay behind the hand rails—it's a long way to the bottom! This is the perfect spot to bring a picnic lunch to, and spend some time at.

The top of the bluff is very wide, and the trail swings to the left on top of it. It swings back to the right, past a break in the bluff, then continues on along the top of the bluffline—all of this area for quite a while is a major SSS! The features of the bluff as well as the view just keep getting better and better. Especially the bluff. To me, this part of the bluff is just as interesting as the Pedestal Rocks bluff. It's kind of hard to describe it—you'll just have to come on out and have a look.

The trail continues on top of the bluff, to the left and up into a ravine. By 1.4 the bluff has pretty much broken up, and the trail works its way up the ravine. It swings around the head of the hollow to the right, then levels off and comes to an intersection at 1.8—this is the Pedestal Rocks Loop. TURN LEFT and follow the old road just a few feet, then TURN RIGHT off of the old road onto trail, back to the trailhead at 1.9.

If you do both loops together, you'll hike about 4.3 miles total.

Agency List #2

Hawksbill Crag Trail

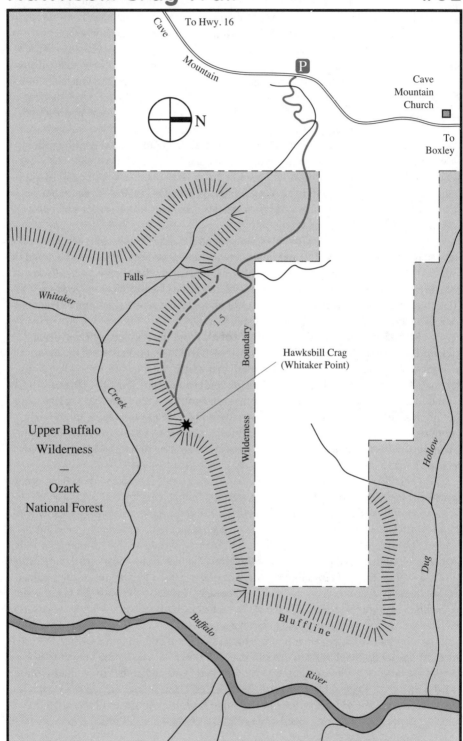

To Hwy. 16

Cave Mountain

P

Cave Mountain Church

To Boxley

N

Falls

Whitaker

Boundary

1.5

Hawksbill Crag (Whitaker Point)

Creek

Wilderness

Upper Buffalo Wilderness

—

Ozark National Forest

Hollow

Dug

Buffalo

Bluffline

River

Hawksbill Crag Trail—3.0 miles round trip

Hawksbill Crag is one of the most recognizable spots in Arkansas. It's an amazing rock outcrop that sticks out from the top of a tall bluff, and is usually photographed with hikers on it. It is located in the 14,200 acre Upper Buffalo Wilderness Area of the Ozark National Forest, near the Buffalo River. There is a well-used trail that runs from the parking lot on out to the Crag. *VERY CROWDED TRAIL*, especially on weekends.

To get to the trailhead, begin at Boxley Valley in Buffalo National River, at the intersection of Hwy. 21 & 43. Head south on Hwy. 21, 1.2 miles. Just before the highway crosses the Buffalo River TURN RIGHT on a dirt road—it literally heads straight *up* the hillside! (We heard a rumor in 2021 that the first mile may be paved in the future, but who knows.) Follow this road 'till you pass Cave Mountain Church and cemetery on the right (5.4 miles from the Hwy.). Continue past the church for another .6 mile to the (expanded?) parking lot. Boxley quad. A normal car can usually make this drive.

From the parking lot the trail heads into the woods (the first half mile may change with a new parking lot). It drops down the hill slightly, crosses a small stream, then switchbacks down a steeper hillside. It crosses the stream again, then runs level out to a "Wilderness" sign and some blue blazes—these mark the wilderness area boundary. Red blazes (also purple) mean private property—steer clear of them. From here the trail continues out on the level, into the wilderness area, winding around as it drops down some. During leaf-off you can begin to see out into the Whitaker Creek drainage.

The trail swings back to the left, drops down to and across a small stream at 1.0. There are a couple of great SSS waterfalls just downstream from here that you might want to look at—a really neat area in the springtime. In fact, this is a great spot to explore around a while either on your way in or out. Be careful though—the rocks can be slick and the landing is a hard one!

From the stream, the trail swings left and up, onto an old road bed, and follows it to the right and on the level for a while. At one spot, the trail eases over close to the edge, near some boulders and a nice view. But for the most part, it stays back away from the edge for safety reasons. Eventually, the trail leaves the roadbed to the right, and drops down to the edge of the bluff. It turns to the left and continues on along the rim and a terrific SSS view. At this point you can look ahead and all of a sudden, there it is—Hawksbill Crag—one of the most major SSS's in Arkansas! *Please be careful* in this area—if you go to the edge to have a look and slip, you'll probably die.

Whitaker Creek, which is what you are looking down on when you are on the Crag, is a terrific place to explore if you have the time. The best way to get down into it is via a break in the bluffline, about a third of a mile west from the Crag. It's a steep descent, but once you get down, is well worth it. You should hike both up and downstream on the creek (it empties into the Buffalo River)—there are some nice waterfalls up in the headwaters. Spend some time hiking along the base of the bluff that the Crag is on too—it's a pretty spectacular bluff even from below!

The total length from the parking lot to the Crag is 1.5 miles. To get back to the trailhead, return the same way that you came. If you want a really scenic trip back, stay on top of the bluffline (below the main trail) back to the waterfalls mentioned earlier, then go upstream a hundred yards back to the main trail—you'll have a wonderful SSS hike along the rim, with great views down into Whitaker Creek.

By the way, you cannot see my cabin from the Crag, but you can see a barn and house on the distant hillside, which are owned by an original 1800's homestead family.

Agency List #4

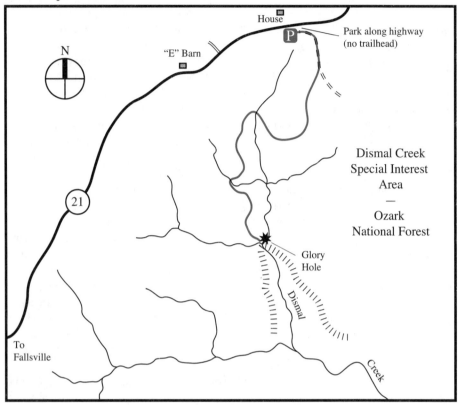

Glory Hole—1.9 miles round trip

This is another neat little spot that many have visited, but most couldn't find—until now. The trail is an old road that drops down the hill to this most unique spot. A creek has actually drilled a large hole through the roof of a big overhanging bluff, and the creek pours right down through the roof. It's a pretty remarkable thing to see when the water is running well! ***VERY CROWDED TRAIL***, especially on weekends.

To get to the spot to begin this hike, take Hwy. 16/21 east out of Fallsville (a National Scenic Byway) for 5.7 miles. Here you will pass a red barn on the left that has a large, white "E" on the side of it. Go .5 miles past this barn, just past a dirt road that leaves the highway to the left, and pull off opposite a house that is up on the hill to the left—there will be a mailbox at the driveway to this house just across the road from you. Park here along the paved shoulder—there isn't much room on weekends though. (If you come to the Cassville Baptist Church, you've gone .7 of a mile too far. This pull–off is also 2.3 miles west of Edwards Junction) Fallsville quad.

The route to the Glory Hole begins right there as a jeep road that heads down-hill slightly into the woods and to the left (probably won't be marked or signed). Follow this road as it levels off and swings to the right, then straightens out. You could drive this road if you've got a 4wd vehicle, but the walk will be better for you! At .3, there is a lesser jeep trail that forks TO THE RIGHT—take this fork (the main jeep road contin-ues straight ahead). This faint trace heads down the hill, eventually swings back to the right and crosses a creek (the one that makes the Glory Hole) at .7. Stay on the road as it heads downstream. (Or if you want some adventure, and want to see several other waterfalls, just follow the creek all the way there!)

The roadbed gets chocked with pine saplings, but you can make your way along it. It drops on down the hillside, swings back to the right, then left, and eventually ends abruptly at .9—this is a good sign, for the Glory Hole is just beyond! From this spot, head down the hill, off to the left a little, through a small bluff area, and you'll come out in a wet, fragile, glade area. (The "Hole," will be off to your left— ***be extremely careful!!!***) To get down underneath the bluff, make your way over to the right (try to go around the glade please), 'till you see the spot near a couple of large rocks where you can get down. This is a terrific area, with lots of big boulders and bluffs—a major SSS. Head back the same way that you came in—perhaps take the creek route!

Agency List # 4

Kings River Falls Trail #38

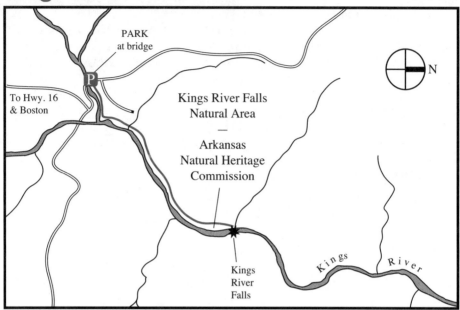

PARK
at bridge

P

To Hwy. 16
& Boston

Kings River Falls
Natural Area

—

Arkansas
Natural Heritage
Commission

N

Kings
River
Falls

Kings River

Kings River Falls Trail—1.7 miles round trip

This short, easy to hike trail will take you to the waterfall that is pictured on the cover of this book. The spot is an "Arkansas Natural Area," and is administered by the Natural Heritage Commission. Many people find this trail difficult to get to, but it's real easy if you follow these directions: From the used–to–be community of Boston on Hwy. 16 (between Fallsville and St. Paul), go north on County Road #3175 (gravel) for two miles, then turn right as the road forks on CR#3415. Stay on this road 2.4 miles (it gets rough in a spot or two, but don't give up), 'till you come to a "T" intersection, and turn left on CR#3500. Go a couple of hundred yards and park at the trailhead, which is located at the bridge that goes across Mitchell Branch. (This trailhead was built in 2009—the old one next to the crumbling barn is no longer there.) Weathers quad.

This is an easy, level trail (perfect for kids) that is marked with blue blazes. The trail begins at the parking area and heads downstream along the top of a small levy, and follows in between the creek (on the right) and hay field/fenceline (on the left). It comes alongside the Kings River and follows the field to the left, then crosses a small stream. Parts of the old trail were washed away by the river so the trail was moved up onto the edge of the field here and continues downstream. There is an old rock wall part of the way that defines the hay field. Besides tons of wildflowers that carpet the area in the spring, there are lots of wild azaleas around too. Stay next to the river, and you'll eventually come to the Natural Area boundary sign—the wonderful waterfall and pool are just beyond at .85. There is a small side creek coming in from the left there that has some nice waterfalls once in a while. The immediate area of the big falls was once used as a grist mill site—can you spot the marks carved into the stone?

This area is pretty nice all around—plan to spend some time here! To return to the trailhead, head back upstream the way that you came in.

Agency List #39

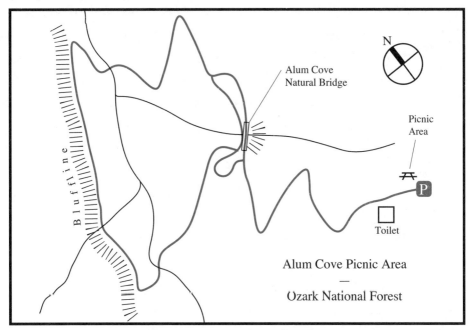

Alum Cove
Natural Bridge

N

Picnic
Area

P

Toilet

Alum Cove Picnic Area
—
Ozark National Forest

Bluffline

Alum Cove Trail—1.1 miles

This wonderful little trail visits one of the largest natural rock bridges in this part of the country. It loops around past a nice bluffline too. There is some tall timber, and lots of flowers, including a rare variety of Shooting Star. This trail is located in the Ozark National Forest. There is a picnic area here, but no camping is allowed.

To get to Alum Cove, take Hwy. 7 south out of Jasper. Turn right on Hwy. 16 towards the community of Deer. After about a mile turn right off of Hwy. 16 onto Forest Road #1206. Take the forest road to the next sign and turn right. Deer quad.

The trail heads on down the hill, and switchbacks down 'till it reaches the natural bridge—of course an SSS (there are several benches along the way). You can walk right out on top of the bridge—it's 130 feet long and 12 feet thick. During the wet season there is a waterfall or two that pours into the open area behind it. The trail loops on down underneath the bridge too. This is where the bridge is most impressive. I took a photograph from this spot one time of the *sun* rising underneath the bridge!

From the base of the bridge the trail continues on down the hill a little and crosses a stream, then works its way up the other side to a wonderful bluffline. The first thing that you see along the bluff is a cave entrance. It doesn't go in very far, but it does have two different entrances and is a neat little spot. All of this area is an SSS!

The trail turns right at the bluff and follows it along for a while. The bluff is made from sandstone (so is the natural bridge), and so has been easily carved out by eons of wind and water. At one point the bluff splits and you can walk behind it. In many spots the bluff is covered with lots of lichens, mosses and ferns. During the wet season, there is a nice waterfall that pours over the bluff. All too soon the trail leaves the bluff, drops back down to and across the small stream, and heads back up to the other end of the natural bridge. Follow the trail back up to the trailhead.

Agency List #4

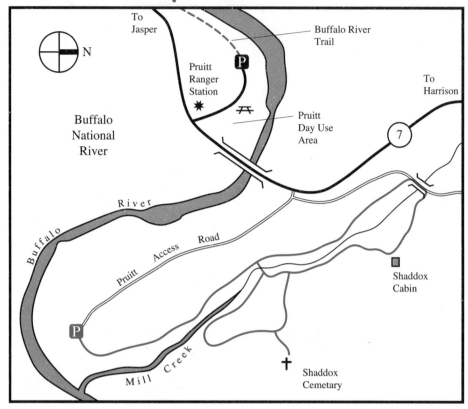

Mill Creek Loop—2.2 miles round trip

If you are traveling down National Scenic 7 Byway between Harrison and Jasper, you should stop at Pruitt and hike this short trail. It is located at Buffalo National River, just off of Hwy. 7 at the lower end of the Pruitt river access. It is easy to walk, and goes through a variety of forest and stream environments, not to mention a couple of historical spots.

The trailhead is on the north side of the river (turn right at the "Pruitt Access" sign). Go down to the access area and find the trailhead sign—park off to the left. The sign reads "Mill Creek Trail—1 mile loop" (it's actually 2.2 miles). Jasper quad.

The trail takes off level from the trailhead beside the Buffalo River. This is a nice, easy, level walk for the most part. It swings to the left and begins to follow Mill Creek, a quiet medium–sized creek. The trail runs through a pretty open bottomland hardwood forest. It veers to the right and rises up over a small bluff, then down to a trail intersection on the other side. The sign reads "Low water trail—turn right (across river), High water trail—straight ahead." The creek here is pretty wide, and usually you'll have to wade the shallow water if you want to go across. You'll have that option on the way back, so for now we'll go STRAIGHT AHEAD.

The trail continues alongside the creek until it comes to a dirt road—TURN RIGHT on the road and cross Mill Creek on a low cement bridge. Just across the other side, TURN RIGHT off of the road onto the trail again—there is a sign.

This section works its way downstream and gradually uphill, and heads up to the Shaddox cabin. This structure has actually been recycled. It was built using the logs from an old log home which stood near this site. Re–use of old buildings was characteristic of thrifty Ozarkers. The trail crosses in front of the cabin, and then works its way back down the small hill again. It swings through the forest and comes to a trail intersection—go straight and you'll end up back at the creek crossing. TURN LEFT for the continuation of the trail.

The trail goes through an old grown–up field, and under a power line, then back into the woods, and to another trail intersection. TURN LEFT, and a short spur leads up the hill to Shaddox Cemetery. This one is larger than most you'll see in the area. Ezekiel Shaddox, the builder of the original log house, is buried in this cemetery. When you are finished looking around, head back down to the trail intersection and continue straight ahead.

This section gradually comes down off the hill, through the woods and back to Mill Creek It turns right and heads back upstream alongside the creek. At one point, a step has been carved out of a giant tree that fell across the trail and embedded itself part–way into the earth. Soon after, you'll reach the point where you either cross Mill Creek, or continue on back to the cement bridge (if the water is too high).

Agency List #17

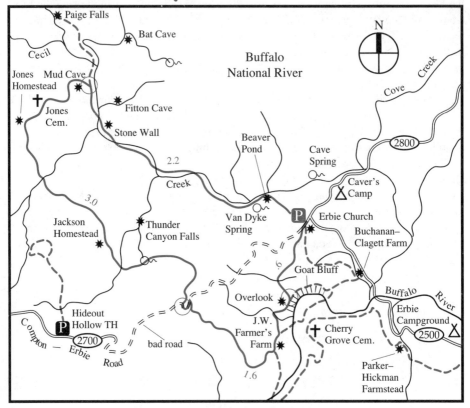

Cecil Cove Loop—7.4 miles

This scenic trail runs along Cecil Creek (crossing it several times), then loops back up high on a bench and drops down to the Buffalo River and Goat Bluff—there are lots of SSS's along the way. It visits many historical sites too. Camping is allowed. All of the trail is located in Buffalo National River. Jasper and Ponca quads.

The trailhead is located on the other side of the Buffalo River from Erbie Campground, and just across the road from the old Erbie Church. There are several ways to get to this area, but the old route from Compton via the Compton-Erbie road is NOT RECOMMENDED. #1) From Hwy. 206 at Gaither, take the Erbie Cutoff Road/NC#2825 south (next to the water tower, paved, then gravel) for 2.2 miles then TURN RIGHT onto NC#2800 (gravel) for 5.6 miles to Erbie. #2) From Hwy. 7 at Marble Falls take NC#2800 (gravel) west 7.4 miles to Erbie. #3) You can also get there by fording the Buffalo River from the Erbie Campground area (but only when the River is low!).

The trail begins off to the right of the toilets, and heads downhill on an old road bed. It eventually leaves the old road TO THE RIGHT and continues down the hillside. At .3 it comes to a beaver pond and dam, which is actually the water from Van Dyke Spring that emerges from the base of a bluff just upstream. You can cross the top of the dam, or cross the small stream below it. The trail heads upstream to the left along the spring pool (you don't cross Cecil Creek yet), past Van Dyke Spring at .4 on the left.

The trail continues on up the valley, passing through the middle of an old corn field. Cecil Creek is just off to the right. This is a nice, level, easy walk.

The trail comes alongside the creek for a time, then swings away through an open forest. There are lots of rock piles in here—these were once cleared to create a field.

At mile 1.0 the trail crosses Cecil Creek for the first time. This spot is home to countless smooth rocks of all sizes that have been polished by the creek for ages. After the crossing, the trail heads off into the woods, still on the level, through some scrub trees and cedar thickets, and away from the creek. At 1.2 it comes back alongside the creek for a brief period, than back away from it again.

At 1.4 the trail crosses the creek again. Once on the other side, the trail turns right and continues upstream. And it passes another SSS area—where a bluff comes down into the creek. As the trail goes on, it passes through several more cedar thickets. Sometimes the trees are so thick that they form a canopy over the trail—kind of like walking through a green tunnel! The trail rises up onto a high bank, looking down on the river. Then it comes down to and crosses the creek for the third time at 1.8.

Back into the scrub timber the trail heads, then comes out alongside not only the creek but right next to one of the best rock walls that I know of in the Ozarks. Although this isn't really a "natural" thing, I'd have to consider this spot an SSS. The main thing that strikes me about this wall is that it's so wide and stable. It was built by pioneers who cleared the creekside woods for use as a field (the remains of the homesite are across the creek).

Just past the wall, the trail drops down to and crosses the creek at mile 2.0. It goes up onto a bench and gets away from the creek—you won't see the creek again. So if you are going to do the entire loop and need to get water, now is the time to do it!

The trail swings to the left, and climbs up the hillside to a trail intersection at 2.2. (Just off to the left of this trail intersection is the site of a former church—only a few foundation rocks remain now.) A lesser trail turns to the right—it is a primitive route (not really a trail) that makes its way up a hill to a spectacular waterfall area— Broadhollow Falls. We're going to continue on the main trail, and continue *up* the hill on an old woods road. And I do mean *UP*. This begins a rather long and steep climb.

At the first turn in the trail you can see a bluff area straight ahead—this is actually Mud Cave, a spot where the churchgoers went to hold services during the heat of summer. The trail continues *up* the hill, and during leaf–off there are some nice views back up into the headwaters of Cecil Creek.

The trail does level off somewhat, swings back to the left, then back to the right again, and then eases up the hillside some more. There are several lesser old roadbeds and gullies that intersect the trail—just continue on what you perceive is the right track.

After another little climb, at 2.7 we come to the Jones Cemetery. From here the trail continues on uphill just a little, winds around, then comes next to a couple of old log structures. Just beyond at 2.9 there is an intersection—turn right for a short walk to the middle of the old homestead of William J. Jones. There is about half of the chimney and the rock foundation left. You can tell that this was once a large home.

Back at the trail intersection, the main trail TURNS LEFT and continues. It's a pretty easy walk now for a while. Soon the Faddis–Keaton homestead appears off to the right, marked by a rock wall along the trail. There are some wonderful old oak trees here, and one of the biggest walnut trees you'll ever see. And the trail crosses a spring– fed stream here too—probably one of the reasons why they choose this spot to live!

The trail is on an old roadbed, and it sort of meanders around through the woods, crossing several small streams. One of these streams, at 3.4, is an SSS area that is full of giant boulders. During the wet season there are lots of waterfalls here. Eventually the trail heads up the hill, then continues on the level again.

Once up on the level, you will pass another old homestead — the Franks–Jackson place. What a neat spot to live. It sits on this narrow bench, with a great view out to the rest of the world, and even a spring for water.

At 4.3 there is another SSS — an area of boulders that in spring would reveal a lot of tumbling waterfalls. This is a good spot to stop and survey the country around you. Soon there is a bluffline that appears just above the trail. And lots of moss–covered rocks. We'll follow this bluffline to the nose of a ridge, as the trail curves around to the right at 5.0 and is now facing the Buffalo River Valley.

During leaf–off you'll be able to see the fields down on the river at Erbie, and a dirt road comes into view below — we intersect with that road at 5.2. TURN LEFT on this road, and walk down it for a short distance. (This is the Compton/Erbie road — if you turned right you'd come out at Hwy. 43 at Compton.)

After about 800 feet, TURN RIGHT onto an old road at 5.4 — it is blocked with large rocks, but there is no sign. (You can continue down this road for a short cut — it's just over a mile back to the trailhead — but you'll miss some nice SSS's.) The main trail eases up the hill, then levels off for a short time, passes a spur that goes to the right up to an old homesite, and begins to drop down the hillside. It passes under a powerline, and also by a wonderful display of worn out tires! The hill gets pretty steep and rocky at times, but you have a nice view of the opposite hillside across the river.

The trail makes a turn back to the left and goes through pine woods on a little lesser grade at 6.2, then resumes its downward trend and finally comes out to a "T" intersection at 6.4. This is the old J.W. Farmer homestead.

The trail that we have intersected is the Old River Trail, which runs from Ponca to Erbie. This is the main horse trail through the area. If you turned right you would be going towards Camp Orr. We want to TURN LEFT at this intersection. Just past a wood spring house, the old road that we've been walking on continues straight ahead and slightly downhill, but we want to TURN LEFT off of the old road onto a trail into the woods.

The trail continues on the level between some "pancake" bluffs on the left and a field on the right. Then it swings away from the field, crosses a small stream, then makes its way up a hillside. And this hillside is the beginning of a large SSS. There are lots of slab rocks and wonderful old, twisted cedar trees everywhere. The trail does get a little steep though. It finally levels off at 6.7. There are some great views of the Buffalo River and the fields along it at Erbie.

At 6.8 we come to a "T" trail intersection. The main trail TURNS LEFT. (To the right is the *Goat Bluff Trail* — it runs along on top of "Goat Bluff" for a third of a mile — lots of great views and twisted old cedars — an SSS all the way). The trail runs pretty level through a cedar thicket with a large field off to the right. At 7.1 it comes alongside a rock wall.

Soon the trail comes out onto the park road at 7.3. (This is the road that you would have taken if you wanted to take the short cut while back up on the hill.) TURN RIGHT and walk down the road, and by 7.4 you will come to the trailhead and will have finished the Cecil Cove Loop!

Agency List #17

Koen Interpretive Trail   #39

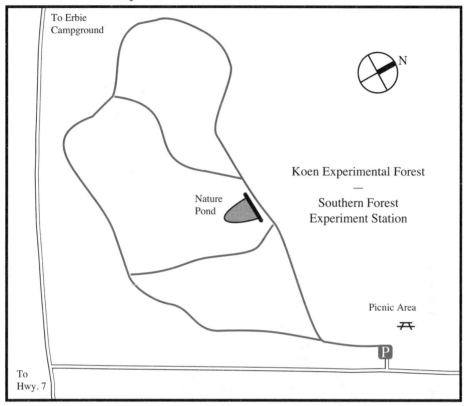

Koen Interpretive Loop—.5 mile

If you are looking for a nice leisurely stroll through a variety of tree species, this is the trail for you. There are at least 34 different kinds of trees and other plants identified along this short loop. To get to the trailhead, turn off of Hwy. 7 about 2.3 miles south of Pruitt at the Erbie Campground sign, go less than a half mile and turn right. After a couple of hundred yards, turn left into the trailhead parking area. There are several picnic tables here, and also benches scattered along the trail. Jasper quad.

The Henry R. Koen Experimental Forest was established in 1950 to develop scientific principles of forest management and to define and evaluate land management concerns. There is a great deal of research that has been and is going on in this small tract of land. Mr. Koen was Supervisor of the Ozark National Forest from 1922—1939.

There really isn't much of a description that I can give you here—you just need to get out and walk this one. Be sure to pick up a trail guide that is available at the trailhead—it describes all of the plant species that are highlighted. These include: black cherry, winged elm, prickly pear, red mulberry, plume grass, common persimmon, box elder, winged sumac, wild plum, honeylocust, sycamore, white ash, mockernut hickory, shortleaf pine, pitch pine, eastern redbud, black locust, black raspberry, buckbrush, Indian cherry, black walnut, eastern white pine, Virginia pine, sassafras, tulip poplar, loblolly pine, eastern red cedar, flowering dogwood, hackberry, chinkapin oak, summer grape, chokevine, blackberry and southern red oak.

Agency List #4

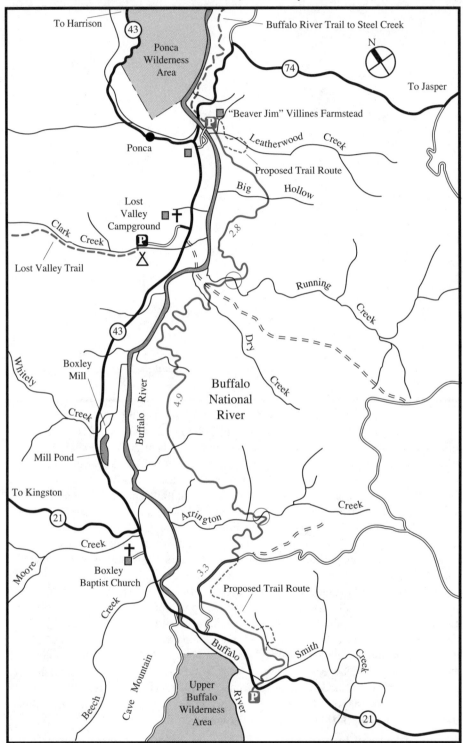

Buffalo River Trail—South Boxley to Ponca—11.0 miles one way

This is the beginning of the Buffalo River Trail, one of the longest in Arkansas. The first stretch winds around the hills on the east side of the Buffalo River, giving views of the river and historic Boxley Valley seldom seen. It ends at the low water bridge at Ponca, where the rest of the trail continues on to Pruitt, a total length of 36.5 miles (see next page). The trail is not blazed. Boxley, Murray and Ponca quads.

The trail begins at the South Boxley Trailhead, which is located on Hwy. 21, 1.1 miles south of where it crosses the Buffalo River—turn right off of the highway and into the parking area. This is also the site of the original Whiteley homestead.

From the parking area, cross the highway and follow a road through a gate and across Smith Creek (may be a wet crossing). TURN LEFT off of the road just past the creek, and skirt the left side of a large field. The trail continues to the right along the left side of the field, at the base of a steep hillside, then begins to head up the hill, and swings steeply back to the left along the nose of a ridge. It soon tops out and levels off. It comes to a much larger field at .6—go into the field and TURN RIGHT (a new section of trail *may* be built in the future to bypass this field area—see map). Follow along the right (uphill) side of this field (lots of great SSS views!), 'till the end at 1.7 and TURN RIGHT onto a county road. Follow this road to where it is woods on both sides (new stretch would rejoin here) and at 2.2 and TURN LEFT off the road onto trail.

The trail heads down the hillside, then levels for a while through a great beech forest, winds past several SSS waterfall "mini canyons," joins an old road trace, and finally leaves the trace TO THE LEFT and comes to Arrington Creek at 3.3, an SSS. It crosses the creek, then another smaller one (SSS too!), then heads *up* the hillside. It finally levels out and soon joins an old road trace at 4.1—TURN LEFT and follow this road. It's level walking for a while—stay on the main road trace—past several springs and an old homesite area. When you come to an SSS spot where a spring comes out of the base of a giant, moss–covered boulder on the right at 5.6, the trail leaves the main road trace TO THE LEFT just *after*, and heads down the hillside on a lesser road trace.

It soon swings to the right, crosses a small creek, then becomes real trail again, and goes along the top of a bluff, and a great SSS view at 6.0. It continues along the edge of a steep hillside, working in and out of several draws, and eventually drops down to and across Dry Creek at 7.6. From there it heads uphill just a little, goes across a road, picks up a short stretch of old road trace (past an old homesite and above Pearly Spring), then turns back to the right on plain trail and runs alongside and above Running Creek, which it crosses at 8.2. From there it heads to the right, then swings left and goes *up* the hill. It continues mostly on the level for a while, along the edge of the hillside (great SSS views all along). See the entrance road to Lost Valley across the way at 9.1.

The trail works its way around the head of Big Hollow on an old road trace, and remains pretty level. It passes a cave entrance and two giant sink holes at 10.3 (100'+ across—SSS!), then swings around to the left and begins a *steep* descent down the middle of a narrow ridge—you can look out ahead and see Ponca, and even glimpse Roark Bluff in the distance. The trail crosses an elk path, then continues down to the low water bridge across the Buffalo River at 11.0.

For a detailed description of this hike, get my *Buffalo River Hiking Trails* guidebook—see page 190.

Agency List #17

Buffalo River Trail (Ponca to Pruitt) #13

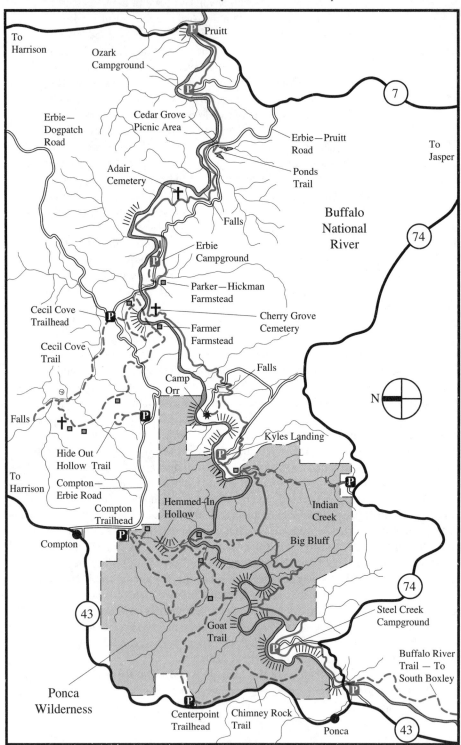

To
Harrison

Pruitt

Ozark
Campground

7

Cedar Grove
Picnic Area

Erbie—
Dogpatch
Road

Erbie—Pruitt
Road

To
Jasper

Adair
Cemetery

Ponds
Trail

74

Falls

Buffalo
National
River

Erbie
Campground

Parker—Hickman
Farmstead

Cecil Cove
Trailhead

Cherry Grove
Cemetery

Farmer
Farmstead

Cecil Cove
Trail

Falls

Camp
Orr

Falls

N

Kyles Landing

Hide Out
Hollow Trail

To
Harrison

Compton—
Erbie Road

Indian
Creek

Compton
Trailhead

Hemmed-In
Hollow

Big Bluff

Compton

74

Steel Creek
Campground

43

Goat
Trail

Buffalo River
Trail — To
South Boxley

Ponca
Wilderness

Centerpoint
Trailhead

Chimney Rock
Trail

Ponca

43

72

Buffalo River Trail—Ponca to Pruitt—25.5 miles one way

This is one of the longest trails in Arkansas, and one of the most scenic! There are several stretches of the trail complete now, but there may be more in the future. The trail in the Park is currently completed from S. Boxley to Ponca (see page 71), this stretch from Ponca to Pruitt, and from Woolum to Hwy. 65, just past Tyler Bend (see page 83). Plans for the rest of the trail are not complete at this time—check with the Park Service office in Harrison for the latest information. I will give you a brief description of the section from Ponca to Pruitt here—for a *complete*, mile–by–mile description of this section,, get my **Buffalo River Hiking Trails** book (see page 190). Ponca and Jasper quads.

There are a lot of access points on this trail. Besides Ponca and Pruitt, you can join the trail at Steel Creek (campground, canoe access), Kyles Landing (campground, canoe access), Erbie (campground, canoe access), and Ozark (campground, canoe access). A wonderful opportunity that this trail gives you is to hike part of it upstream, then get in a canoe and float back to where you started (or canoe down and hike back up). This would give you the best of both worlds—being able to see this terrific country from below and above.

This section of the Buffalo River Trail begins at Ponca (take Hwy. 43 south out of Harrison), across the old low–water bridge, and on the other side of the Buffalo River, through a gate. Park in the parking area before you cross the bridge though. A word of warning here—if you plan to be on the trail overnight, don't park your car here—take it on into Ponca—the river could come up and sweep it away!

The trail takes off to the LEFT. It crosses under the highway bridge, then heads out into a cedar thicket, with a couple of large beech trees here and there, and basically follows the river downstream. The trail is not marked with any type of blazes, although for the most part it is easy to follow. There are many great views along here, of the river, the bluffs along it, and of the hills across the way. The trail eases up the hill to some bluffs, through a neat split in one of them at 1.2,—an SSS—then back down again. There are a lot of SSS's along this stretch. It eventually heads on towards Steel Creek Campground at 1.6—turn left to go into the campground area, but the main trail continues STRAIGHT AHEAD. One of the highlights here is Roark Bluff, which is just across a large field and on the other side of the river.

The trail swings to the right past the campground, crosses the access road to the Steel Creek area, and comes to a spur to the trailhead there at 2.0 (outdoor phone located at the group of buildings at the far end of the field). A lot of times you can spot elk in the fields here, so be on the lookout for them. From the trailhead the trail takes off uphill, up a series of steps, and past some real nice moss–covered rocks. It heads *up* the hill, goes around a Ranger residence (which can be seen down below), levels off, then drops on down to and across Steel Creek at 2.6. Steel Creek forms the boundary of the Ponca Wilderness Area. This is one of the finest wilderness areas in the state, and includes such wonderful things as Indian Creek, Hemmed–In Hollow and Big Bluff. It contains 11,300 acres, and we'll be in it almost all the way to Kyles Landing.

Once across the creek the trail heads uphill again, winds around through some nice stuff, and comes out to an incredible SSS view at 3.4 where, if the climb hasn't taken your breath away, the view certainly will. It's a panoramic view of the river, the Steel Creek complex, all the bluffs in the area, and the hills beyond. The river makes a wide sweeping curve below you and heads out of sight around a corner downstream.

73

Buffalo River Trail—Ponca to Pruitt (cont.)

From the viewpoint the trail heads uphill very steeply, then swings left and levels off. It eventually makes its way to the end of the hill, and works on down some and turns back to the right. At 4.6 the trail is right on the edge of the hillside (actually on top of a giant bluff), and another spectacular SSS viewpoint. You are looking squarely at Big Bluff in front of you and just off to the left.

The trail heads, then levels off and begins to descend. It passes an SSS waterfall area, crosses a horse trail road, then goes down to and across Beech Creek at 5.6, another SSS area. From there the trail heads uphill, swings around level to the left, then works its way steeply up a hill to a roadbed intersection at 7.0—TURN LEFT. The roadbed heads mostly level to a trail intersection at 7.4—this is called The Slaty Place. The main trail TURNS RIGHT and heads to Kyles Landing (the left turn goes on down the hill to the river at Horseshoe Bend—1.9 miles, and on to Hemmed–In Hollow).

The trail on to Kyles is pretty easy. It's mostly level, for quite a while, then eventually begins to wind its way down the hill. At 9.0 there is a wonderful SSS view down into Indian Creek. From there it continues to drop down to and across Indian Creek at 9.4 (and leave the Ponca Wilderness Area just beyond). If you have the time, I would definitely recommend a side trip up into Indian Creek, especially if there is water running. Square foot for square foot, I think that this little area is the most scenic spot in Arkansas. Besides the tumbling creek that has several nice waterfalls during the wet season, there are some great bluffs and other rock formations. There's even a spot where a section of the creek comes out of the mouth of a cave up on the canyon wall. It's very lush, with lots of ferns, wildflowers and mosses everywhere. (The terrain is rough and slippery—not maintained nor recommended by the National Park Service.)

Back on the main trail, bear to the LEFT (past a lesser trail that goes up the creek) 'till you come to an intersection. The main trail goes to the RIGHT, and heads uphill on an old road (*grey rock*, the famous canoe dumping spot on the Buffalo, is down the trail straight ahead, and off to the left on a spur trail). The road soon levels off and drops back on down to another trail intersection—TURN RIGHT. Just beyond at 9.8 there is another intersection—the main trail TURNS RIGHT. (If you went straight here you'd come out to Kyles Landing a couple of hundred yards ahead.)

The main trail heads up along Bear Creek, crossing it three times. It heads up the hill, through a rocky SSS area, and crosses the Kyles Landing access road at 10.6. After crossing the road, the trail turns to the right and climbs up some, eventually swinging back to the left and a nice view out over Buzzard Bluff—an SSS. Beyond you'll see some paint blazes—these mark the boundary of Camp Orr Boy Scout Camp.

The trail heads downhill, then swings sharply back to the right (there is a lesser trail here that takes off to the left and goes down to the Boy Scout Camp), down to and across Shop Creek at 12.0. Like many in the area, Shop Creek is dry much of the year. When there is water here, this is a definite SSS. There are lots of large boulders just tossed about in the creek bed. A little ways beyond there is an off–trail SSS, down on the creek to the left—a wonderful waterfall—worth a side trip.

The main trail heads uphill a little, around the hillside, and drops down to and across Rock Bridge Creek at 12.4, then over to and across the road down to Camp Orr at 12.6. It drops down to Dry Creek at 12.9, then climbs up some. It levels off for the most part and gets pretty easy for a while, crossing a couple of small streams. At 13.6 there is a trail intersection. It's a short spur that joins up with the Old River Trail. (This is the horse trail that follows an old road 18 miles from Ponca to Erbie, and crosses the

74

Buffalo River 20 times—great summer hike.) The main trail goes STRAIGHT AHEAD.

The trail comes right next to the river at 14.0, and begins a 1/2 mile SSS area—lots of bluffs and waterfalls, and the trail even goes right up through the bluff at one point. There are many waterfalls up to the right in this area too. Once it tops out and leaves the bluff area, it winds out through the woods pretty level, then intersects with a park service road at 14.9. TURN LEFT and follow the road downhill, past the Cherry Grove Cemetery at 15.0. Just beyond the cemetery, the trail leaves the road TO THE RIGHT. It goes through a cedar grove, comes alongside the river, and a neat spur trail at 15.6—an SSS.

It goes up and around this bluff area, turns right and crosses through between some fields. The trail eventually comes out to the road and the Parker/Hickman Farm site at 16.0. TURN LEFT on this road and go through the farm complex and a gate. This is a neat spot, and is the oldest standing homesite in the Buffalo area. The main trail TURNS RIGHT after the gate and follows the fence row. It follows a small stream, then intersects with a road—TURN LEFT and follow the road across the creek. Soon beyond, the trail leaves the road TO THE RIGHT, and passes an old oak shingled smokehouse off to the right. It then swings back to the left some and eventually heads up and over "Tornado Hill." It's very rocky in places. As the trail heads down the hill, the view is wonderful, and all of the moss–covered rocks about qualify as an SSS.

From there the trail drops down further, comes alongside a nice little slickrock area, and crosses the Erbie Road at 17.0. There is a trail intersection just beyond— TURN RIGHT to continue on the main trail to Pruitt (turn left to go into the Erbie Campground). The main trail swings around the river to the left, runs on an old roadbed for a while, then leaves it at 17.6 TO THE RIGHT. From here the trail pretty much follows the river downstream, back up on the hillside. It joins a road or two for short distances. It's pretty easy hiking.

There is a trail intersection at 19.0—a little spur trail to the left leads a short ways to Adair Cemetery. Some of the graves date back to the 1840's, and include at least one Confederate soldier. The main trail GOES STRAIGHT. It passes through an old farmstead area, then plunges back into the woods again. It continues to wind on around, mostly out of sight of the river. At 19.7 there is a great SSS waterfall area. Beyond there are some great views as the trail overlooks the river at several points. It dips down to and crosses several smaller creeks. Then the trail runs through the Cedar Grove Picnic Area at 21.2. There are a couple of tables here and a real nice view up and down the River (just across the road there is a short trail that visits two neat ponds—worth a side trip).

From the picnic area the main trail continues along the river, working its way in and out of several draws. At 22.5 it crosses a nice SSS stream area. At 22.9 the trail comes into one end of Ozark Campground. It crosses the road and continues on into the woods up and around the campground, heading towards Pruitt.

From the campground the trail heads uphill some, then winds around through the woods, mostly away from the river again. It crosses a road at 24.0, and wraps around a neat spring–fed pond at 24.3. It climbs up some from there, then begins to head on down the hill, once again overlooking the river. The trail eventually comes out and ends at the upper river access picnic area at Pruitt at 25.5, which is located on Scenic 7 National Scenic Byway.

Agency List #17

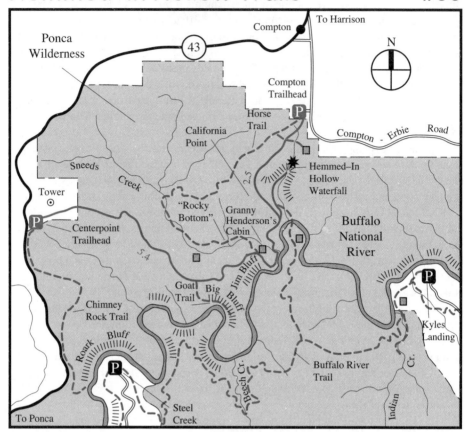

Hemmed-In Hollow—5.0 miles round trip

This is one of two trailheads that will take you down into the famed Hemmed–In Hollow at Buffalo National River, and to the tallest waterfall between the Rockies and the Appalachians. It's the Compton Trailhead. This is a *steep* trail, both going in and especially coming out, but if you can handle it, you will be rewarded greatly! We are going to go in and out the same way, but I'll briefly describe the way out to the other trailhead (Centerpoint Trailhead), which also gives you access to the Goat Trail on Big Bluff. For a complete description of all this area, get my book ***Buffalo River Hiking Trails*** (see page 190).

To get to the trailhead, go north out of Ponca on Hwy. 43 for 8.3 miles, then turn right at the community of Compton. Continue on a dirt road for another .8 mile, then turn right at the sign—the trailhead is just down this road. There are two trails that begin here. The one on the right is mainly a horse trail, but can be combined with our trail for a nice loop. The trail on the left is closed to horses, and is the quickest (steepest!) way to get to Hemmed–In Hollow (it is 2.5 miles to the falls). All of this trail is inside the Ponca Wilderness Area. Camping is allowed. Ponca quad.

This area is great for dayhiking—a quick jaunt down to the falls and back. But *let me warn you*—the hike out on this trail will humble even the greatest of hikers. It is very steep, no matter which way you hike out. Be sure to plan the entire day, carry lots of water, lunch, extra snacks, and a first aid kit. Better yet, spend the night, or two, or three. Take your time and enjoy this place. *No camping near the falls, though.*

We will take the trail on the left. It heads out into a scrub forest and swings around to the right, then begins to drop down the hill. By .7 the trail has leveled off and comes to an intersection. (A left turn will take you over to Wild Vic's Cabin, a neat little mountain hut. A right turn will take you up to the horse trail that goes back to the trailhead.) GO STRAIGHT at this intersection to continue with the main trail.

As the main trail works its way down the hillside, you can look back to the left and begin to see the bluffline that forms Hemmed–In Hollow. There are some pretty steep spots here, and the trail isn't in very good shape, so be careful. During leaf–off the views just keep getting better—the river, the bluffs, even the old Lockhead barn down at Horseshoe Bend is visible. At 1.5 there is spectacular SSS view of the waterfall.

The trail continues down the hillside to a trail intersection at 1.8. If you turn right here you'll head off towards Jim Bluff, Sneeds Creek, Big Bluff, and the trail out to Center Point Trailhead (described in a minute). To get to the falls, TURN LEFT here. The area above this is known as California Point, so for the sake of clarity, we'll call this intersection the "California Point" intersection.

The trail doubles back to the left, passing through an SSS forest of beech trees. At 2.3 we intersect with a trail that heads to the right, down to the Buffalo River at Horseshoe Bend—it's an easy downhill walk of about a half–mile. The main trail continues STRAIGHT AHEAD. There is an SSS just beyond—two waterfalls. The trail heads up the hill beyond them and at 2.5 ends at the base of Hemmed–In Hollow falls—177' tall, and of course an SSS. Return to the trailhead the same way that you came in, for a total hike of 5.0 miles.

If you would like a longer outing, we'll hike out a different route, and will end up at the Centerpoint Trailhead—it's still pretty steep. Go STRAIGHT AHEAD at the California Point intersection (instead of turning right to get back to Compton). The trail drops down to and across Sneeds Creek—TURN LEFT there and go over to the Buffalo River. The trail follows upstream for just a little while, then comes to an intersection (Jim Bluff is straight ahead on the river. Also the Old River Trail crosses the river here and heads upstream to the Ponca bridge)—TURN RIGHT and head up the hill to another intersection at 4.4—the mileages from now on *include* the distance from California Point intersection to the falls and back. (Just off to the right here is Granny Henderson's cabin, an interesting historical spot with a great SSS view.) At this intersection you can either turn right and make a loop up Sneeds Creek via the horse trail back to the Compton Trailhead (a total loop of 8.6 miles), or go STRAIGHT AHEAD up and out to the Centerpoint Trailhead, which is what I'll describe.

The trail continues up the hill on an old road, and I do mean *up* . It levels off some, then more up, and at 5.2 you come to an intersection with the Goat Trail that goes on out to Big Bluff—the main trail continues STRAIGHT AHEAD on the old road. (Big Bluff, 440' tall, is a dangerous spot, but is also one of the most impressive SSS's in Arkansas! It's about a quarter mile to the left down to the bluff—*unofficial trail, and no camping.*) The main trail out continues uphill, but not nearly as steep. Bear right at 6.1 and then again soon after, and stay on the old road. It does get real steep again at one spot, but finally levels off somewhat at 6.9. From there it's mostly a gradual climb (lots of great leaf–off views back to the left) out to the Centerpoint Trailhead, which makes the total hike 7.9 miles. This trailhead is located on Hwy. 43, 3.5 miles from Ponca.

Agency List #17

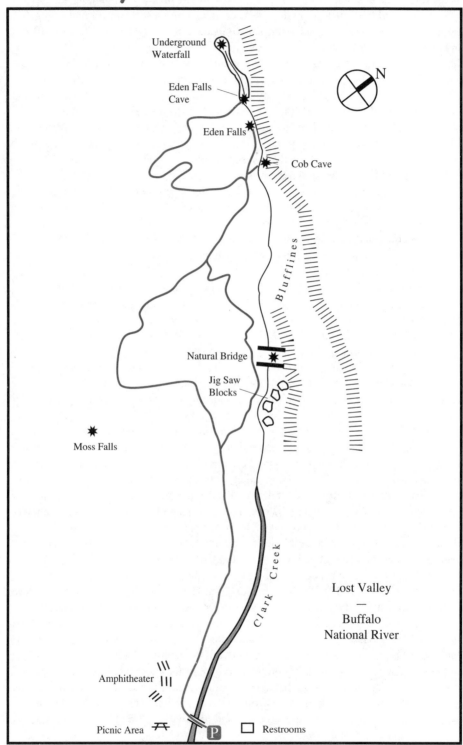

Underground
Waterfall

Eden Falls
Cave

Eden Falls

Cob Cave

N

Blufflines

Natural Bridge

Jig Saw
Blocks

Moss Falls

Clark Creek

Lost Valley
—
Buffalo
National River

Amphitheater

Picnic Area

P

Restrooms

Lost Valley Trail—2.3 miles round trip

This little area is one of the special places in the world. Calling it an SSS is an understatement! This popular trail is short, and for the most part, very easy to hike. Although the last section of trail does get pretty steep as it climbs up to a cave—which reminds me—be sure to bring a flashlight (one for each) if you wish to go into the cave.

The trail is located at Buffalo National River, at the Lost Valley day use area (camping is no longer allowed). To get there, turn off of Hwy. 43 between Boxley and Ponca onto NC#1015 at the big brown sign, and follow this road to the end. There are picnic tables, water, phone, restrooms, and a Ranger's residence. Osage S.W. quad.

The trail begins by crossing over Clark Creek (which eventually empties into the Buffalo River). This is the creek that the trail will follow up into its headwaters. The first half–mile or so is on a wide, level trail. It's a nice stroll that passes some large trees, including sweet gums, cedars and my favorites, the giant beeches. The creek is a typical babbling brook, with lots of smooth rocks for a floor. It does dry up once in a while though—springtime is the greatest here!

The trail forks at .7—TURN RIGHT, and you'll head on over to the creek where the trail comes to some huge stone blocks. These are called "Jig Saw Blocks," and you can probably figure out why. It looks like they fell off of the bluff just behind them—that would have been interesting! Just beyond, the trail comes to the Natural Bridge on the right. All of this is an SSS. When the water is running good, this is a magical little spot. When it's almost dry, you can actually hike through the bluff, and come out on the other side upstream.

Continue on up the trail (bear right at the next two forks), and you'll find yourself standing at the base of a 200–foot bluff, and Cob Cave at 1.0, of course another SSS. This is the giant overhang that you can hike back into. It is named for corncobs that were found there many years ago—left by Indians. At the far end of this spot is Eden Falls, which is a spectacular waterfall. The falls come out of Eden Falls Cave, which we'll hike up to in a minute. There are lots of mosses, ferns and other lush stuff around the base of these falls.

No matter what time of year you are here, you're sure to find something that interests you. Spring is great of course. But so is fall, with all the colored leaves. And even the dead of winter is nice. One hint for popular times—come during the week to avoid the crowds!

To get to the cave, go back down the trail to the first intersection that you come to, turn right, and follow the trail *up* the hill. It's a short but steep climb, and the view back behind gets better with every step. The trail ends at the cave at 1.1—use some caution here, 'cause it's pretty narrow and it's a long drop! Eden Falls Cave isn't very large or long, but it does have Clark Creek flowing out of it, which makes it special indeed, and an SSS. This is of course what makes Eden Falls that we just saw from below. It's not an easy crawl to get back into the cave. But you get in, you'll be rewarded, 'cause the creek also forms a waterfall *inside* the cave—it's about 35 feet tall.

To get back to the campground, just head back the same way that you came in, only bear right at all intersections (you'll hike a short stretch of trail that you didn't hike on the way in, and pass "moss falls" on the right, an SSS). Soon you'll be back at the trail fork at 1.6, and from there it's a nice level stroll home, making a total hike of 2.3 miles.

Agency List #17

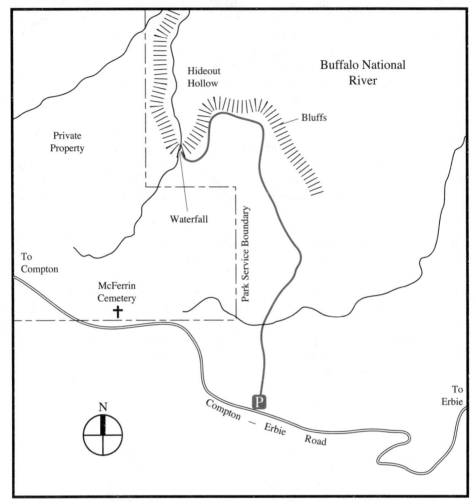

Hideout Hollow Trail—2.0 miles round trip

This is a wonderful little trail that takes you into a large bluff and waterfall area. It is often overlooked by hikers, since it is one of the lesser–known trails in the Buffalo National River trails system—you won't see many other folks here. It is one of my favorite trails. The hike is pretty easy, with only a few ups and downs. Camping is allowed. Ponca quad.

To get to the trailhead, which is called the Schermerhorn Trailhead, go north out of the town of Ponca on Hwy. 43 for 8.3 miles, turn right at Compton and go 3.5 miles. You'll see the trailhead on the left just after you pass the National Park Service Boundary sign. (The road continues down the hill, very rough at times, and goes to the Cecil Cove Trailhead, and across the Buffalo River to the Erbie Campground.)

I knew Jim Schermerhorn many years ago. He was one of the most advanced cavers that ever lived in Arkansas. He was also a terrific filmmaker, and did a lot of work in caves in Arkansas, as well as around the world. He died much too young. This trailhead was named after him.

From the parking lot the trail takes off straight out into the woods (be sure that you get on the correct trail, which is on the left—a "volunteer" trail or two leave the parking area too, but don't go anyplace). It works its way down a hill and across a small stream, then eases its way up the other side, passing beneath a powerline. There is one spot where the trail goes next to what I call an "N" tree—a tree that in its early years probably had another tree fall on it and bent it over, then it continued to grow up, forming an "N" shape in its trunk.

The hillside gets kind of rocky, and there are some nice large trees scattered about. The trail continues up the hillside gradually, then levels off, then rises up just a little, up and across a flat–topped ridge. It begins to head down the hillside through a thick stand of trees, several of them nice large pines, then goes through an area with lots of rock outcrops. In this area you'll be able to look out and see the emerging drainage area in front of you. Soon you come out on top of the edge of a tall bluff at .8 miles, and have some great views into and across this hollow—Hideout Hollow, and off to the right into the Cecil Creek Valley. This spot, from this point on up the drainage, is a major SSS. And in my opinion, the area is one of the best kept secrets of the Buffalo Area, so lets not tell anyone else!

One of my favorite sights is the large, apartment–sized rock across the way that has broken off from the bluff—it has some giant pines sprouting from it. It's a difficult thing to try and find your way down into this hollow, and I won't tell you how, but if you make it, you are in for some wonderful stuff.

The trail turns to the left here, and continues along on top of the bluff. A word of caution—there are lots of tall bluffs in this area, and if you have little ones with you, please keep a hold on them at *all* times. There are a couple of signs of past man in here—a small rock structure and a couple of old car doors. The trail runs back away from the bluff a little, and you can begin to hear water, a sign that neater stuff is ahead!

The trail passes through a cedar grove, where there isn't much of a definite trail tread—just follow along the best you can. Also in this area is the intersection with the return loop that we passed earlier—it's not too noticeable, but we'll find it on the way back.

The trail goes downhill just a little ways to a creek. This is the head of Hideout Hollow, and down below the trail is the large waterfall that we've been hearing. Of course all of this is one big SSS. There are also some other lesser falls both below the trail and a couple of hundred feet upstream too. It's rather thick across the way, but you can work your way around to get a better view of the big falls, and the bluffline that you've been walking on. Looks like a great place to "hide out" don't you think? The end of the trail is right at 1.0 mile from the parking lot.

To return to the trailhead simply go back out the same way that you came in, making it a nice two-mile hike.

Agency List #17

Buffalo River Trail (Woolum to Highway 65)   #14

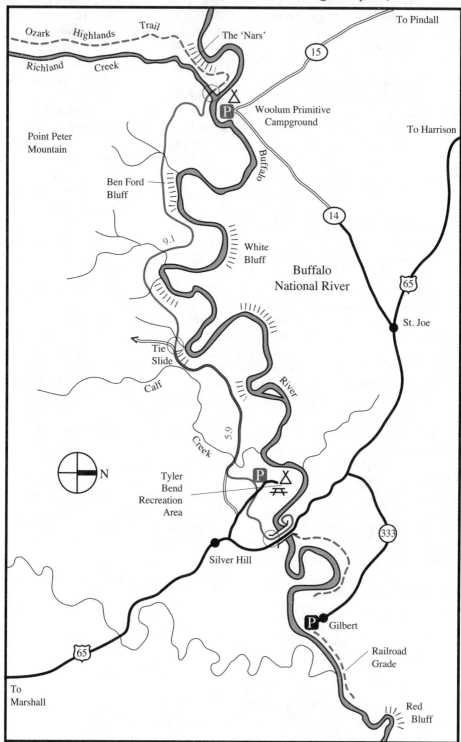

Ozark Highlands Trail

The 'Nars'

Richland Creek

To Pindall

15

Woolum Primitive Campground

P

Buffalo

To Harrison

Point Peter Mountain

Ben Ford Bluff

9.1

14

White Bluff

Buffalo National River

65

St. Joe

Tie Slide

River

Calf

5.9

Creek

N

Tyler Bend Recreation Area

P

Silver Hill

333

P Gilbert

65

Railroad Grade

To Marshall

Red Bluff

Buffalo River Trail—Woolum to Hwy. 65—15.0 miles one way

This is another sleeper trail—it has some tremendous scenery, but because access to the upper end of the trail is limited, it won't get a great deal of use. It begins in the Richland Creek Valley, just across the Buffalo River from Woolum (this is also the end of the Ozark Highlands Trail, which extends 165 miles back to Lake Ft. Smith State Park), runs across the tops of many bluffs that overlook the river, goes through Tyler Bend Park, and comes out onto the Hwy. 65 bridge over the Buffalo. This section may someday connect with the Boxley–Pruitt section, and continue downstream to Hwy. 14. It will also be part of the trans–Ozark Trail that will extend 1,000 miles across Arkansas and Missouri to St. Louis. Someday. The trail is located in Buffalo National River.

Getting to the beginning of this section can be a bit of a challenge. The easiest way is to go to the Woolum access on the Buffalo River (turn off of Hwy. 65 at Pindall or St. Joe to get there). This area has primitive campsites and canoe access. Then you have to wade the Buffalo River. It is a wide crossing, that can be anywhere from knee–deep to over your head. If you are lucky, you can talk someone with a canoe there into running you across. Confusing intersections are marked—white for the BRT, yellow for horse trails, and yellow for horse/hiker trails. Snowball and Eula quads.

The only other way to get to the beginning of this section, is to drive in from the other end of the Richland Valley, on a dirt road. If you come in from Snowball, you'll have to ford Richland Creek once. If you come in from the Richland Creek Wilderness Area, or Lurton, you'll have to ford Richland Creek twice.

So OK, here we go. The trail begins just across the Buffalo from Woolum. You want to go across Richland Creek. It is often knee–deep or less, *but can be dangerously deep!* Then cross the large field and head for the trail on the other side. The trail leaves the valley at .2, and heads *up* the hillside on some steps. It is pretty steep for a little while, and the trail switchbacks to the left. It eventually levels off somewhat, and you are looking down on the river. The views, especially during leaf–off, are good. There is an SSS view at .5. Just beyond, the trail swings back to the right, away from the river. It works its way up and along the top of the ridge. This is part of Point Peter Mountain.

As the trail levels off on top at 1.0, there are several sinkholes next to the trail. Must be a cave around somewhere. It crosses a seep, and continues on the level, across the wide hilltop. At 1.2 there is an intersection. The trail/road to the right is a horse trail, and swings back down to Woolum. There are two trails/roads to the left that you can take. The one on the left is level and again is a horse trail (blazed yellow). The one on the right, which goes uphill just a little, is also a horse trail, but is the one you want. So at the intersection, TURN LEFT and then TURN RIGHT (follow the BRT signs).

The trail stays on the old road for a while, and pretty much just makes its way around Point Peter Mountain, staying up high . There are some good views along here during leaf–off, and an old homesite or two, plus an old car body, complete with tail fins. The trail runs along fairly level, with some up–and–downing. Then at about 2.7, it turns to the left, and begins a plunge down towards the river.

It does get steep at times—aren't you glad you're hiking it downhill! When you reach the bottom and level out, you come next to a little bluff–lined stream at 3.4, an SSS. You stroll along this pleasant creek, 'till you cross it at 3.5. This is Ben Branch.

Just around the corner there is an intersection. The main road heads uphill to the right. There is a lesser road that takes off to the left, down towards the river. There is also a path that goes STRAIGHT AHEAD and level—this is the one you want. After less than 100 feet, TURN RIGHT onto plain hiking trail.

The trail heads up a small drainage, and gets a little steep as it swings back to the left. It levels off shortly, and from here on for a while it is just a wonderful hike. As it swings around to the right, there is a spur trail at 4.0, that leads a few feet out onto the edge of Ben Ford Bluff. This is the first of many SSS views that you have. The river sprawls out below you in both directions (White Bluff looms above the river downstream). There are fields as far as you can see. And the immediate area around you has lots of craggy bluffs. It's time to drop your pack and take a break.

From the viewpoint, the trail continues along the top of the bluffline. There are lots of nice views. At 4.4 a road comes near the trail off to the right. There is an old field out there too. Just beyond, there is an unofficial spur trail to the left that leads out onto a "slice" of bluff—another SSS. The trail stays along the edge of the hillside for a little while longer, then swings back to the right, and leaves the river behind. It heads up a hollow, right next to a nice field on the right. It leaves this field, then comes alongside another, smaller one. At 4.8, just as the field ends, the trail intersects with a road—TURN LEFT on this road.

This begins another road section, but at least this part of the road is moss–covered. There is a lesser road that takes off to the right just ahead, but ignore it. At 5.1 there is a fork in the road—take the RIGHT HAND fork. It runs along on down the hillside to the bottom, where it comes out into a giant valley at 5.5, and another road. TURN RIGHT, and continue on the valley road.

At 6.0 you need to TURN LEFT onto a road. Just down this road is where you will get back on "real" trail again—it takes off to the right. The trail crosses through the bottomland, across Hage Hollow Creek, then begins to work its way up a small hollow. At 6.3 it joins an old, narrow, grown up road and heads steeply uphill. At 6.5 the trail leaves the road TO THE LEFT, and continues out through the woods, but still climbing.

It switchbacks a time or two, and finally swings over to the edge of the hillside, and overlooks the river at an SSS view. The trail eases up the hill, levels off, then begins to descend. It lands at another SSS view, then continues *down* the hillside.

At 7.1, the trail crosses Whisenant Hollow, which is a small stream, then heads up the other side. It gets real steep as the trail switchbacks to the right, then to the left (if its real wet, you may hear and see a waterfall off in the woods). At 7.3 all is well again, as the trail has leveled off, and there is a spectacular view—you are now standing on those massive bluffs that you've been looking at.

And this is just the beginning. There are three SSS viewpoints right in a row. Each has a little different view of the bluffs and the world below. These bluffs are typical Buffalo River bluffs—a sheer face of solid limestone, painted with shades of grey, black, white, disappearing down into the forest below. Wish I had wings.

The trail begins to drop off the hill a little, swings to the left, and then back to the right. At this corner there is one last SSS view of the bluffs. From here the trail continues to drop down the hill, crosses a small creek, then runs up a short hill and veers off to the right. At 8.2 the trail goes across a dirt road and continues into the woods, veering off to the right some. A vast field comes into view on the left, and the trail stays in the bottom for a while. At 8.7 the trail TURNS RIGHT up a gravel creek, then leaves the creek and heads uphill to the left.

It climbs up the hillside, swings back to the left, then back to the right. The last part gets steep, but during leaf–off a view opens up to help you manage the stress. The trail runs along the top of the ridge, veers away from it for a little while, then back to it. It runs on the left side of the hill, then comes to an SSS view at 9.1 that is also a historical spot—the "Tie Slide." Way back when, as the mighty white oak trees in this area were being cut down to be made into railroad ties, this spot was used to "slide" the logs, down along a cable, to the gravel bar below. At the Tie Slide, the trail hits a road—TURN LEFT onto the road (it will follow this road for quite a while).

The road swings to the right, away from the river for a short distance, then rejoins the edge of the hillside. And at 9.7, there is a cleared trail spur off to the left—it is a terrific SSS area! This is one of the ten best views on the river. Craggy bluffs, twisted cedars, the river and valley below stretching out forever. Yea, it's an SSS alright. And down below, somewhere among the crags, is Peter Cave. Enjoy it while you can, 'cause there aren't many more views of the river for a while.

From here the trail remains on the road, and runs along level. During leaf–off, you may be able to look out to the right and see the Calf Creek drainage. You'll be crossing Calf Creek in a few miles. At 10.3 the road forks. The left fork will take you down towards Cash Bend on the river. Take the RIGHT FORK for the main trail. There are several lesser roads that intersect with the one you are on—stay on the main road.

By 11.3, the trail hits bottom and begins a long, level walk through several grown–up farmsteads. There is a pond on the right. In the late and early spring the honeysuckle perfume makes this a very pleasant hike. There is a hill and bluff off to the left that come into view—you'll be climbing up that hill shortly. The bluff is up on the River View Trail at Tyler Bend.

You'll pass the remains of the Arnold house at 12.0. Then Calf Creek comes right up to and below the road on the left. You get a good look at the hillside you're about to climb up too. At 12.3 you cross Calf Creek. This is a wide, gravel–bottomed crossing, that is usually about mid–calf deep (but can get much deeper).

Past the creek, the road winds through a field. Just as the road enters woods again at 12.5, the trail leaves the road to the LEFT, and heads up the hillside into the woods as dug trail. It climbs on *up* past great view of the Calf Creek Valley. At 13.0 it comes to the Collier Homestead, and connects with the River View Trail, which goes 1.5 miles to the left (past a nice overlook), on down to the Tyler Bend Visitor Center. To continue with the Buffalo River Trail, TURN RIGHT.

The trail goes over to the Collier Homestead Trailhead at 13.1. You are now in the Tyler Bend area. There are four short trails in the park, and all of them connect to the Buffalo River Trail. For a complete description of these trails, see page 86.

The Buffalo River Trail swings around the right side of the parking area, crosses the paved entrance road to the park, and continues out into the woods. It intersects with the Spring Hollow Trail at 13.5 (turn left for it). The main trail GOES STRAIGHT. It gradually climbs up to and around the head of a hollow, and comes to the Buck Ridge Trail at 14.1 (turn left for it). The main trail TURNS RIGHT and heads out across the head of another hollow.

At 14.6 it comes to the Rock Wall Trail. The main trail GOES STRAIGHT, and heads down the hillside towards Hwy. 65. Before it gets there, it makes its way down the hill some, passes under a powerline, then drops down to and across a small stream twice, and finally comes out at the end of the Hwy. 65 bridge over the Buffalo at 15.0. The BRT is now complete 28.6 miles downstream (south side) to Hwy. 14—maps and descriptions are included in the ***Buffalo River Hiking Trail****s* guidebook starting with the #5 edition.

Agency List #17

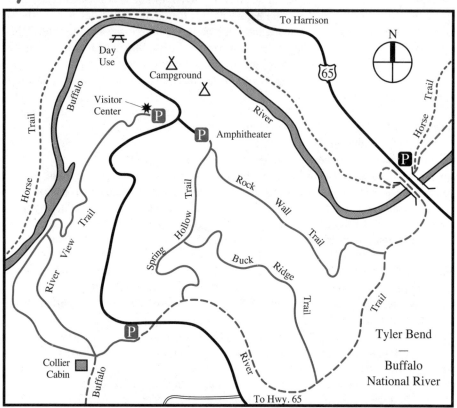

Tyler Bend Trails System—.9 to 4.0 miles

Tyler Bend is one of the main visitor facilities on the Buffalo River. There is a nice Visitor Center and museum there, as well as campgrounds, picnic areas, and canoe access. Tyler Bend is located off of Hwy 65 between St. Joe and Marshall, just south of the Hwy. 65 bridge across the Buffalo. There are three trail parking areas—one off to the left as you begin the drive down the hill to the Visitor Center, the Visitor Center itself, and just beyond the Visitor Center on the right, at the Amphitheater.

There are four trails in the park, and all of them connect with the Buffalo River Trail, and to each other. You can make several different lengths of loop hikes by connecting these trails. Snowball quad.

RIVER VIEW TRAIL

River View Trail to Collier Homestead Trailhead—**1.4 miles**
River View/Spring Hollow Trails Loop—**2.9 miles**
River View/Buck Ridge Trails Loop—**3.8 miles**
River View/Rock Wall Trails Loop—**4.0 miles**

I'll begin with the River View Trail, which begins right at the Visitor Center. It is certainly the most impressive, as it has some great views of the river valley. It visits the Sod Collier Cabin, and comes out at the Collier Homestead Trailhead. You have the option of making a loop hike out of it by connecting with the other trails.

The trail begins to the left of the Visitor Center, and takes off to the left into the woods. It drops down alongside one of the many large, open fields, and follows it. As you come to the end of the fields, you can look out through the cane and see the Buffalo River. At about .3 miles the trail crosses a little wood bridge that spans a small creek. The trail swings on around to the left, and begins a gradual rise up into a hollow, away from the river.

The trail continues to ease on up the hill, then at .7 miles it drops down just a little and crosses a small creek, and then turns back to the right and continues to head up the hill. It swings back to the left, then tops out and levels off at .8 at a wonderful view point. The view down to the river and upstream is just terrific. There are lots of old, twisted cedar trees hanging out here.

The trail turns to the left and continues along the ridgetop, heading uphill—lots of nice views. At .9 there is a trail intersection. One trail goes steeply up the ridge. This trail levels off on top and comes out at the Collier Cabin. If you were just going to do this trail and return to the Visitor Center, I would certainly recommend that you take the main trail (to the left) on the way up (less steep), then come back down the steep trail.

So TURN LEFT here, and continue on the main trail. It makes its way gradually up into the hollow, and eventually tops out at 1.3 at the Collier Cabin. This is a very well preserved structure, and like most of the homesteads in the area, there are a lot of flowers and herbs surrounding the home in the spring and summer.

There are several things that happen here. The Buffalo River Trail intersects here (it's about a half mile straight ahead from the cabin down to the Calf Creek Road—see page 83 for the description of that trail). If you wanted to loop back and go down the steep trail that we were at a minute ago (past a nice overlook), turn right . The main trail TURNS LEFT at the cabin and continues on across the top of the ridge to the Collier Homestead Trailhead at 1.4. This short stretch of trail is handicap accessible.

If you want to continue hiking from this spot and do a loop back to the Visitor Center, then continue from the Trailhead across the paved road and into the woods—this will be on the Buffalo River Trail. In .4 miles you will intersect with the Spring Hollow Trail. Turn left and follow it .9 miles down the hill to the amphitheater (you will intersect with the Buck Ridge Trail after .5 miles), then on around another .2 miles back to the Visitor Center. Your total loop this way would be 2.9 miles.

Or, from the Spring Hollow Trail intersection, continue along the Buffalo River Trail for .6 miles to the next intersection, which will be with the Buck Ridge Trail. Turn left and follow the Buck Ridge Trail to an intersection with the Spring Hollow Trail after .8 miles. Turn right and follow it .4 miles to the Amphitheater, then on around back to the Visitor Center. This would be a 3.8 mile loop.

Or, from the Buck Ridge Trail intersection, continue along the Buffalo River Trail .5 miles to the next intersection, which will be with the Rock Wall Trail. Turn left and follow the Rock Wall Trail down the hillside, along the rock wall and .9 miles to the Amphitheater, then on around back to the Visitor Center, making a 4.0 mile loop.

SPRING HOLLOW TRAIL
Spring Hollow Trail to Buffalo River Trail—**.9 miles**
Spring Hollow/Buck Ridge Trails Loop—**2.7 miles**
Spring Hollow/Rock Wall Trails Loop—**2.9 miles**

This is a fine little trail that follows Spring Hollow, and the little stream in it, from the wide–open fields in the valley, up to the Buffalo River Trail at the top of the hill. The first .5 mile section is nearly level and is an easy hike. The next section climbs up the hillside. Most folks will connect with the other trails in the park for a loop hike of up to 2.9 miles.

The trail begins at the Amphitheater parking lot, and makes its way off to the right as it enters Spring Hollow. The trail stays down in the bottom for a while, crossing a creek and passing by an old log structure. There is a long, narrow old field just across the way. At .5 miles it intersects with the Buck Ridge Trail, which goes to the left. TURN RIGHT and continue up Spring Hollow.

The trail crosses the stream twice—there are lots of delicate wildflowers along the way during the springtime. It swings back to the left and begins a pretty good climb out of the hollow. It makes a couple of sweeps across the nose of the hill, and finally intersects with the Buffalo River Trail. It's .9 miles back to the Amphitheater.

Turn right to take the Buffalo River Trail upstream to Woolum, to get to the Collier Homestead Trailhead, or to hike the River View Trail back to the Visitor Center. Turn left to take the Buffalo River Trail on to Hwy. 65, or to loop back to the Amphitheater via either the Buck Ridge or Rock Wall Trails.

BUCK RIDGE TRAIL

Buck Ridge Trail to Buffalo River Trail—**1.2 miles**
Buck Ridge/Rock Wall Trails Loop—**2.6 miles**

This trail begins at the Amphitheater and follows the Spring Hollow Trail for the first .5 miles. It TURNS LEFT at the intersection, crosses a small creek, and then begins a winding climb up the hillside to Buck Ridge.

As it gets near the top, the trail swings to the right around Buck Point. Then it levels and heads out across a flat and over to the middle of Buck Ridge. It continues down the middle of the ridge, climbing up a small hill a time or two. It swings around the head of a steep hollow to the right and intersects with the Buffalo River Trail.

Turn right at this intersection to take the Buffalo River Trail over to the Spring Hollow Trail, to the Collier Homestead Trailhead, or to take the River View Trail back down to the Visitor Center. Turn left if you want to take the Buffalo River Trail on to Hwy. 65, or to connect with the Rock Wall Trail and loop back to the Amphitheater.

ROCK WALL TRAIL—to Buffalo River Trail—**.9 mile**

This neat little trail heads out from the Amphitheater across the right side of the large open field that sprawls out to the Buffalo River. It heads into the woods and soon comes alongside a wonderful example of a pioneer wall—built by the early settlers of the area from the rocks that they had cleared from the field. This rock wall, though not particularly tall or sturdy, is one of the longest rock walls that I know of along a hiking trail. The only longer one is up on Hare Mountain on the Ozark Highlands Trail.

The trail follows the rock wall for a half mile. Along the way you'll find lots of wildflowers in the springtime, and near the end of it there are a couple of nice bluffs. Just as the trail gets to the end of the wall, it veers off to the right, then crosses a creek and begins a long climb up the hillside. About halfway up the hill, right in an opening, the trail turns sharply back to the left. As it nears the top of the hill and the end of the ridge, the trail turns back to the right, goes through a low spot in the ridge (a "saddle"), and drops down to an intersection with the Buffalo River Trail. Turn right at this intersection to take the Buffalo River Trail on to Woolum, or to connect with any of the other trails in the park. Turn left to take the Buffalo River Trail on to Hwy. 65.

Agency List #17

Indian Rockhouse Loop—3.0 miles round trip

(turn page for map)

Buffalo Point is the most developed public area within Buffalo National River. Besides a Visitor Center, there are several campgrounds, cabins, a restaurant, picnic areas, river access, and a number of hiking trails. Most of these trails just connect facilities, but one, the Indian Rockhouse Trail, is a wonderful three–mile loop into a scenic area, and visits one of the largest bluff overhangs that I know of in the Ozarks.

Buffalo Point is located off of Hwy. 14, between the turnoff to Rush, and the Hwy. 14 bridge over the Buffalo River. Follow the signs—the road is all paved. The main trailhead parking area is located just past the Visitor Center. You can pick up a trail booklet there that is keyed to identification signs along the trail. Cozahome quad.

The trail begins *across* the road from the trailhead, and heads down an old road. The return trail comes in from the left just as you start down the hill. Near the bottom of the hill, the trail turns to the right and follows beside a small creek. The first sign that you come to is "Poison Ivy." That is fitting, since a lot of you that hike this (and any other trail for that matter) will get poison ivy—so be careful—there is a lot of the stuff out here in the woods. Please excuse me for chuckling—I'm not allergic to it!
The next sign is "Ferns and Mayapples." You should come in late April and May to see these. The trail continues on, and passes a small bluff to the right. "Smooth Sumac" is next, and in late September and early October this stuff turns a wonderful color. Just beyond, the trail leaves the old road bed that it has been following and is plain trail now.

Next is the "Sinkhole Icebox" on the left. A nice spot to be in the heat of summer! Be careful not to slip in. This is an SSS. The trail continues on fairly level, out through and past our next sign "Hardwood Forest." Then the trail begins to drop off down the hill just a little, past the "Cedar Glade" sign. Just after, be sure to TURN LEFT down the hill on a slab rock. And the trail keeps going *down* for a little while, and swings around to the left.

Then we encounter another SSS, a wonderful waterfall. The trail actually crosses under it, then swings back to the right. This is one of the largest waterfalls in the area. The bluff that forms the waterfall is pretty neat too, and the trail follows it to the "Bluff Mammals" sign.

The trail heads on down the hill, past the bluff, and comes alongside the small creek that formed the waterfall. Then we pass "Abandoned Mine," and you can see the remains of a small zinc mine. Down to Panther Creek we go, as the trail turns to the left and begins to follow the creek upstream. This is a nice little creek—we'll see a lot of it.

There are lots of bluffs around, on both sides of the creek, as you pass the "Moist Bluff" sign. But the real treasure in this area is the creek. This is probably one of the best streamside walks in the state. But not for long, as the trail soon eases up the hill to "Small Cave," another SSS area. It's a neat little cave, with a sinkhole coming into the ceiling at one point. If it's hot, this is a great place to hang out and cool off at.

Just past this cave you come out onto an old paved road—TURN RIGHT on this road, and you will come to an intersection. The main trail continues STRAIGHT AHEAD on the old road, but if you are getting tuckered–out, you can turn left and head up a pretty little side stream for a short cut to the return loop.

The main trail crosses Panther Creek, and heads up a hill (still on the old road), then levels off and looks down onto the creek. You will pass Pebble Spring, which you'll visit on the return loop. Just beyond, you'll cross a rock slab, which is nice during the wet season. Then the trail passes by the "Calamint" sign, and another trail intersection (it's another short cut over to the return trail—stay STRAIGHT AHEAD to get to the Indian Rockhouse).

At the "Sculptured Bedrock" sign you'll encounter another SSS which is worth a closer look. Just past this area, the trail crosses Panther Creek. The "real" return loop takes off to the left here—continue on STRAIGHT AHEAD for the main trail (still on the old road). It will head up another short but steep hill, level off, then drop down again, to a trail intersection. If you are really adventurous, you can turn right here and head off to Bat Cave. This is a tough hike up a steep hill and down the other side to the cave. It will add nearly 2 miles to your hike.

The main trail goes STRAIGHT AHEAD at the trail intersection, crosses Panther Creek, and heads right up to the Indian Rockhouse. This is a marvelous place, of course a major SSS. There is a large sinkhole in the roof to the right, a creek running through the back of the overhang, and just lots of neat stuff for you to explore. There are even some genuine cave formations here—the "stalactites" point down from the ceiling, "stalagmites" are growing up from the floor, and there are "curtains" and "flowstone" along the wall. I'd plan to spend an hour or more here. And if you don't do anything else, just sit down against the back wall and absorb the place a little. It's one of Arkansas's great thinking spots.

After a good rest, you're ready to head back to the trailhead. Begin by going back the same way that you came, across the creek and past the trail to Bat Cave. Just before you cross Panther Creek again, TURN RIGHT at the intersection, and follow the trail upstream. It crosses a bridge, and comes to the Sculptured Rock area that we saw from the other side. Then it meets up with a short spur trail that drops down to Pebble Spring, another SSS. The main trail swings to the right, up a small hill and then levels off. After a little ways you come to another wonderful sculptured rock area on the creek—this area wasn't seen on the trip in from the other side, and I would definitely rate it as an SSS! A cool spot to spend some time.

Just beyond is a trail intersection. Back to the left is the way that you came in. TURN RIGHT at this intersection to continue with the main trail out. This is the "Natural Bathtub," another SSS. The trail follows this small stream up the drainage through a cedar glade. It crosses the stream at a pretty little spot, heads *up* the hill a little, swings back to the right and levels off.

It continues up the drainage, with the little stream down off on the right, past the "Watershed" sign. Here it gets more serious about climbing up the hill, and in fact does just that—CLIMBS. Up several switchbacks it goes, to an intersection. The left fork goes over to the old "Fossil Quarry," a short walk. The main trail TURNS RIGHT and continues up the hill on an old roadbed past the "Dogwood" sign.

As the trail tops out, you pass through a wooden gate, cross an old road with another wooden gate off to the left, and continue into the woods on level trail (you are now alongside the paved road that you are parked on). You will shortly come out at the trailhead where you started. What a great hike!

Be sure to check out the large trail sign at the trailhead—it shows the other trails in the park (the Overlook Trail is nice). And stop off at the Ranger Station for information. Ask about their summer hikes (they have one that visits a wild cave).

Agency List #17

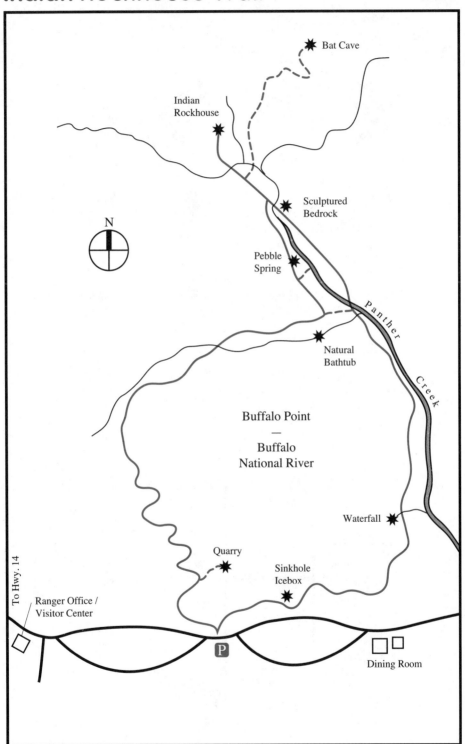

Rush Mountain Trail

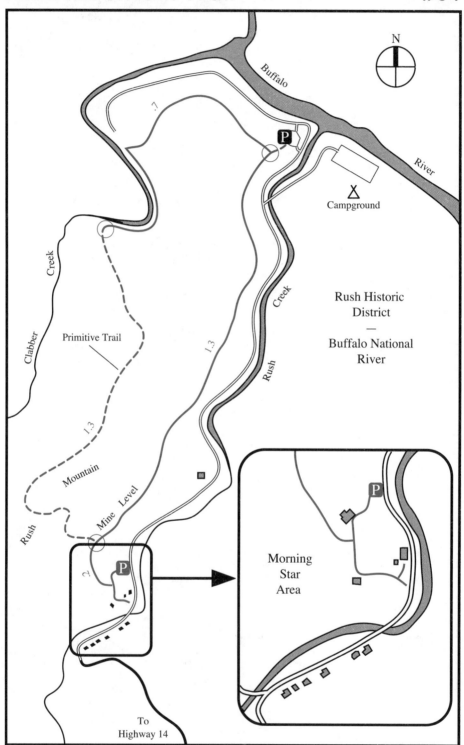

Buffalo

River

N

P

Campground

Creek

Clabber

Primitive Trail

Rush Creek

Rush Historic
District
—
Buffalo National
River

.7

1.3

1.3

Mountain

Mine Level

Rush

.2

P

P

Morning
Star
Area

To
Highway 14

Rush Mountain Trail—3.6 miles

Rush is an old mining town, a ghost town if you will, that was first opened up in the 1880's when zinc ore was discovered. The community that was built up around the mines endured until the 1960's. Some of the buildings still exist today, and two different trails visit the area. One of them, the Morning Star, is a short loop. The other, the Rush Mountain Trail, is a longer trail that goes past many of the old mines, loops around and goes *up* and over Rush Mountain. All of this area is now part of Buffalo National River. Rhea Valley quad.

A word of caution: *Do not enter any of the mines.* Many of them are *very* unstable. The mine entrances are usually fenced off, so be sure to *stay out of them.* Most of the old buildings are fenced off too.

To get to Rush, turn off of Hwy. 14 between Yellville and the Hwy. 14 bridge over the Buffalo River (it's well marked) and follow the paved road to the entrance to the Historical District (road turns to gravel). As you enter the District, you'll pass a row of old buildings off to the right, and just beyond on the left is the trailhead parking area. Down this road is the campground, picnic area and canoe access to the Buffalo River.

From the trailhead, the trail heads up the hill as a nice wide, graveled path (this is actually the main tailings pile for the area). It winds its way up through the ruins of the Morning Star Processing Mill. Just beyond this area the trail levels off and then forks (the short Morning Star Trail goes straight ahead, then loops back to the parking lot). The Rush Mountain Trail TURNS RIGHT and begins to climb up the hill.

This trail goes up the hill on an old road that leads to the "mine level." On the way up is an unmarked intersection of a trail that turns to the left—this is the return loop of our trail, and I recommend that you hike this in a counterclockwise direction. There is also a path that takes off to the right and goes out to a rock pile—these rocks were blasted out of the mines to get to the ore. It's kind of a weird sight to see such a pile of rocks right in the middle of all the forest.

The main trail continues up the hill at a steep pace, but not for long as it soon levels off at the mine level, and turns right. You can see entrances to the old mines scattered all about here. As I mentioned before, most of them are gated and have warning signs on them. Just as you pass the second gated area there is a spur trail that goes off to the right and runs out on top of another tailings pile.

This entire hillside is pretty much dotted with mine entrances and small tailings piles. The views up and down the valley below are quite nice, especially in the early morning during leaf–off. At about .5 mile there is an old mine car off to the right of the trail. This is the type of car that was used to bring the crushed rock out of the mines.

The trail leaves the road and becomes just trail at one point, then returns as an old road again, passing a few more mines. Near the entrance to one of the mines are the remains of a wooden structure. It eventually heads down the hill and leaves the mine level behind. As it's on its way down, the trail leaves the old road TO THE LEFT and continues on as just plain trail. If you stayed on the old road it would come out on the main road that is visible off through the trees.

The trail sort of up–and–downs a little through a forest of scrub trees, and at about the one mile point it runs along on top of a small bluff—the main road is visible just below. Beyond this a ways the trail swings to the left and begins a real steep (but not too long) climb up the hill. It passes several more tailings piles and spots where it looks like mines were started, but never really developed.

The trail levels off, then begins to drop down the hill and comes to a trail intersection at 1.5. (Turn right to go to another parking area by the river and toilets.) TURN LEFT to continue on with the rest of the trail to Clabber Creek, the Monte Cristo Mine, and the loop back to the main trailhead (up and over Rush Mountain). The remains that you see from this intersection are those of the White Eagle Mine—this is one of the earliest mines in the area—dating back to the 1880's.

From the White Eagle Mine the trail heads uphill just a tad but mostly level. During leaf–off you can see the Buffalo River down below. The trail swings around the hill to the left. At this point you've got a good view of the river valley downstream, and you leave the river, and begin to work your way up the Clabber Creek drainage towards the Monte Cristo Mine.

The hardwood forest is wide open, and the trail passes by a hand–dug hole off to the right. Soon after, the trail drops down to and intersects with an old road at 1.9. TURN LEFT on this road, which heads uphill just a little, up to the base of a nice bluff that overlooks the creek.

And at mile 2.0 you come to the Monte Cristo Mine, which appears to be the most developed of any of the mines—at least it has more dugout entrances than the rest! There is an old engine in front of the mine that dates from a 1960's mine reopening. This area is definitely an SSS—the bluff up above and the view of the creek below is great.

Past the mine the trail continues on the level and swings around to the right. You can see another bluffline up above the trail to the left. At 2.2 the trail leaves the road TO THE LEFT. (It does continue just a little further and then enters private property.) The section of trail from this point back to the trailhead is a rough, *steep* little trail that I would advise only those in good shape to try (shown on the map as a primitive trail). If it's not for you, then simply turn around and backtrack to the trailhead.

This woods trail is supposed to be marked with white blazes, so be sure to look for them as you climb up. The trail climbs up the hillside, and at 2.5 actually goes up through a break in the bluffline that I mentioned earlier. This spot is a minor SSS, and is a great spot to stop and catch your breath.

Once through the bluff, the trail continues uphill steeply, but soon levels off and continues along a fairly level bench for quite a while. Lots of good views through the trees during leaf–off. All too soon this bench peters out, and the trail climbs up again and heads for the ridgetop of Rush Mountain.

At 2.9 the trail reaches the ridgetop, TURNS RIGHT and begins to follow the ridgetop. From here you'll have views off of both sides of the mountain. By 3.0 the trail is going uphill some, and the road from the highway down into Rush becomes visible off in the distance.

As the trail swings around to the left of the ridge, it takes off to the left and begins its descent back down to the trailhead. This gets real steep at times, but usually is just heading down through a rocky, cedar glade. And it is usually easy to follow. The trail lands on an old road and follows it for just a hundred feet or so—be sure to TURN LEFT off of the road—and continues downhill through a rock wall.

After a nice tunnel made by a thick cedar grove, the trail comes out and lands on an old road at 3.5—this is the end of the loop—TURN RIGHT, and you will drop back down to the trailhead at 3.6 miles.

Agency List #17

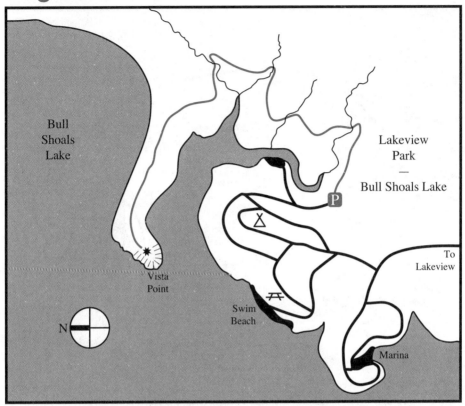

Dogwood Nature Trail—3.0 miles round trip

This trail winds through the woods just above Bull Shoals Lake, and ends at a spectacular set of bluffs that disappear deep into the waters. It is located at Lakeview Park, just outside the community of Lakeview, near Bull Shoals Dam. There is a brochure about the trail available at the entrance station. Bull Shoals quad.

Find your way to the trailhead at the back of the park. The trail heads down a flight of steps, quickly levels off behind several houses, then eases up the hill. It drops down the hill as it swings back to the left, then crosses the first of several small streams. It heads back uphill a little, swings around the hillside as it levels off, then drops back down into another small ravine. It does this four times. There are numerous trees that have name tags telling what they are—some interesting ones! Mile 1.0 is just beyond the one marked "Eastern Red Cedar." And just beyond that at 1.1, there is a trail intersection, and an SSS view of the lake! TURN LEFT here and head down the narrow ridgetop (be sure to watch for this turn on the way back). The views on both sides are great, and the trail passes through a nice cedar glade.

The trail drops down the hill some to the low spot in the ridge, just above the lake—you can see the dam to the left. It heads back up the hill, levels off, and comes to the end of the trail at 1.5. This is a terrific spot, a definite SSS, with craggy bluffs and a wonderful view. Return to the trailhead the same way that you came (unless you want to swim!), and remember to make the right–hand turn back at the other end of the ridge.

Agency List #21

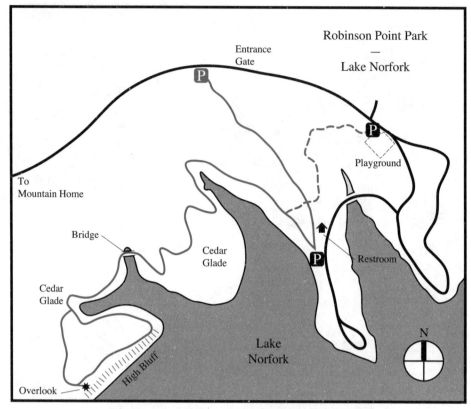

Robinson Point Trail—3.3 miles round trip

This National Recreation Trail, just outside of Mountain Home, winds around the shores of Lake Norfork, and has a spectacular view of the lake from high atop a terrific bluff area. It also visits some stands of very old, twisted cedar trees that have a great deal of character. And in the springtime, there are lots and lots of wildflowers scattered all along the trail.

This trail is part of the proposed 84–mile trail around the lake that will some-day be connected with other trails to form a 1,000–mile system (the first section of it was just built and begins at the dam—see page 99). This "trans–Ozark" system trail will connect NW Arkansas with St. Louis (and will include the Ozark Highlands and Buffalo River trails in Arkansas, and the Ozark Trail in Missouri). Contact the Corps office in Mountain Home if you would like to volunteer to help make this dream trail a reality!

The trail is located at Robinson Point Park on Lake Norfork, and is operated by the U.S. Army Corps of Engineers. This is a favorite park for boaters and campers, and does get a bit crowded during the summertime! To get to the park, head east out of Mountain Home on Hwy. 62 about 8 miles from the square and turn right on Hwy. 295. The trailhead is located on the right, just before you get to the entrance gate of the park.

The trail takes off on an old road behind the sign. It winds around through the rocky forest, heading downhill somewhat, and comes to a trail intersection at .3. The lesser trail to the left heads back to the playground area of the park. An un-maintained trail goes to the right—this is actually a cutoff trail that comes back in at another section of this trail. We want to go STRAIGHT AHEAD here, as the trail curves to the right some. It will come out behind a toilet building—you want to TURN RIGHT, just past a sign that shows this trail on it, and head into the woods.

The trail from this point on is marked by yellow blazes on the trees. It runs along just above the shore of the lake in the woods. At one point you've got an open view out across the lake. The water is usually pretty clear. As it gets near the back of the cove, it turns to the right and heads uphill on a pretty steep grade for a short distance. Just as it tops out and turns to the left at .7, the un-maintained cutoff trail that we passed earlier comes in from the right. The main trail is level for a while, then eases up the hill some, and curves around to the left. It drops down and crosses a small drainage that has a pretty nice waterfall on it during the wet season.

From there the trail runs along level, crosses an old road, then heads out into a cedar glade. These twisted old trees are pretty thick through here. It swings over to the right (be on the lookout for deer—I've seen lots of them in this area), then turns to the left and drops on down the hill. As it turns back to the right, there is an SSS view out across the lake at the 1.0 mark. The trail makes its way along the shore, heading up another cove, to a neat bridge across a drainage. It heads back down for another great view of the lake, then up the hill just a tad to the right, then a sharp turn to the left and down into and across a wider drainage that is usually dry. (When the lake is really high, there may be standing water here.)

From there the trail heads across a steep hillside to a "T" trail intersection at 1.4—the trail splits and makes a loop here. We're going to TURN RIGHT and head uphill (we'll end up back at this spot). It winds up back and forth, then levels off and swings back to the left, as it rises just slightly across a wide ridgetop. At 1.6 there is a minor SSS—a neat rock garden surrounded by large trees. Just beyond we intersect with a short spur trail that takes off to the right and ends up at a wonderful SSS view area. This is the main reason for hiking this trail—it is such a great spot. The handrails prevent getting too close to the edge. The bluff here drops right on down into the lake. This is a high bluff that looks out over a large chunk of Lake Norfork.

To continue with the trail, go back to the intersection and bear right. It begins to drop just a little, then swings on over to the bluff for another great SSS view at 1.7. Here you get a good view of the craggy limestone bluff that you were standing on a few minutes ago. It begins to really drop down the hill now, down through a thick cedar area that has the best examples of these old twisted guys I've ever seen—of course an SSS. The view is still wonderful too—but be careful, there's no handrail! Watch for a sharp left turn in the trail, as it continues down the hill and away from the bluff.

The trail levels out some, and you get a view of the cove out in front. It drops down some to and across a small dry drainage, then back up just a little. As the trail turns sharply to the left, it gets steep for just a short period, then intersects with the trail that we came in on and completes the loop at 1.9. TURN RIGHT at this intersection and return to the trailhead the same way that you came—a total trip of 3.3 miles. You can take the cutoff trail that I pointed out if you want to, but remember that it is not maintained.

Agency List #21

97

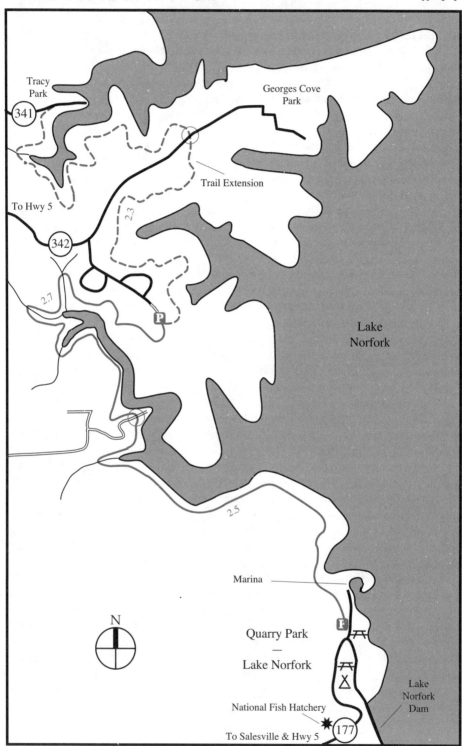

Tracy
Park

341

Georges Cove
Park

Trail Extension

To Hwy 5

2.3

342

2.7

P

Lake
Norfork

2.5

Marina

N

P

Quarry Park
—
Lake Norfork

Lake
Norfork
Dam

National Fish Hatchery

To Salesville & Hwy 5

177

Lake Norfork Trail—5.2 miles one way

This is the first stretch of the Lake Norfork section of the Trans–Ozarks Trail to be built. This trail system will someday connect the Ozark Highlands Trail, parts of the Buffalo River Trail, a new trail across the Sylamore District of the Ozark National Forest, and this Lake Norfork Trail, with the Ozark Trail that will someday run across Missouri. This will create a connected trail system of nearly 700 miles! The Lake Norfork Trail will eventually be 84 miles long (will be done *SOON* we hope!). This 5.2–mile stretch, which begins at the dam and runs along the lake shore, was built in 1993. Another 4 miles will be built in 1994 (shown as dotted line on map). Since things will be changing so rapidly, be sure to check with the Corps of Engineers office in Mountain Home for the latest information. Norfork Dam North and Mountain Home East quads.

The trail begins near the Lake Norfork Dam. To get there, take Hwy. 5 south out of Mountain Home to the community of Salesville. Turn east on Hwy. 177 and go about two miles to the picnic area, which is just before the highway crosses the dam—turn left onto the road that goes to the marina, and the parking lot is just on the left. The trail heads off across a narrow field, up into a cedar thicket. It eases up the hill just a little, then runs level through a rocky area. It crosses a utility access road at .3, goes across the end of an old camping area, and heads into the woods again on the level. It crosses a couple of small drains, then works its way down the hillside to the lake shore.

It curves around to the left, heading back into a large cove, and passes mile 1.0. The trail will be working its way around this cove the entire time. There are constant leaf–off views through the trees all along this trail, out over the lake. The trail runs close to the lake some, but most of the time it is up on the hillside a bench or two, where the walking is easy. It passes one SSS waterfall, then mile 2.0. It swings back to the left around a tiny cove, then dips down and crosses the creek that feeds it at 2.3. From there it swings back to the right and heads uphill across a steep, viney, thorny, rocky hillside.

As the trail tops out around the nose of a ridge at 2.5, there is a great SSS view across the lake, and some nice rock formations. It crosses a dirt road just beyond, then heads down the hill some, crossing a creek at 2.7, an SSS. The trail gets real close to the lake for a while, skirting along the side of private property, past mile 3.0. It heads out across a flat, then swings back to the left around the very tip of the big cove. It crosses the feeding creek at 3.5—be careful through here, it is a briar jungle!

The trail heads up the hillside, crosses a flat, then goes up some more, and turns back to the right. It runs down a little ridge, then swings back to the left and heads downhill. For some reason, this area is my favorite part of the trail. It levels out, crosses a side creek, passes mile 4.0, then swings to the right and crosses a larger creek, an SSS area. It continues turning to the right and heads uphill a little, then swings back to the left across the nose of a ridge. It works its way back up into a drainage, crosses a usually dry creek at 4.3 (another SSS area), then heads to the right towards the lake.

It eases up the hill some and swings to the left, climbing steadily. As it curves to the right, it passes mile 5.0. Just a little more climbing, then it levels off and heads across a big flat as it curves to the left—lots of giant oaks here, an SSS area! For now, the trail ends at 5.2 at a gate at the end of a subdivision. It is OK to park here. As soon as the next stretch of trail is constructed, it will continue across the oak flat, make its way around several hillsides, cross a couple more streams, and eventually end up near the Georges Cove Recreation Area. From there it will hug a few more hillsides above the lake, and head towards the Tracy Recreation Area. From there, on to Missouri!

Agency List #21

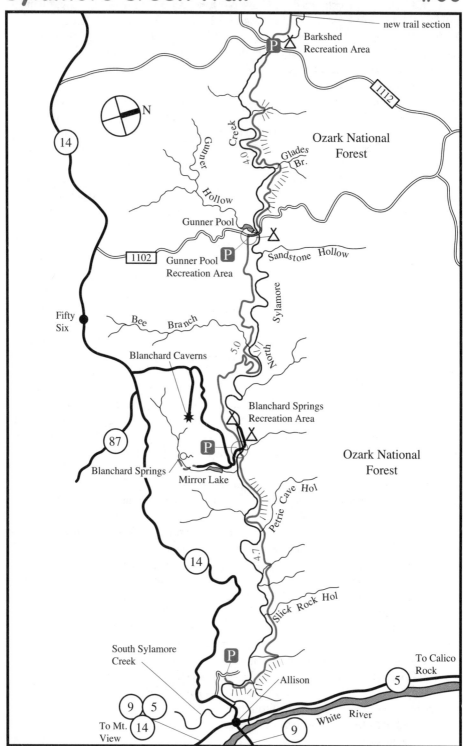

Sylamore Creek Trail—13.7 miles one way

This is one of the most scenic backpacking trails in the state. It follows North Sylamore Creek the whole way—a crystal clear, spring–fed, beautiful stretch of water—and winds around past painted limestone bluffs and big trees. There is something very special about this trail. Sylamore, Fifty–Six and Calico Rock quads.

You can access the trail at four points—Barkshead, Gunner Pool and Blanchard Springs campgrounds, and at the main trailhead, near Allison, where we will begin our hike. You can hike any of these sections individually, but I strongly recommend that you do the entire trail so that you can see everything! To get to this trailhead, take Hwy. 14/9 north out of Mountain View to Allison, turn west on Hwy. 14, cross over South Sylamore Creek, and just as the highway begins to head up the hill and to the left, TURN RIGHT onto a dirt road that heads over the bank. This road will take you about a half mile through private property to an open field—park at the signboard on the right in the field. You are past the private property now, and all but a tiny section of the trail is located on the Ozark National Forest.

The trail begins to the left of the signboard and runs along the fence line there down towards the creek. You can look up the valley and see bluffs on yonder hill—we'll be hiking along the base of them shortly. At the end of the fence, it TURNS LEFT, crosses a horse trail on a diagonal, and crosses Sylamore Creek (first of three crossings—the other two are on road bridges) on a series of boulders (tricky crossing during high water). It goes up a flight of steps, turns left and heads upstream—nice view up the valley. The trail is marked with white plastic diamonds. It quickly runs up to and alongside our first bluff, and our first SSS at .4. There is an overhang there that has a terrific waterfall pouring over it during real wet periods. And as is typical of the bluffy spots around here, it is moist and lush at the base, with mosses and ferns growing wild. This scene will be repeated many, many times. In fact, just beyond, it's even nicer, and the trail crosses under a waterfall area on bedrock—can get slippery!

Next we pass through an SSS area of old, twisted cedar trees. They are thick in here. Up on the bluff you may see more waterfalls, and there are some good views out to the right, down onto the creek. The trail runs along pretty much level, hugging the base of the fern–lined bluff, with a little up–and–downing. You can look back and see the field and the trailhead downstream. The bluff is undercut in several places, and during a big rain, the trail will actually pass behind waterfalls pouring off of the bluff.

We leave the bluff area and head towards the edge of a field, and cross a small stream at 1.1. Just beyond we cross another trail—continue STRAIGHT AHEAD. Just beyond that, there is an SSS glade area that is stacked up with reindeer lichens, and great views. In fact it goes through several of these areas. At 1.5 it crosses another small creek—an SSS area with waterfalls both above and below the trail. Beyond it passes through more cedar glade areas—some of the slabrock trail can get slick.

The trail turns to the left, then drops down to and across Slick Rock Hollow at 1.9—a neat SSS area just below the trail—a beautiful waterfall that dumps into a pool. This is a great spot to sit a spell. Just across the creek, the trail forks—TURN RIGHT and head uphill just a little. It swings to the left and heads across another SSS glade. As the rock slab/glade area heads on down the hill, the trail TURNS RIGHT and takes off on the level. It passes through more glades, (lots of wildflowers and cactus), does more up–and–downing (some of it steeper), and crosses several more small streams with waterfalls, one of them Petrie Cave Hollow.

We drop down the hill, pass by a small field, then come alongside Sylamore Creek at mile 3.0. This is one of the clearest streams that you'll ever see. A little ways beyond we come to a massive chunk of bluff that arches out over the trail—an SSS! This is easily the tallest bluff that we've seen—great area for a rest stop and a little exploring. The bluff veers away from the trail, then visits again as the trail continues along in the sandy bottoms.

At 3.4 the trail joins a road—TURN RIGHT and run along it as it joins another one, then leaves the road shortly beyond TO THE RIGHT—there are karsonite posts with a hiker symbol marking the way. The trail continues on the level through a grown up field, then forks again—TURN RIGHT (if you hit the creek at any of these spots, then you've missed the turn). The trail comes right next to the creek at 3.9, and at the base of a bluff too—of course an SSS area. Just beyond there is a wooden bridge over a spring—a lush SSS area of thick mosses and ferns.

The trail swings away from the creek and passes lots of big, towering oak trees. Soon you may hear the hum of the sewage treatment plant across the way—this is for the Blanchard Springs Caverns complex. The trail remains fairly level and crosses a steep hillside, looking down on the Sylamore. Across the way is also where Blanchard Spring empties into the creek (actual spring is a mile away). At 4.7 the trail comes into the parking lot to the swimming area at Blanchard Springs—TURN RIGHT and go across the creek on the bridge, then across the road and through the picnic area and around the restroom to the large trail sign. This is a great campground/day use area. You should drop your pack and wander over to the other end of the picnic area to Shelter Cave—it's one of the most beautiful bluffs in the world!

The trail here begins on a sidewalk, then leaves it to the left and begins a steep climb up the hill to the left. It levels off a time or two, past a cedar glade, and past a spur trail to the right that goes down into one of the campgrounds. There are lots of neat cedars in this area, and some big pines too. The trail levels off and runs along the edge of the hillside—some nice views to the right during leaf–off. It drops on down some, across a small drainage, then runs level again to a nice SSS view at 6.1. There are some neat boulders scattered around too. During leaf–off this is a terrific walk!

At 6.4 the trail hits a roadbed—it TURNS RIGHT and heads down the old road, steeply at times. It swings around, and goes through an open area on a long rock slab, then leaves it to the right. Just beyond at 6.8 the trail passes through the remains of the Claudis Mitchell homestead. The trail drops a little further down, swings to the left and levels off through a narrow open area. It comes alongside the creek for a nice SSS view upstream. (When I worked at Blanchard Cave in 1973, before this trail, I used to hike up the creek to this spot and camp—my first nights alone in the wilderness!)

Just beyond, the trail swings to the left and continues along the creek. The trail passes a grown–up field on the left, then crosses Bee Branch Creek at 7.7—there is a tremendous bluff just across the Sylamore—an SSS. The trail heads up some, then eventually swings back to the left and climbs up through another great SSS area at 8.0 of cedar trees, glades and broken bluffs. There are some great views too. This is a pretty good climb. The trail levels off, and does some up–and–downing as it crosses a steep hillside. There are some terrific views up and down the creek below during leaf–off.

At mile 9.0 we intersect with a road—TURN RIGHT and head steeply down the road for a hundred yards, then TURN LEFT off of the road, back into the woods on trail again. Soon after there is a neat moss–covered bluffline that forms a wet–weather waterfall—all of it an SSS. The trail passes under a powerline, then at 9.5 comes right out to the edge—it's a long drop straight down into the creek—an SSS area for sure! Great views up and down stream. You can even look across and see the Sandstone Hollow Scenic Area drainage come in downstream (a great place to explore if you're camping in the area). *Be careful here*—a fall would be fatal.

After this dramatic trail spot, the trail runs level on out to FR#1102 at 9.7, TURN RIGHTS and heads down the road through Gunner Pool Recreation Area (site of CCC Camp Hedges in the 1930's). Follow the road across Sylamore Creek, and a little ways beyond, then leave the road TO THE LEFT, at the trail signboard. From here the trail continues alongside the creek—a nice walk. Then it heads away from the creek and up the hill to the right. At 10.2 it levels off at a wonderful SSS view area—up and down the creek. The trail heads up through a split in a bluffline here—one of the most unique spots on the entire trail, then follows along the base of the bluff for a while—all of it an SSS. Along the bluff you may see some actual cave features that have formed—flowstone that hugs the bluff. There's even a "column," about two feet tall.

The trail drops down some, through a rocky area, and out of sight of the creek. At 10.8 there is another SSS bluffline, with more cave formations. Just beyond, another, much larger bluff comes into view above the trail. At 10.9 the trail actually goes under the bluff—an SSS. Soon, we cross Glades Branch Creek—there is usually lots of water in it. The trail gets pretty rocky as it continues up the hill past some cedars and broken bluffs, then levels off. It goes into and out of a small ravine, then up to and around the nose of the hill and around to another SSS bluff area at 11.4. It's very steep down to the water! There are some terrific views here.

At the end of the bluffline the trail heads up a flight of steps, then into and out of another ravine, and around another nose of a ridge, and good SSS views during leaf–off. The trail heads on down the hill, across a small creek, then back uphill again. As it tops out there is an SSS view at 11.8 back downstream of the big bluffs that we hiked past. It goes in and out of another ravine, then joins an old roadbed at 12.0, and drops downhill just a little, then continues as plain trail.

It works its way down and back into a neat SSS area on a little creek at 12.3. It crosses the creek and continues along the bluff on the other side. It leaves the bluff area and winds on around out through a much less steep forest, crossing several old roadbeds. It works its way up the hill, then levels off. The hillside does get a little steeper, but the trail remains fairly level. It does some up–and–downing, across several tiny drainages, then heads down the hill steeply and comes alongside Sylamore Creek again near mile 13.0. Then it does some more up–and–downing, past smaller bluffs, and finally out to FR# 1112 at 13.6—TURN LEFT and head down the road to Barkshead Campground, ending at 13.7. There is a wonderful little swimming area here on the creek—right alongside a bluff. It's an SSS as well as a great place to jump into after a long, hot hike. I must tell you, though, the water is cold!

To get to Barkshead, from Fifty–Six, go west on Hwy. 14 four miles, turn right on FR#1115 (Cartwright Road, County Road 56), and follow it three miles to Barkshead. For shuttle service, check with Cody's in Fifty–Six at 870–757–2270

NOTE: This trail has just been extended upstream for an additional 10 miles, and connects with the Ozark Highlands Trail near the Leatherwood Wilderness Area.

Agency List #8

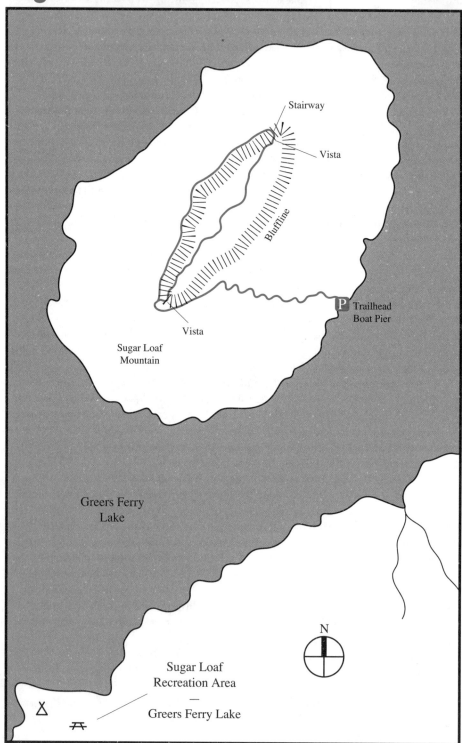

Stairway

Vista

Bluffline

P Trailhead
Boat Pier

Vista

Sugar Loaf
Mountain

Greers Ferry
Lake

N

Sugar Loaf
Recreation Area
—
Greers Ferry Lake

Sugar Loaf Mountain Loop—2.0 miles

This is one of the most unique trails in the state—it's built on an island! Right in the middle of Greers Ferry Lake. Naturally you have to have a boat to get to it, but it is worth the extra trouble because it just happens to also be a very spectacular trail, with lots of towering bluffs, twisted old cedar trees, and great views. It was the first trail in Arkansas to be designated as a National Recreation Trail. It's a pretty good climb to get the 560 feet to the top, but once you're up there, it's all down hill back to your boat. Fairfield Bay quad.

The best place to access this trail is via the Sugar Loaf Recreation Area on Greers Ferry Lake. From Heber Springs, take Hwy. 25 south for 8 miles, then go west on Hwy. 16 for 11.9 miles to Hwys. 92 & 337 for 2.7 miles to the park. Sugar Loaf Mountain is located northeast of the park—it's pretty easy to spot, and is a short boat ride away. The dock trailhead is located on the southeast side of the island.

The trail begins off the end of the dock, and heads up the hill to a signboard. This trail gets a lot of use, especially in the summer, so the trail is rather wide in places. It swings back and forth on up the hill, leveling off here and there. You will see several signs that indicate how far up the hill you are—these relate to elevation gain and not mileage. There are also several benches along the way. During leaf–off the views behind you get better through the trees as you go up. The trail runs along level under a bluffline for a while, and at .5 it heads back uphill. In fact it goes right up through a split in the bluff—an SSS area. On top of this spot, the trail forks—TURN LEFT (we'll come back down from the right fork).

The trail runs along the base of a craggy, lichen–covered bluff—all of this area for a while is an SSS. This is also the first views, during leaf–off, of the other side of the lake down below. There are some neat old cedar trees hanging around, and the trail actually goes under the bluff at one point. It heads down some steps, and continues along the bluff. You get a chance to look real close at the bluff, and can find lots of interesting stuff there. Still an SSS. At .8 the trail heads uphill, across a wooden walkway that hugs the bluff, now level. At .95 the trail climbs up a great set of steps—winding around through the bluff as it climbs. At about 1.0, it gets really narrow. The view is beginning to get spectacular. Still an SSS. It levels off briefly, and the view is stunning! So are the rock formations. It's spots like this that command us to build trails.

The trail climbs up further, and at 1.1 levels off again. A spur to the right reveals another spectacular view. There is more climbing, but not too much, as the trail does level off finally and runs down the middle of a widening ridgetop. There are some great oaks up here, as well as old, twisted cedars, and ferns and cactus plants. The elevation is 1,001 feet, about 560 above the lake. Towards the end of the ridge is another spectacular SSS view at 1.3. And then the trail drops down the hill, on another set of steps, through one last SSS. Just beyond, at 1.4, is the intersection with the loop—TURN LEFT for the half–mile trip back down to the boat dock. The total loop distance is just under 2.0 miles. When it's real hot, there's nothing quite like coming off this trail and jumping into the lake!

There are several short nature trails at the Greers Ferry Visitor Center, which is located on the other side of Heber Springs. The Visitor Center itself is a great place to check out.

Agency List #22

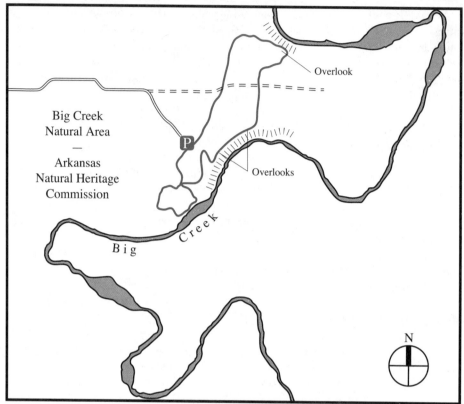

Big Creek Natural Area
—
Arkansas Natural Heritage Commission

Overlook

Overlooks

Big Creek

N

Big Creek Loop—2.6 miles

This out–of–the–way loop trail is located in the Big Creek Natural Area, one of 52 such special areas that have been designated and are managed by the Arkansas Natural Heritage Commission. They are sort of like mini wilderness areas. The Commission has a booklet that is keyed to the 34 numbered stops along the trail, and is available from them (see agency list). These mostly point out different types of trees, vines, and other plants and neat stuff. This trail has some spectacular views of Big Creek, and visits numerous ecological neat spots. Floral quad.

To get there, take Hwy. 110 east out of Heber Springs about 9 miles to Wilburn, then turn left on Tylar Road (dirt), go .8 and bear right at the fork (Central Chapel Road), go 1.4 and continue straight through intersection (Natural Area sign here), go .3 and turn left onto lesser road (sign), go .4 and stay left away from farmhouse, go .3 and turn right (sign) to the parking area .4 ahead—for a total of 3.5 miles from Wilburn. Most of this dirt road is OK, but I probably wouldn't take a new vehicle in here 'cause it might get scratched.

The trail begins here and continues down the road past the parking lot. It drops down the hill and to a signboard—TURN RIGHT here and continue downhill on the road. The trail is marked with blue blazes. There are some nice, big rock slabs both above and below the trail as it drops down the hill, then levels off and swings back to the left. The numbered signs begin with one of these rocks, as it points out Poison Ivy and Virginia Creeper, two common vines growing on them. The trail levels off for good and winds around in the bottom. Just before it crosses Big Creek at .5, the trail leaves the road and TURNS LEFT, then heads uphill past markers 11 & 12, an SSS area.

It soon leaves the creek area and heads up the hill to the left. It gets pretty steep in a few spots. At .7 there are more slab rocks along the trail, and some nice large trees as well. Not too far beyond, the trail comes out back at the signboard—TURN RIGHT here for continuation of the main trail. It runs basically level for a while, some up–and–downing. It dips down and crosses a tiny drainage at .9, then eases up on the other side, bears to the right and passes through a nice glade. At one time there was a sawmill operation here, and you might be able to spot some of the sawdust. A little ways beyond you see lots of blue–green mossy clumps covering the ground—these are Reindeer Lichens (stop 21).

The trail curves back to the left and soon comes to a short spur trail at 1.0 that goes over to the right to the first of three spectacular SSS views. That's Big Creek that you're looking at. There are lots of neat old twisted cedars along the top of the bluff—and that stuff hanging off of them is another lichen called Old Man's Beard. From the overlook the trail continues on through the woods, back from the edge a little, winding around just slightly uphill. During leaf–off you would have a pretty nice view all through here—much of it an SSS view. There are several large pine trees, and scattered patches of wildflowers along the trail.

At 1.2 there is another spur trail to the right that goes out to the second overlook—of course an SSS—the view is wonderful. Of special note here also is the poison–ivy–like vine that is growing on top of the bluff. It is actually Aromatic Sumac, and is not harmful, and its berries can even be used to make a lemonade–like drink.

The trail swings up the hill a little and to the left, away from the creek area. At 1.4 there is an intersection—TURN LEFT onto road and then immediately TURN RIGHT off of road (if you continued straight on this road, eventually turning left off of it, it would take you .6 miles back to the parking lot). The trail eases on down the hill, jogs to the right, then left, crossing a tiny creek. It heads uphill just a tad, then turns to the left. It drops on down a little to the third spectacular SSS overlook at 1.7. All though all three overlooks are terrific, I like this one the best. The bluffs are made of sandstone, which breaks off irregularly, creating those jagged edges.

From the overlook the trail heads gradually uphill some, swinging back and forth. It levels off on top and passes through mile 2.0. Just beyond, you hit the shortcut road—go STRAIGHT ACROSS the road. The trail winds around, mostly level, but dropping just slightly. At 2.4 there is a tiny drainage, then the trail heads uphill some, then levels off. At 2.6 the trail comes out and ends at the parking lot.

In case you aren't able to get the booklet, here are the numbered stops: #1, poison ivy & Virginia Creeper; #2, Bracken fern; #3, Dogwood; #4, Lichens; #5, Sweetgum; #6, Red Mulberry; #7, Partridgeberry; #8, American Hazlenut; #9, Switchcane; #10, Musclewood tree; #11, Christmas fern; #12, Red Maple; #13, Wahoo shrub; #14, Mockernut Hickory; #15, Farkleberry; #16, White Oak tree; #17, Shortleaf Pine tree; #18, Black Oak tree; #19, Winged Elm; #20, Sawmill site; #21, Reindeer Lichens; #22, Eastern Red Cedar; #23, Blackjack Oak; #24, Post Oak; #25, Downy Serviceberry; #26, Aromatic Sumac; #27, Old grown up fields; #28, Northern Red Oak; #29, Elephant's Foot wildflower; #30, Muscadine vine; #31, Rattlesnake–master wildflower; #32, Devil's Walkingstick; #33, Winged Sumac; #34, Blackgum.

Agency List #39

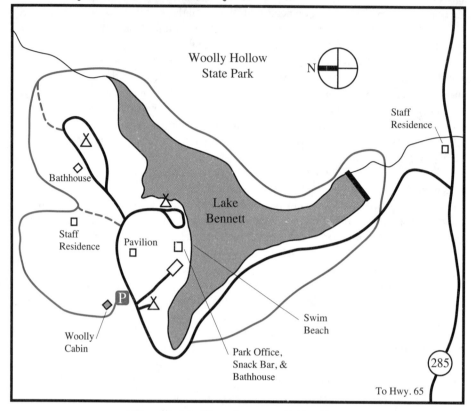

Woolly Hollow Loop—3.5 miles

This is a fairly easy–to–hike trail that loops around Lake Bennett at this State Park. It visits a number of hillside glades, To get there, take exit 125 off I–40 at Conway, then go 12 miles north on Hwy. 65 to Hwy 285 (one mile north of Greenbrier), take Highway 285 east for 6 miles to the park entrance. There are some nice campsites in the park, as well as a Visitor Center, covered pavilion, swimming beach, and showers. We're going to combine two trails for this hike—the newer, short Cabin Trail, and the Huckleberry Nature Trail. Together they make a fine loop hike. Guy quad.

We're going to begin this hike at the site of the Woolly Cabin, which is on the left as you approach the main park area. This restored cabin was built in 1882, and was moved here from the original site nearby. The trail begins to the left of the cabin, and heads on up the hill. At the top of the hill, the trail swings to the right, alongside a field. There is a bench at .3 if you've already run out of breath! The trail heads back to the right, easing down the hill, past a glade area on the left—lots of wildflowers during the spring and summer. In fact there are quite a few coneflowers scattered around along the trail—these are the tall ones with the big heads, kind of pale purple.

It continues to drop down the hill, past lots of dogwood trees, and a few nice, big hardwoods. There are a few more glade areas too. You may notice a park staff residence off to the right. At .7 there is a trail intersection—TURN LEFT for the main trail (the trail to the right goes back towards the Visitor Center and the beginning of the

Huckleberry Nature Trail). We have actually just joined the Huckleberry Nature Trail, and will be following it the rest of the way. It eases up the hill just a little, then heads down to and across a creek at .9. It goes up just a little, past mile 1.0, and swings back to the left. There is a lesser trail here that takes off to the right and goes down into the campground.

We work our way back up into and down and across another small drainage or hollow at 1.2. And then another one at 1.3. It's a pretty nice hillside all through here, heavily forested with hardwoods. There are scattered wildflowers, too, in the spring and summer, and the leaf–off views during the winter down towards the lake are nice. At 1.5 there is another small hollow. Most of the trail through here is fairly level, with some mild up–and–downing. The trail does drop down some to and across a small creek at 1.6—this neat little area is an SSS. And we are now in the bottom. It's pretty jungle–like in here, thick with growth, and there are some nice, large trees scattered about.

At 1.7 there is another trail intersection—the right fork goes into the camp-ground, we want to TURN LEFT. This will take you over to a wonderful bridge across a creek at 1.8. This is one of my favorite spots on this trail, and a definite SSS—lots of huge trees. The creek is the one that is dammed up to make the lake, which begins just downstream. From here, the trail heads uphill a little, working its way across a steep hillside. The park has posted mileage markers in 1/2 mile increments that begin at the Huckleberry Nature Trail Trailhead—since we didn't begin at this point, they don't per-tain to us. Actually, they are pretty close, 'cause just past their 1.5 mile marker is our 2.0 mile mark—so you can just add 1/2 mile to their markers! The creek below fades away, and at last Lake Bennett comes into view, even during leaf–on. The trail is running pretty level now, but it's real steep down towards the water.

As the trail makes its way on around above the lake, you can look across the lake to the beach, Visitor Center and the hillside that we hiked across earlier. Eventually, the trail swings back to the left, towards the end of the lake. Did you notice how the vegetation changed? It just got a lot thicker—the slope is facing a different direction. At 2.5 there is an open view spot, and you can look right down on the spillway of the lake. During periods of high water this would be really nice. The trail begins to drop down the hill, down to an SSS area just below the spillway—when the water is running this is a great spot! It turns to the left, then right, and goes over to and across two bridges—this area is all an SSS. It swings back to the right, then left and up the hill a little, up to and across the entrance road to the park at 2.7.

Across the road the trail heads up into the woods, swings to the right, left, back to the right, then levels off somewhat at the 3.0 mile mark. It continues pretty level for a while, then at 3.2 hits a short spur trail—this runs straight out just a few feet to a view spot across a "naked" hillside field—it's a nice view. The main trail TURNS RIGHT and heads down the hill at a pretty good clip, then down a set of steps. At the bottom of the hill the trail intersects with the paved road again at 3.3—TURN LEFT and follow the road back to the trailhead, which will complete the loop at 3.5 miles total length.

Agency List #38

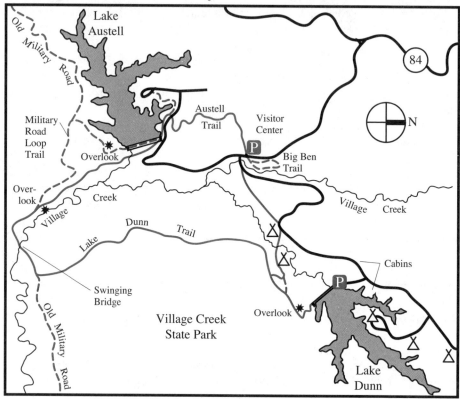

Village Creek Loop—6.3 miles

Village Creek is a special State Park located on Crowley's Ridge over near Memphis. The diverse fauna, flora and especially the geology of the area make this a terrific place to visit. In fact, the Park has been included in the State system of Natural Areas. This loop is actually a combination of several of the Park's trails. There is a wonderful Visitor Center there that should be your first stop. There are several campgrounds, cabins and even two lakes for boating and fishing. To get to Village Creek, take exit #242 off of I–40 (just east of Forrest City) and turn north onto Hwy. 284, and follow it 11 miles to the entrance to the Park. Turn right and head down to the Visitor Center, then turn left onto the road that goes to Lake Dunn. This road winds around through the Park, and finally you turn right off of it to the Lake Dunn Dam, where the trailhead is located. Wittsburg quad.

We're going to start off hiking the Lake Dunn Trail. It takes off across the top of the dam. The view of the lake is great. At the far end, the trail turns to the left, drops down to the shore, then heads uphill to the right. There is a bench and overlook spot just up the hill, as the trail levels off. At .3 the trail hits an old roadbed and TURNS RIGHT onto the road (bear right at the next fork too). We're walking down the top of a narrow ridge. There are lots of big trees all along here. At .5 there is a lesser trail that goes to the right down into a campground. Continue STRAIGHT AHEAD on the main trail. Soon there is another trail to the right at .6—we will come up this trail on the return loop. But for now, continue STRAIGHT AHEAD again.

The trail does some up–and–downing, passing lots and lots of huge trees. The smooth–barked ones are, of course, beech trees. There are oaks and sweet gums too. The trail stays pretty much down the middle of the ridgetop, through mile 1.0. It goes by several old grown–up fields. For the most part, it's a nice, wide trail all through here on the old roadbed, and there are steep ravines dropping off from either side. This is a very pleasant hike, on through mile 2.0. There are several SSS areas because of all the giant trees.

At 2.3 the trail hits the Old Military Road (built in 1829) and TURNS RIGHT. We're down in the bottoms now. Just beyond there is a man–made SSS—a swinging bridge across Village Creek. The trail continues along the roadbed, swings to the right, then begins to head uphill. At 2.6 you get a good look at the unusual layer of topsoil found here, called "loess," as the roadbed has cut into it. Near the top of the hill at 2.7, there is a trail intersection. This is the end of the Lake Dunn Trail, and the beginning of the Military Road Loop. TURN RIGHT off of the road and get on real trail—this is the Lower Loop (the road route straight ahead is the Upper Loop, and less scenic).

This route heads on over to an SSS overlook area. Then it drops on down the hill and comes alongside Village Creek at 3.0. This is one of the more scenic areas in the trail—lots of SSS areas—take your time and have a good look around. It winds around to a "swampy pond" area, crosses the creek, then runs below the dam across a meadow. It turns to the left and heads up the dam.

Once up on the dam we intersect with the Military Road Upper Loop at 3.7—TURN RIGHT for just a few feet, then TURN LEFT off of the dam and head into the woods. It winds around just under a road, across a couple of bridges, then crosses a road and continues into the woods. We are now on the Lake Austell Trail, that will take us to the Visitor Center. It crosses some more bridges, then at mile 4.0 passes a spur trail that goes to the picnic area to the left. TURN RIGHT, head up the hill and cross the road. It heads down into some deep woods, into a little SSS ravine area full of moss and giant beech trees. It crosses the creek on a bridge, then heads upstream—this is a good spot to stop and spend some time.

The trail heads out of the ravine and up the hill. It soon levels off and runs down the middle of a ridgetop. It swings over to a field area, then back into the woods. Soon the trail begins to descend, at first gradually, then steeper. The Visitor Center comes into view. And at the bottom of the trail there is a trail intersection—continue STRAIGHT AHEAD, across a bridge out into the parking lot at 4.7. If you haven't done so already, now would be a good time to take a break and stop in at the Visitor Center. There are lots of interesting things to see and do in there, and you can even get a snack! (Just across the road is the Big Ben Trail, which is a short loop that visits some huge beech trees—highly recommended.)

At the parking lot, turn right and head out to the far end of it, then get on the main road that you came in on and TURN LEFT towards Lake Dunn. About 200 feet after you cross the bridge there, TURN RIGHT and head out across an open field on a faint old road trace. This will take us over to the campground. At 5.3 head on through the campgrounds to the back right corner of the figure 8 setup. At 5.6 TURN RIGHT onto the Lake Dunn Trail between campsites #23 & #24. It heads up the hill, past some terrific beech trees, and reconnects with our loop on top. TURN LEFT and head back to the trailhead. (You've done this section before!) Mile 6.0 is at the overlook spot with the bench that looks down on the dam. The total distance for the hike is 6.3 miles.

Agency List #35

Bear Creek Trail

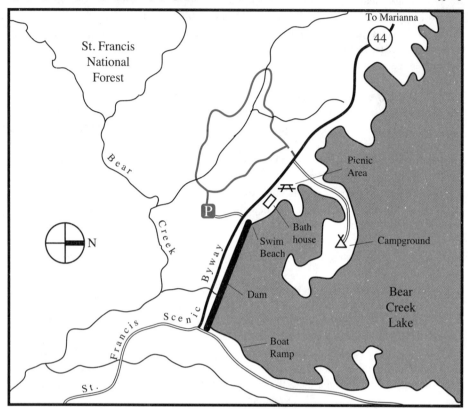

Bear Creek Loop—1.0 miles

This is a wonderful, wonderful trail that winds around past huge trees and lots of giant grape vines. It's out of the way, but worth the effort. In fact, I consider this entire trail an SSS! Take Hwy. 44 east out of Marianna (a National Scenic Byway) to the Bear Creek Recreation Area. Just before you cross the dam of Bear Creek Lake (opposite the beach), turn to the right and head down the access road to the trailhead. You are on the St. Francis National Forest, and this area is actually part of Crowley's Ridge. It's kind of strange to see such forested hillsides here that rise up out of the Mississippi River Delta.

There are numerous numbered posts along the trail—these point out the different species of trees that are found along the trail. If you get a chance, stop in at the District Ranger's Office on the way out to the trail and pick up a copy of the brochure that explains them. I will list these trees at the end of this description. La Grange quad.

There is a spur trail that goes from the trailhead on down to the trail—TURN RIGHT and follow the trail around to the right, across a bridge, and up the hill. It soon tops out and runs along a narrow ridge—lots of huge trees and vines. At an intersection the main trail TURNS LEFT and runs down another narrow ridgetop (the trail to the right just goes out to the highway). It swings around to the right, and drops down to and across the first of several bridges. It winds around in the bottom to another bridge across the main creek, then eventually swings up into another ravine and climbs the hill. All along the trail you'll see wonderful big trees. At one point the trail goes right between two of the largest.

When the trail tops out it hits an old roadbed and TURNS LEFT, and runs along the top of a narrow ridge for a hundred yards or so. There is a timber cut area on the right that is growing up. This is quite a contrast to the huge trees on the other side. The trail bears to the left, past a bench, and goes along the center of another narrow ridgetop. There are some pretty nice views down into the ravine below. At the end of the ridge there is a set of steps that takes you swiftly down to the bottom again and across two long bridges. Pause for a while here 'cause the end is near. A little ways off of the end of the bridges is the spur trail back to the trailhead. The total distance is about a mile.

This trail is surfaced with a special type of gravel—very fine, crushed rock. All of the gravel was hauled in and spread by hand. There are 275,000 pounds of it on the trail! It took me 1007 trips with a wheel barrow to complete the task.

The numbered posts are not in any order, but the numbers do correspond to the order of the trees in the brochure. Here is a list of the trees, by post number, not the order of the posts (are you confused yet?):   Agency List #7

#1	American Sycamore
#2	Red Buckeye
#3	White Oak
#4	Northern Red Oak
#5	Chestnut Oak
#6	Sugar Maple
#7	Flowering Dogwood
#8	Eastern Hophornbean
#9	Cucumbertree
#10	Black Walnut
#11	Yellow Poplar
#12	Sweetgum
#13	Winged Elm
#14	White Ash
#15	American Beech
#16	Black Cherry
#17	Sassafras
#18	Cottonwood

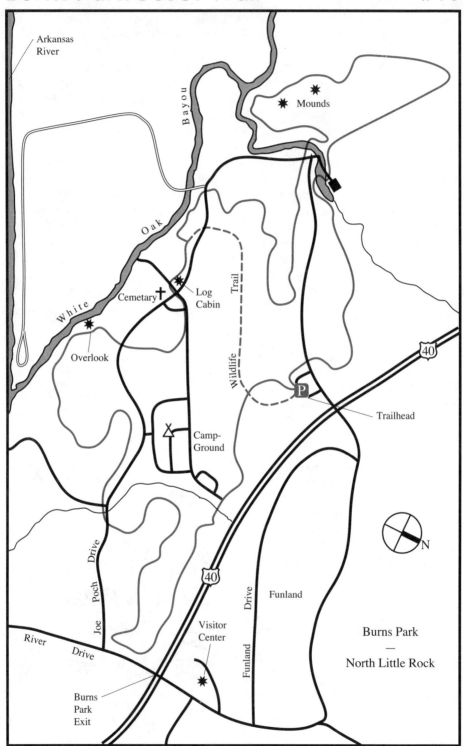

Arkansas
River

Bayou

Mounds

Oak

White

Cemetary

Log
Cabin

Wildlife Trail

Overlook

P

Trailhead

Camp-
Ground

40

N

Poch Drive

Joe

40

Funland Drive

Funland

River Drive

Visitor
Center

Burns Park
—
North Little Rock

Burns
Park
Exit

Burns Park Scout Loop—8.3 miles

I wasn't going to include this trail in this book—until I hiked it, and discovered that it's a pretty darn nice trail. It winds around through Burns Park, which is the large city park on the edge of North Little Rock. This is really a dayhiking trail, although there is a campground at the park, inside the loop. This trail is mainly used by the Boy Scouts. It's a pretty easy trail to hike, with a few climbs here and there. I hiked this trail during the month of May, and made a note on my tape recorder that it was the "sweetest smelling trail that I had ever hiked"—lots of blooming things along the way!

To get to the trailhead, take the Burns Park Exit off of I–40 (exit #150), go past the Visitor Center and turn left on Funland Drive, then left again when it "T" intersects, cross over I–40 again, and pull into the parking area just beyond on the left. It is marked with blue Boy Scout blazes (an eagle). N. Little Rock quad.

The trail begins at the back of the loop, and heads on down the hill through the woods. It goes up a hill and to the left—TURN LEFT at the top and continue down the middle of the ridge. It works its way on down the hill, near the I–40, through some nice woods. It crosses a little–used paved road, across a small bridge, and runs out across bottomland. There are lots of wildflowers and big trees in this area. The trail turns sharply to the right at 1.3 and runs alongside River Drive, then turns back away from it.

The trail heads up into the woods, does some up–and–downing, swings back to the left and crosses Joe Poch Drive. It crosses through a lowland area, heads up some and crosses a dirt road at 2.2. It runs along just above the road, then swings back to the left, up and around the hill. The woods are pretty nice through here. It swings back to the right, fairly level, then comes to an SSS view at 3.0, overlooking White Oak Bayou.

It heads down the hill, across the road, winds around through level bottomland, past several benches, and a couple of small bridges. At 3.5 the trail hits a paved road—TURN LEFT and hike down the road (archery range is just across the road—don't go that way!). Continue on the road, past a restroom on the left, *across* Joe Poch Drive, then TURN RIGHT and head on over to a log cabin at the corner—a historical SSS.

The trail takes off from the back corner of the cabin lot and heads off into the woods. Soon we come to an intersection at 4.0—the main loop TURNS LEFT (turn right for the "Five Mile Loop," via the Wildlife Trail, back to the trailhead). This less–used section of the trail swings around to the right, past White Oak Bayou again, and crosses Joe Poch Drive again. It eases on up a hill, then back down and across a bridge. It turns to the right, then back to the left, and runs level through a picnic area.

It crosses another paved road, then goes through a man–made SSS area just below a covered road bridge. On the other side it swings right briefly, then sharply back to the left and follows an old roadbed. It leaves the road TO THE LEFT, and winds on around through the bottomland, past a bluffline. It winds on around, past a couple of Indian Mound areas off to the right—its pretty thick in here, and the trail is hard to follow in spots. It finally comes out to a jeep road—TURN RIGHT and follow this road (bear left at the road fork beyond). It comes back out to the Covered Bridge at 7.3—turn left and go across the wonderful pavilion in the water, then TURN LEFT on the paved road for just a hundred yards, then TURN LEFT again, back into the woods.

The trail follows an old road trace, then TURNS RIGHT and heads up on plain trail, and eventually comes out to a paved road—the trail crosses it and swings to the left and comes out at the trailhead at 8.3.

Agency List #40

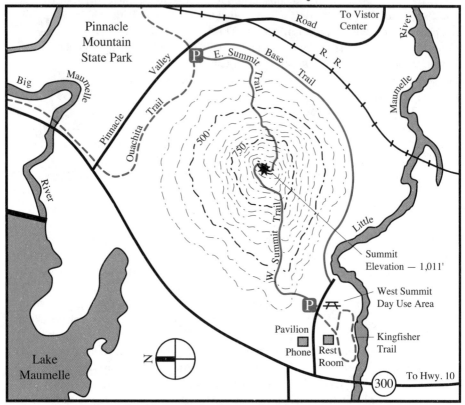

Pinnacle Mountain Summit Loop—2.6 miles

This is the steepest hiking trail in Arkansas—it climbs up the standing spine of Pinnacle Mountain—the views and rock formations are simply spectacular! We'll combine three trails to make a loop through Pinnacle Mountain State Park, which is located just outside of Little Rock. Take exit 9 off of I–430 to Hwy. 10, then west 7 miles to Hwy. 300, turn right and go 2 miles north to the park. The trailhead is located in the picnic area on the right. (Be sure to hike the Kingfisher Trail too, which is located just across the lot.) There is no camping in the Park, but it does offer a whole host of educational opportunities, and great exhibits at the Visitor Center. A parking fee may be required—check with the office. The park closes at 10pm. Pinnacle Mountain quad.

The West Summit Trail is blazed with yellow blazes. The trail begins up a flight of steps, and heads uphill rapidly—get used to this! It switchbacks its way on up the hill, passing a couple of information signs along the way. The trail is pretty easy to follow—in fact it's pretty much a trail highway with all of the traffic that it receives. There are several areas where other beat–down paths take off, but be sure to follow the yellow blazes and you'll be just fine.

By .4 the trail has swung over to the right edge of the mountain, then back to the left again, and comes to our first major SSS at .5—a boulder field. There isn't really a trail through this neat area, but rather arrows and blazes painted on the boulders to show the way as the trail heads up through the area. Towards the top, you can look back and see a sprawling Lake Maumelle. Back to the right again the trail goes, on over to the edge of the mountain—this SSS view area reveals most of the known world below! From here on up is all one big SSS. You are basically heading up the solid–rock spine of the mountain. Take plenty of time to rest through here, and enjoy the view.

As the trail continues *up*, there is a series of rock slab steps just away from the edge. Finally, the trail swings over to the left and levels off somewhat—gosh, we must be near the top! One more little rise up brings us to a sign at .7 that confirms this. (On my first trip up this trail, one hot and humid August morning, I encountered "Mable the Mountain Dog," who had just completed her second summit—needless to say she was in better shape than me).

At the sign the trail splits, and is blazed yellow both ways. The left trail is just a short spur that goes on out a hundred yards to a wonderful SSS view. We're going to take the right trail, and head just a little further up to the high point on the mountain. Congratulations, you made it!!! Now it's time to take a break, enjoy the nearly 360 degree view of the Arkansas River area to the front, and the Ouachita Mountains back behind. A great spot to watch the sun do its thing at rise or set. This is the end of the West Summit Loop part of the trail—a nearly 700 foot climb up from the parking lot.

To continue with the loop, look off to your left and down—you'll see the red and white blazes that signify the beginning of the East Summit Loop Trail. This area is **very** steep, and there are no steps—you just make your way down the sheer rock face. The trail turns into boulder field as it continues downhill. There is a nice sharp bluff that sticks up to the right. The view on the way down is great, and all of this area is an SSS. As you continue down through the boulder field, it may be easier walking to stay along the right side. Did I say that this area was steep?

Towards the bottom of the boulder field at .9, the trail swings to the right, still continuing down the hill at a sharp incline, but more on dirt trail now. And just when your knees are about to give out because of the severe descent, the trail levels off as it turns back to the left on an old road. The forest is mostly pine now. Just beyond the 1.0 spot, the road splits—be sure to follow the blazes and TURN LEFT. It's a nice gentle walk through here along a fairly level bench. Soon the trail swings back to the right, and drops down to another bench, which is near the bottom.

The trail passes through an open area, then eases down just a little more, then at 1.4 comes to an intersection and a trail sign (the East Summit Trail parking area is just off to the left). We'll TURN RIGHT and continue with the loop on the Base Trail. The hike from this point back to the trailhead is an easy stroll through a mixed hardwood/pine forest. It is blazed with green paint.

The trail eases uphill just a tad, crosses the same open area that we did before, and at 1.6 crosses a small footbridge. We come alongside a large powerline, then head back into the woods to the right. The trail does some easy up–and–downing as it goes through rocky areas laced with some nice older pines and oaks. At 1.9 there is a bench next to the trail—a great spot to stop and look around. Soon after, at the 2.0 mark, the trail heads downhill some, then quickly levels off in the bottom, as it swings to the right. At 2.3 you come alongside the Little Maumelle River. This area from here on to the end is subject to some flooding—if the trailhead area is flooded, then this area will be.

There are some terrific, huge cypress trees along the river here, which makes this area an SSS. And the end of the parking lot comes into view. The river swings off to the left, and the trail does the same, crossing a bridge at 2.5. As you enter the parking lot, TURN RIGHT and follow the road back to the trailhead at 2.6.

Agency List #33

Cedar Falls Trail

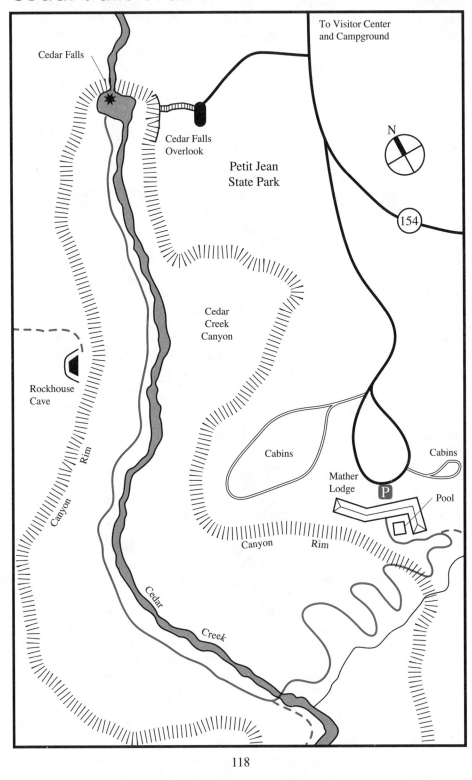

Cedar Falls

Cedar Falls Overlook

To Visitor Center and Campground

N

Petit Jean State Park

154

Cedar Creek Canyon

Rockhouse Cave

Canyon Rim

Cabins

Cabins

Mather Lodge

P

Pool

Canyon Rim

Cedar Creek

Cedar Falls Trail—2.0 miles round trip

Petit Jean State Park has a number of trails—I've included two of them here—the Seven Hollows Trail (next page) and the Cedar Falls Trail. Two other trails here are especially worth taking the time to hike—the Cedar Creek Self–Guiding Trail and the short little trail into the Bear Cave area. Stop at the park Visitor Center to obtain more information about these two trails. The Park itself is one of the most popular in the system, with complete facilities including a lodge, restaurant, cabins, swimming pool, camp grounds, and a lake. Much of the park was built by the CCC's back in the 30's. Some of the finest examples of their work can be found here. A parking fee may be required—check with the office. Adona quad.

The Cedar Falls Trail is one of the most used trails in the state, and with good reason, since it takes you to one of the most impressive waterfalls in this part of the country! The area is also an ecological garden—lots and lots of neat plant life. The trail begins at Mather Lodge. It drops on down a steep hill, crosses Cedar Creek, then heads upstream to the waterfall. There is lots to see all along the way. One word of caution— the last part of the hike out is pretty tough, and is not recommended for anyone with problems climbing hills.

The trail begins through the archway at the lodge, with an SSS view out in front of you visible right off the bat. It goes to the left, around and below the swimming pool. The trail is marked with sort of orange/peach colored paint blazes. Just beyond the pool there is a trail intersection—a white–blazed trail (a Boy Scout trail that loops around through the Park) takes off to the left and heads over to the Bear Cave area—go STRAIGHT AHEAD at the intersection and head down the hill.

As the trail switchbacks down through giant boulders and next to a tumbling stream, make sure that you stay on the trail—there are lots of opportunities to short cut, which as you can see has 'caused quite a bit of damage in the past. This entire hillside area is an SSS—just beautiful. Especially when there is water in the stream! See if you can spot the brightly–colored lichens on the rocks. There are some nice big pines around as the trail finally hits bottom, levels out, and comes to the bridge across Cedar Creek at .35. The bridge at this location has been washed out a time or two. The current bridge was constructed so that it can be retrieved if washed out, and put back together. By the way, please appreciate the amount of work that went into putting this bridge in—*all* of it was carried in by hand!

Once across the bridge, TURN RIGHT and head upstream. (A lesser, yellow– blazed trail heads downstream to some other neat areas, including the "Blue Hole.") The hike upstream is an easy one, with SSS areas at almost every turn—the creek is wonderful, the steep hillside on the left has several boulder fields or "rock glaciers," and numerous large oaks and sweetgum trees tower overhead. At .7 you step across a lesser creek on some boulders—look for waterfalls here during the wet season.

At almost the 1.0 mark, there is another "rock glacier" up the hill on the left, and some bluffs become visible ahead. You should begin to hear the rumbling of Cedar Falls. This is truly one of the best SSS's in Arkansas—the wide falls pour 90' into a large pool of water. Sorry, swimming isn't allowed.

The trail ends here, and after an hour or three of taking it all in, you should head back out the same way that you came in. Take it easy on the hike back up the hill—if you go slow, you'll probably see a lot of neat stuff that you missed in your rush to get down the hill to the falls. The round trip is just over 2 miles total.

Agency List #32

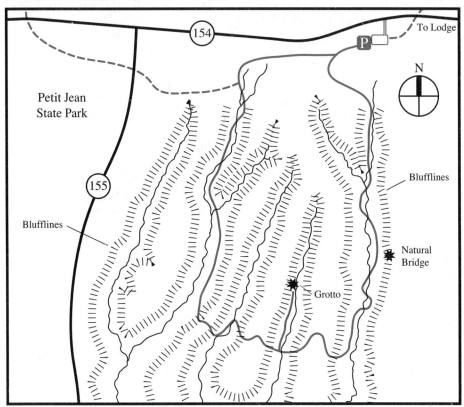

Seven Hollows Loop—4.2 miles

This is one of my favorite trails in the state. It's got tons of bluffs, boulders, wildflowers and waterfalls. This is an SSS nearly every step of the way! The bluffs there are made out of Hartshorne Sandstone. This rock contains hard iron deposits which have caused it to weather at varying rates and created a wide variety of colors and patterns on the rock faces. Although we'll only visit four of the seven hollows, you'll get an eye full. The trailhead is located on Hwy. 154, just west down the highway from the Mather Lodge (and Cedar Falls Trail) turnoff. A parking fee may be required—check with the office. Adona quad.

The trail takes off next to the signboard, and is marked with blue blazes. The Boy Scout Trail that winds through the park comes through here too, so you will also see some white blazes for it. Soon there is an intersection—TURN LEFT (we'll return from the trail on the right). There are some rocks off to the right that are covered with thick mosses. It begins to head on down the hill, past a huge SSS rock. It swings back and forth some, and comes alongside a small stream.

Soon the bluffs begin to appear on the right. At .5 there is a spur trail that goes to the right into a wonderful SSS canyon area—worth a look see. The main trail continues down the hill and crosses the creek. You get a good look at the main bluffline across the way—an SSS, and there are a couple of little spur trails that go over to it. At .7 the trail crosses the creek again, coming closer to the wonderful bluffline. There are several cave-looking overhang areas on the bluff that might require a look see.

The trail crosses the creek again, and soon the bluffline of the left comes into view. There is also another little canyon area across the way—another SSS. The trail is above the creek now, looking down on it. We cross a small stream that comes in from the left. There are some nice big trees through here. In fact, a couple of them have grown around big rocks—an SSS. The bluff next to us disappears and reappears again several times, each time getting neater looking.

The trail heads uphill some, past an SSS giant rock area at 1.1. It drops back down the hill, around more huge SSS boulders. Then at 1.3 the trail passes under the Natural Bridge on the left, which is of course just spectacular—an SSS. The trail drops down the hill as the bluff gets larger and more solid. It comes alongside the creek at an SSS there—a waterfall and some boulders. It crosses another small stream, runs up a little to an SSS bluff area, then drops back down to and across the creek at 1.5—an SSS.

The trail continues along the base of a smaller bluff, then crosses the creek twice more, quickly, for the last time. We are at the base of the bluff again, and there are big trees and ferns hugging it through here—an SSS at 1.7. At the end of the bluff, the trail turns sharply up TO THE RIGHT and climbs up through the bluff and curves back on top of it. It swings around to the left through a beautiful glade area full of wildflowers and thick mosses—an SSS for sure. We'll pass through several of these areas—be on the lookout for large collared lizards—they sometimes get up on their hind legs and run off! The trail drops on down the hill through another glade just past mile 2.0, and runs on top of another bluff. It quickly turns back TO THE RIGHT, drops down through the bluffline, and across a creek to an intersection at 2.1.

The main trail continues STRAIGHT AHEAD up the hill, but we're first going to take the spur trail to the right. This will take us about 200 yards to "The Grotto," one of the most scenic spots that I know. There is a large overhanging bluff on one side that curves into the creek and connects with the solid bluff on the opposite side—and the creek spills over all this into a pool—a terrific SSS area!!!

The main trail heads up the hill to the right, on top of the bluff through another SSS glade area, then swings up into the woods to the left, leveling out. It heads downhill, through another glade area, then turns back TO THE RIGHT and drops down into the next hollow. It crosses the creek at 2.5, continues upstream just a little—this is another SSS area—then it heads up the hill out of the hollow. It curves back to the right, uphill, passing through more SSS glades.

The trail works its way uphill some more, then eases into another hollow, just below a bluffline. At 2.9 the trail goes over a 50' long rock slab, which is actually a low natural bridge, and an SSS. Just beyond there is a narrow little canyon, another SSS, and the trail turns left at the far end of it at mile 3.0 and drops on down the hill. The trail runs pretty level now in the bottom, crosses a small creek, and just upstream there is an SSS canyon area. The trail swings away from it, continues up the hollow, and crosses a creek several times—SSS areas on both sides. If fact, these are the tallest bluffs that we've seen. At 3.8 the trail intersects with the Boy Scout Trail (it turns left)—continue STRAIGHT AHEAD.

The trail leaves the bluffline, swings to the right and climbs up the hill through several more SSS glades, past mile 4.0. It is up on top now. Just beyond is the loop intersection—go STRAIGHT AHEAD back to the trailhead at 4.2.

Across the highway from the trailhead is the Bear Cave Trail—a most unique rock formation that I highly recommend you go see!

Agency List #32

Mt. Nebo Trails

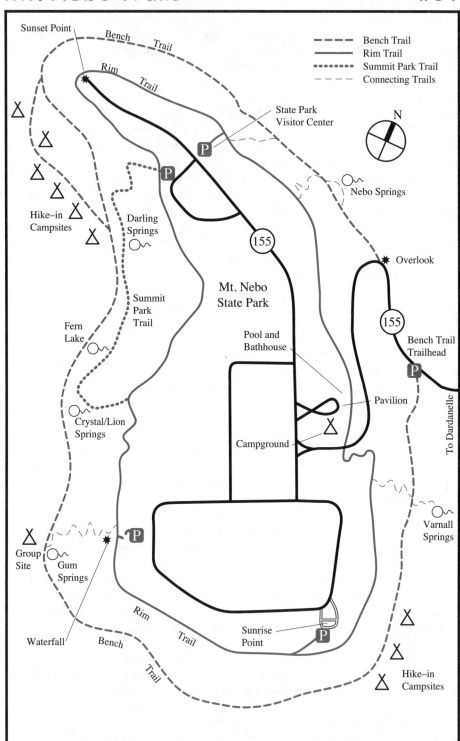

Sunset Point

Bench Trail

Rim Trail

State Park
Visitor Center

N

Nebo Springs

155

Hike–in
Campsites

Darling
Springs

Mt. Nebo
State Park

Overlook

155

Summit
Park
Trail

Fern
Lake

Pool and
Bathhouse

Bench Trail
Trailhead

Pavilion

Crystal/Lion
Springs

Campground

To Dardanelle

Group
Site

Gum
Springs

Varnall
Springs

Waterfall

Bench
Trail

Rim
Trail

Sunrise
Point

Hike–in
Campsites

Legend:
- Bench Trail
- Rim Trail
- Summit Park Trail
- Connecting Trails

Mt. Nebo Trails System—1.0, 3.4 & 4.0 mile loops

Mt. Nebo State Park sits atop the majestic mountain that rises 1800 feet out of the Arkansas River Valley near Russellville. There are a lot of spectacular views and geological formations along the many trails there. We're going to visit the three longest—the Rim, Bench and Summit Park trails. Besides a campground, there are many cabins at the park, and since there are terrific sunrise and sunset viewpoints, you should plan to spend the night. A parking fee may be required. Adona quad.

To get to Mt. Nebo, take exit 81 off of Interstate 40, go south on Hwy. 7 through Russellville to Dardanelle, turn right onto Hwy. 22 west, then turn left on Hwy. 155 south—the last couple of miles up to the top is *very* steep and winding—not recommended for a large RV on a hot summer day. Turn right once you get into the park and stop at the Visitor Center. That is where we'll begin our first hike on the Rim Trail, which is the most spectacular of these trails.

RIM TRAIL LOOP—3.4 miles total. This trail circles the mountain on top of, and sometimes at the base of, the bluff that runs the entire way. You would expect some incredible views, and you would be right! The trail is a historical one too—it was actually built in the 1890's, when the mountain was a booming resort center. There are many access points to this trail, and we are going to begin at the Visitor Center. It is marked with yellow blazes.

The trail begins off the back of the Visitor Center, runs down a flight of steps to an intersection—TURN RIGHT (we'll finish from the left). It soon drops on down steeply through the bluffline, then levels off and passes a spur trail to the left that drops down further to Nebo Springs—continue STRAIGHT AHEAD. It eases up the hill just a little, up against a bluff, past an SSS view, then on up the hill some more. At .6 it passes "Buzzard Roost," an overhanging bluff SSS. During leaf–off there are some nice views, and the lake you're looking at is Lake Dardanelle on the Arkansas River.

Just beyond the trail goes next to the swimming pool, across the back of the pavilion at the campground, then heads on over to and across the entrance road at .8. It turns to the left and switchbacks steeply down through the bluff—an SSS. There are several spurs that run out to other viewpoints. It levels off below the bluff and heads over to the right. It continues along the base of the bluff, all an SSS area. And there is a boulder field down and to the left—another SSS. At 1.1 the Varnall Springs Trail takes off to the left (heads steeply down the hill), but we continue STRAIGHT AHEAD along the towering bluff.

Just beyond, there is an oak tree that has literally grown over the trail—you have to duck to pass under it! The trail begins to swing around to the right, and heads uphill some as the bluff gets smaller and more broken. The view opens up too—an SSS. At 1.4 there is a spur that heads back to the left and up the hill to Sunrise Point, a great SSS viewpoint (accessible by car). We go STRAIGHT AHEAD here, mostly level, past lots of rock outcrops, and another SSS overhang area, as the trail swings on around the hillside. We are now on the backside of the mountain, still running next to the bluffline, much of it being an SSS.

At 1.7, after you leave the bluff area, there is an old trail that takes off down to the left (this was the Lower Rim Trail, but is now closed)—STAY RIGHT here. It goes through some broken bluff boulders, then comes out on top, and continues along the left edge around a cabin. There are still a number of private cabins up the mountain, like this one. There are some old, twisted cedar trees along through here too.

At 1.9 it intersects with the Gum Springs Trail (This trail heads steeply down the hill to the left, and soon goes past an SSS waterfall—worth a look during the wet season—then continues down to Gum Springs on the Bench Trail). GO STRAIGHT AHEAD here, up through a parking area, and out the other side. The trail continues along the top, sometimes running across lawns, sometimes through the woods. At 2.2 the Summit Park Trail joins us up from the left—continue STRAIGHT AHEAD. There are more park cabins, lawns and woods, then the trail drops down just a little, and goes over a neat stone bridge at 2.5, then eases back up the hill.

We pass more cabins on the right, and head through the woods to the Summit Park Trailhead at 2.7. It drops down some steps to an intersection—the Summit Park Trail turns to the left here. The Rim Trail continues STRAIGHT AHEAD, coming out into a large open area that it skirts along. Just past mile 3.0 is Sunset Point—a major SSS area that is accessible by car (some incredible views, especially of the sunset of course). The trail swings through it and around the point to the right. It crosses a roadbed and continues swinging around the hillside past several buildings. It eventually comes back to the Visitor Center intersection—TURN RIGHT and head up to the end of the trail at 3.4.

SUMMIT PARK TRAIL—one mile total. This interpretive trail plunges steeply down the hill past lots of geological formations, springs, a lake, and a multitude of natural things for you to look at. There is a brochure available at the Visitor Center that is keyed to the interpretive points along the trail. To get to the trailhead from the Visitor Center, simply go across the road from it, down the park road there for a couple of hundred yards and you'll come to the parking area on the right. The trail takes off on the right, drops down the hill and to the left. It switchbacks on down past lots of neat stuff, on down to the Bench Trail, then back uphill to the left, and on over to Fern Lake. From there it heads steeply back up the hill, past some amazing rock gardens, up to the Rim Trail, then turns left and follows it back to the parking area.

BENCH ROAD TRAIL—4 miles total. This loop trail (a great mountain bike trail) circles the mountain on an old roadbed that follows a level spot or "bench" that is just down below the Rim Trail. Overnight camping is allowed at several primitive campsites along the way—check in at the Visitor Center for a permit. It's a pretty easy trail to hike, with only a few climbs here and there. There are a number of connecting trails that come down from the Rim Trail. The trailhead is located on Hwy. 155 on the way out of the park, down to the right at the first level area.

The trail takes off and follows the old roadbed pretty much on the level. It passes the Varnall Springs Trail, three hike–in campsites, then swings around the hillside to the right. There are some nice rock formations scattered along the way, and the forest is pretty lush. It passes Gum Springs, and the Gum Springs Trail there, a group site, and Fern Lake. Past the lake it heads up the largest hill, and comes to an intersection—the left trail goes on over to more campsites, then rejoins the main trail. There is also a short spur that joins the Summit Park Trail. The trail continues on up the hill, then levels off and swings around the hillside to the right, passing a spur trail that goes up to Sunset Point. It continues on around the hillside on a gentle downhill grade, past Nebo Springs, and finally comes out to Hwy. 155 at a lookout pavilion—continue STRAIGHT down the highway back to the trailhead.

Agency List #31

Cove Lake Loop Trail #22

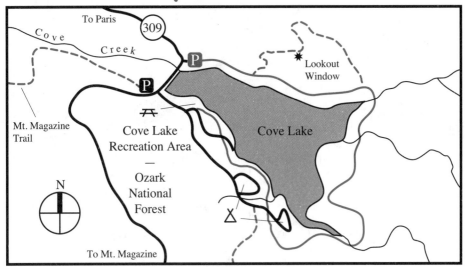

Cove Lake Loop—3.5 miles

Here is an easy loop trail that circles Cove Lake, and makes for a great afternoon stroll. There is pretty good fishing along the way too! To get to the trailhead, take Hwy. 309 south out of Paris about 9 miles to the lake—turn left into the parking area just before you cross the dam. On the far side of the dam is the beginning of the Mt. Magazine Trail (see next page), and a campground. Magazine Mtn. NE quad.

The trail takes off from the parking area and heads along the lake shore. Stop and fish anywhere you like! It comes to the intersection with a blue–blazed spur trail at .2. This spur winds its way a half mile *up* the hill to the "lookout window," a spectacular SSS overlook spot—you can see the top of Mt. Magazine from there (highest point in Arkansas). The spur continues around and down and rejoins the main trail.

From the spur intersection, the main trail continues along the lake. It veers to the left, heads away from the shore a little, and past the other end of the spur trail. At mile 1.0 it crosses a footbridge over a stream. There is a second, more narrow bridge across another stream just beyond. The trail curves to the right some, then left, then skirts the end of a food plot, and continues along through a low, often wet, area.

At 1.4 the trail follows a barbed–wire fence for a short distance, then heads on over to the lake shore again for a moment at 1.6. From there it swings back to the left, away from the lake for a time, then swings back to the right and down to the third bridge at 1.9. The trail eases up onto a bench overlooking the end of the lake, and an SSS at 2.0—a great view of the lake and lots of cypress trees (knees too).

From there the trail turns away from the lake and climbs up a rocky drainage—an SSS (*lots* of moss–covered boulders). It crosses the creek at 2.3, then winds on around, through another SSS boulder area, and comes to pavement at 2.5—it crosses the road, stays on blazed trail that goes down and to the left along the shore, and ends at the boat ramp at 3.1 (you can also turn left on the first road and follow it out to the highway). From the boat ramp parking lot, follow the road out to the highway at 3.3—TURN RIGHT and head across the dam to the parking lot at 3.5.

Agency List #5

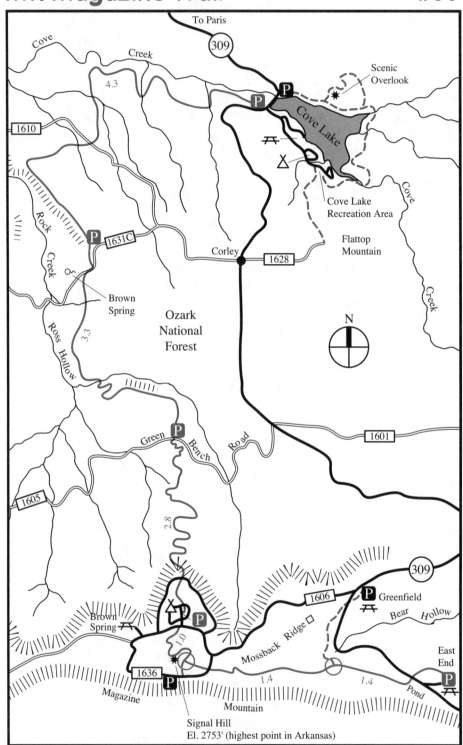

To Paris

309

Cove
Creek
4.3

Scenic
Overlook

Cove Lake

1610

Cove Lake
Recreation Area

Rock Creek

1631C

Brown
Spring

Corley

1628

Flattop
Mountain

Ross Hollow

3.3

Ozark
National
Forest

N

Cove Creek

Green

Bench

Road

1601

1605

2.8

Brown
Spring

1636

1606

Greenfield

309

Bear Hollow

Mossback Ridge

East
End

1.0

1.4

1.4

Pond

Magazine

Mountain

Signal Hill
El. 2753' (highest point in Arkansas)

Mt. Magazine Trail —14.2 miles one way

Here is your chance to climb to the highest point in Arkansas. You can drive most of the way up, but taking this trail from Cove Lake up to Mt. Magazine is a much better way to do it. I was surprised at how scenic it was, even before reaching the top. There are a number of options on where to begin and end this hike, but we're going to do the whole thing, and point them out as we go along. I do recommend hiking this trail from the bottom *up*, so that you can say that you really did climb the highest hill! It is a total elevation gain of 1753'. Camping is allowed along the trail (out of sight of). All of this trail is in the Ozark National Forest, but the top is now Mt. Magazine State Park (479–963–8502)—stop by their great visitor center on Hwy. 309. Blue Mountain quad.

To get to the beginning point at Cove Lake, take Hwy. 309 south out of Paris about 9 miles to the lake—the trail begins at the far side of the dam, at the trailhead on the right. This highway continues on up to Mt. Magazine (it is a National Scenic Byway), and the end of the trail. Also see the Cove Lake Trail on page 125.

The trail begins at the trailhead, across the highway from the campground road, and heads on into the woods. It is marked with white paint blazes. It drops on down just a little and comes alongside Cove Creek. After a short visit the trail swings to the left and uphill. It winds around up into and across a small drainage at .6—lots of rocks and large trees—an SSS. It heads back uphill some again, to the right, and swings around the hillside on an old roadbed. Towards the top, just as the roadbed curves back to the left, the trail leaves it TO THE RIGHT. Just beyond we come to mile marker #1 and level off. There are some nice views during leaf–off.

The trail runs along the top edge for a while, then swings left and drops down to and across another smaller creek at 1.4. It heads up some more to the right, then back to the left on the level. We skirt the edge of an open area, and then enter a thick stand of cedar trees. At 1.8 there is an SSS view off to the right. As the trail swings back to the left and across the ridge there are several glade spots that have lots of nice wildflowers scattered about. It crosses a road, and just beyond is milepost #2. Soon after, the trail leaves an old roadbed that it has been on TO THE LEFT as it heads down hill.

It works its way up hill a little, swings to the right and crosses FR#1610 at 2.6. There is some up–and–downing, across a small stream, and on to milepost #3. It eases uphill a little more as it swings back to the left and comes out at 3.4 to a spectacular SSS view. You are overlooking Rock Creek, and can see all the way up the drainage (Ross Hollow) to Mt. Magazine itself. It's a nice bluffline that we'll follow on up the hill to the left for a while, working our way up the ridge. Just as the trail levels off some, we pass milepost #4. At 4.3 we come to a trail intersection—a spur trail to the left goes a short distance on over to the Corley Trailhead (an optional starting/ending point), which is 1.6 miles by road from Hwy. 309 at Corley. Continue STRAIGHT AHEAD for the main trail.

The trail heads on down the hillside, levels off some, then heads back uphill and intersects with a road at 4.5—TURN RIGHT and follow this road downhill. It stays on it 'till it levels off at 4.8 and then leaves the road TO THE LEFT. The trail passes through a boulder field, comes to milepost #5, then dips down to an SSS stream crossing area. Just beyond, the trail heads through several "regeneration" areas (old timber cuts that have been replanted), joins an old road in the last one, and finally gets back into the real woods again at 5.6. It drops down the hill and turns left in the bottom near a stream, following it up to a crossing at 5.9—a springtime SSS. The trail is beside the stream for just a little bit, then turns to the left away from it and begins to head uphill, as it passes mile 6.0.

It winds on up this steep, rocky hillside, past an SSS rock garden down to the right. As it comes into an open area, the trail turns sharply left and levels off at 6.4. It makes its way around the edge of the hill to the right. The leaf–off views to the left can be pretty nice. It eases up just slightly and away from the edge, past mile 7.0, then heads out to the right across level forest. Down the hill just slightly it goes to an SSS at 7.3—a neat wildlife pond. From there it runs on out to FR#1605 (Green Bench Road) at 7.6. This is another optional start/end spot, and is 1.5 miles from Hwy. 309.

The trail begins to switchback uphill, past lots of great leaf–off views, and finally levels off at 7.9 and joins an old roadbed. Just after it turns and begins to run down the middle of the ridgetop, we pass mile 8.0. At 8.2 the trail leaves the roadbed TO THE RIGHT, and begins to head uphill, swinging back and forth. This is the beginning of a nearly 1000' climb to the top! At 8.8 the trail hits a "T" intersection—TURN RIGHT and continue uphill slightly (the left turn goes down to a wildlife pond). It levels off, goes past mile 9.0, then actually eases downhill just a tad. Then it begins to rise up again, as it swings back to the left.

It gets a little steeper, and passes large trees on its winding way up. This is a prolonged climb, but stay with it, and pause to enjoy the leaf–off views behind you often. At 9.9 the bluff comes into view up to the right. There are a number of steps on the roadbed in this area. At mile 10.0 we pass a registration box, then level off (yea!) and turn to the right. Just beyond the trail crosses FR#1606A (paved). There is a wonderful picnic shelter and incredible view of Cameron Bluff just up the road to the right. The trail heads into the woods, stays mostly level, across another paved road, and comes out to a parking area in the middle of the Cameron Bluff Campground at 10.4 (optional start/end point). TURN LEFT on the road up to the main road intersection at 10.5—the trail continues in the woods across the way as the "Signal Hill Trail."

This trail heads up the hill, not too steep, winds around and finally tops out at the highest point in Arkansas (congratulations, you made it!!!), which is 2,753' high, at mile 11.0. Although the view isn't open, this is definitely an SSS, just because of where you are. From here the trail turns left, then begins to swing down around the hill to the right, past some large oak trees. It levels off and comes to an intersection at 11.4—the main trail TURNS LEFT (a less–used trail) and continues as the "Mossback Ridge Trail" (stay to the right and you'll come out to the paved road in a couple of hundred yards, near the old Lodge site—a parking lot and optional begin/end spot).

At 11.6 the trail crosses the paved road, then goes on fairly level 'till it turns sharply uphill to the left at 11.9, then back to the right and on the level again right at mile 12.0. All along here there is an SSS view during leaf–off. The trail runs along through the open woods, mostly level, and comes to an intersection at 12.8. The main trail goes STRAIGHT AHEAD on to East End Picnic Area (the trail to the left goes .9 mile down to Greenfield Picnic Area). On an old roadbed now, the trail drops down the left side of the ridge to a neat SSS pond at 13.6—TURN LEFT HERE, off of the road and into the woods. It drops down to and across Hwy. 309 at 13.7, then heads out on the level. At mile 14.0 it intersects with an old roadbed—TURN RIGHT and follow this the rest of the way to the Greenfield Picnic Area at 14.2, and the end of the trail.

Agency List #5

Bridge Rock Trail #9

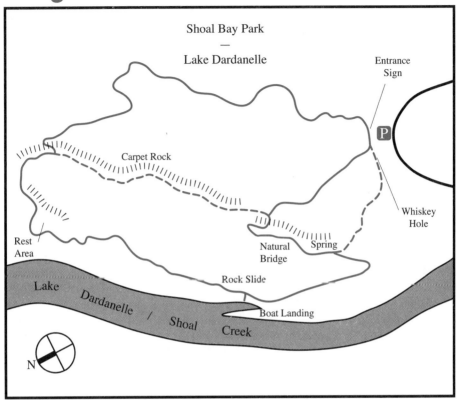

Bridge Rock Loop—.6 mile

This is one of the most scenic short trails in the state. There is a little bit of climbing involved, but it's worth it! The trail is located in Shoal Bay Park on Lake Dardanelle between Paris and Dardanelle, just of off Hwy. 22. From New Baine, go north on Hwy. 197 for 3 miles to the Park entrance and turn right. New Baine quad.

Begin your hike on the trail that heads off directly behind the big sign. It quickly comes to an intersection at .1—TURN LEFT and head down the hill. This area is a major SSS, and you'll find the trail's namesake here—a wonderful sandstone natural bridge. Spend some time here. The trail continues on below the bridge, and comes to another intersection—TURN RIGHT. The trail leads down the hill and to the right, and heads to the lake. At .2, it comes to a boat landing, which makes this trail accessible from the lake. It continues along the lake, past an SSS rock garden, a good view of the lake. Then at .3 it turns to the right, passes the first of several benches, and heads *up* the hill—all of this area for a while is an SSS! And I do mean *UP*. There are several flights of steps as you climb up through the moss and lichen covered rocks.

At .4 there is an intersection—TURN LEFT and continue *up* the hill. (The right fork takes you on over to "Carpet Rock," another SSS area, and beyond to the Natural Bridge.) Just a little more climbing, another bench, then the trail levels out—there are some really nice big pines here. It winds on around through the forest, and eases on down a little, back to the parking lot at .6.

Agency List #23

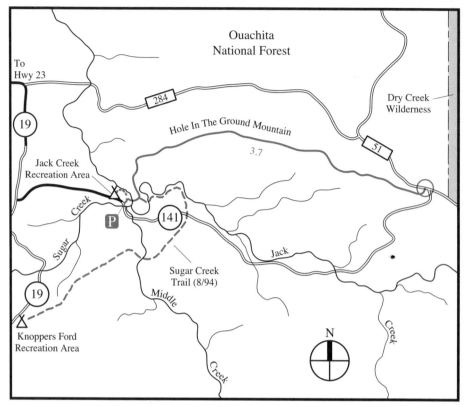

Hole In The Ground Mountain Trail—7.3 miles round trip

This trail is a bit of a sleeper—not too many folks know about or hike it. The first section of the trail looks down into a remarkable horseshoe bend in Jack Creek, and later on there are some terrific views out across the mountains. The first section of this trail gets pretty steep, but does level off on top of the ridge after a while. This is a good trail to use to access the Dry Creek Wilderness nearby if you're looking for a longer hike into the area. It is located on the Cold Springs Ranger District of the Ouachita National Forest, just south of Booneville. (The Sugar Creek Trail was scheduled to be constructed in the summer of 1994—it connects this trail with Knoppers Ford Campground—check with the District Office for information.) Sugar Grove quad.

From Booneville, take Hwy. 23 south 2.4 miles and turn left onto Hwy. 116 east, after .8 miles turn right onto road 19 (will turn to dirt road), after 6.6 miles turn left onto FR#141 (paved) and continue one more mile and turn left into Jack Creek Campground. Go to the end of the road and you'll find the trailhead. This is a small but nice campground with a pavilion, swimming area and neat trail that connects the camp and picnic areas via a lookout over the creek. The campground may be closed during the winter months. If it is, you can park adjacent to the campground, next to the bridge across Sugar Creek on FR#141, and you can camp at Knoppers Ford Campground a few miles away. There usually isn't any water on this trail, so be sure to bring plenty!

The trail begins next to the last picnic table on the right and runs on over to the creek. Jack Creek and Sugar Creek have just come together upstream. If the water is too high to cross, you can go over to the bridge on the forest road and cross there (you will be crossing private property though—be courteous). The trail is marked with wooden markers that are painted white. It crosses a short level area that has lots of nice towering pines in it (The Sugar Creek Trail will come in from the right in this area). But it quickly heads up the hill to the left. As it curves around up on the top of the ridge, you can wander over to the right at .3 and get a terrific SSS view of a hairpin curve in Jack Creek and the bluffs down below. It is pretty steep here, so take your time. Off to the left you can look down on the campground and swimming area.

The trail continues uphill steeply, with some relief at .5, when you cut across the tip of an opening—sort of angle to the right just a little and pick up the trail in the woods. It swings left and right through the timber, with some good views off to the left during leaf–off. Before long the trail levels on a ridgetop and heads over to the right. There is a large clearcut area down below that we'll be hiking just above for a while— this will provide some great open views out across the mountains.

There is some more uphill, and some fairly level, and we pass a 1–mile marker on a tree. The last time that I hiked this trail, I found a cactus in full bloom there. At 1.1 there is one of those SSS views off to the right. This area is rather lush with ferns and wildflowers. And there are more views as the trail heads gradually uphill here and there. It is working its way up near the top of another ridge—this is actually Hole In The Ground Mountain. No, there isn't a giant hole anywhere. I've heard several stories about the origin of the name. I think it comes from the fact that back at the hairpin curve the creek looks as if it has dug a "hole" in the mountain with this curve. You are welcome to hunt for your own hole in the ground!

Eventually the trail tops out up on the narrow ridge, actually heads downhill a little, and at 2.0 it crosses over the ridge to the north side. During leaf–off you get a pretty good view on this side too. The hillside in front is much steeper than the south side. The trail remains fairly level with some uphill as it runs down the middle of the ridgetop some, then off to the left side again, and finally through a rocky area back up on top. At 2.3 another clearcut area becomes visible off to the right, and the trail, still pretty much level, skirts around it. The ridgetop is more flat and open here.

Soon the trail leaves that area, swings back to the left, and crosses a couple of small, usually–dry drainages. At 2.9 there is a small stream that may have a few little waterfalls on it during the wet periods. It tumbles down the hill to the left. The trail crosses an old roadbed, and just beyond is mile 3.0. I saw two of the largest coyotes here that I've ever seen—they looked like wolves. There is a little more uphill, but gradual, as the trail crosses several dry drainages. The hillside below gets pretty steep, then flattens out again.

At 3.7 the trail ends at the intersection of forest roads 141 and 51. The Dry Creek Wilderness Area is just across the road. The District has a map of the area available—there weren't any official hiking trails into it when I did this book, but there are plenty of old log roads to hike on, and there is some pretty neat stuff in there—check with the District for the most current information.

The best way to get back to the trailhead is simply to turn around and hike back the same route—it's mostly downhill, and you'll always see different things!

Agency List #11

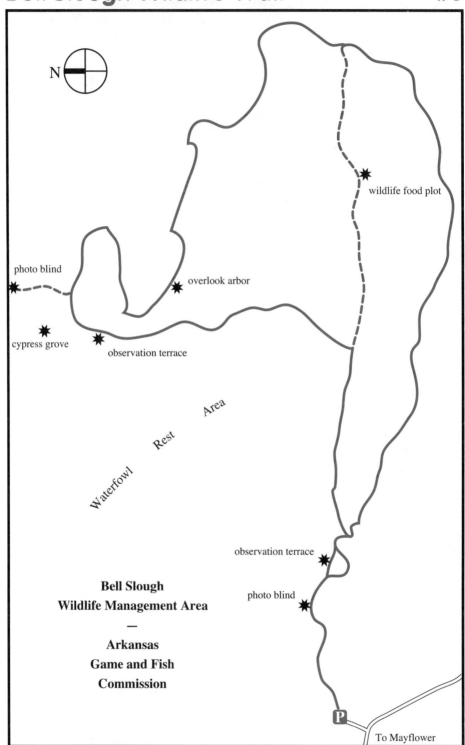

N

wildlife food plot

photo blind

overlook arbor

cypress grove

observation terrace

Waterfowl Rest Area

observation terrace

photo blind

Bell Slough
Wildlife Management Area

—

Arkansas
Game and Fish
Commission

P

To Mayflower

Bell Slough Wildlife Loop Trail—2.3 miles

If you like ducks and other waterfowl, this is a great trail for you. It loops around the edge of an official "Waterfowl Rest Area" where thousands of waterfowl and other wildlife can be seen from the trail, and from specially-constructed photo and observation blinds. The trail is easy hiking, but one note of warning is that the area often floods a couple of times a year and the trail is inaccessible during those times.

To get to the trailhead, take exit #135 on I-40 at Mayflower, then head south on Hwy. 365 through Mayflower. Continue south out of town and turn left onto Grassy Lake Road, which will take you under the interstate, and finally turn left and park at the trailhead.

There are several different ways that you can utilize this trail. You can make a quick hike out to the first photo blind if you don't have much time; continue on the north side of the loop that hugs the waterfowl rest area to the second photo blind (a round trip of about 1.5 miles); or make the entire outer loop, which is what we are going to do.

From the trailhead the trail crosses several boardwalks and soon comes to the first photo blind/observation point. There is a great view out into the rest area from there. Follow the trail to the next observation area nearby, still along the edge of the rest area. Just past this spot the trail actually goes out onto a roadbed—both the roadbed and trail are surfaced with the same material so make sure you stay on the trail and not the road! The trail crosses the road and then splits—the left fork swings out to the north and to the second photo blind, but we are going to take the RIGHT FORK that heads up a little hill and make the entire loop in a counter-clockwise direction.

The trail levels out and meanders through a nice forest, all of it easy hiking. It curves back to the left and comes to an intersection at .8 with a short-cut trail back to the trailhead (it goes past a wildlife food plot)—CONTINUE STRAIGHT ahead. After the trail crosses a small foot bridge, it curves back to the left and climbs up a hill. At 1.2 there is an observation arbor on the left. Lots of wildflowers up on this hill, as well as some great views of the surrounding country side.

From the arbor the trail heads down off of the hill back to the right, then levels out and swings back to the left, where it comes to the intersection with the spur trail out to the photo blind at 1.5. It is just a short hike down to the blind. Back on the main trail, continue STRAIGHT AHEAD as the trail curves back to the left, past a grove of cypress trees that you can see out in the rest area to the right.

The trail runs near the edge of the waterfowl rest area and then heads into the woods again and intersects with the short-cut trail at 1.8—TURN RIGHT and follow the trail back to where the loops come together at the old roadbed. Cross the road and take the trail back past the original photo blind and over the boardwalks to the trailhead, making the total loop of 2.3 miles. If you just did the South Loop (using the cut-off trail), the distance would be about 1.3 miles, and the North Loop would be 1.8 miles. There may be additional trails added so be on the lookout for new intersections.

This fine trail was built from funds received through the special 1/8th cent sales tax, and is one of many "Watchable Wildlife" projects that is constructed and maintained by the Arkansas Game and Fish Commission.

Arkansas Game and Fish Commission, 800–364–4263

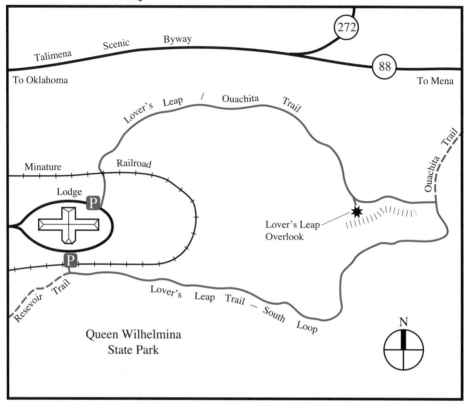

Lovers' Leap Loop—1.1 miles

This short loop is located high atop Rich Mountain in Queen Wilhelmina State Park (lodge and other facilities there), on the Talimena Scenic Drive, about 14 miles from Mena. The trailhead is located behind the lodge, around to the left. Rich Mtn quad.

The trail takes off down a set of steps and crosses miniature railroad tracks, then continues downhill through a lush forest. This first section of the trail is also part of the Ouachita Trail—it's 51 miles to one end of the trail in Oklahoma, and 171 miles to the other end at Pinnacle Mtn. State Park near Little Rock. There are a number of benches along the way, as the trail heads uphill to the Lover's Leap overlook at .3—it's just off to the right, and is a large wooden deck. It's a wonderful SSS view!

Beyond the overlook the trail continues downhill to the point where the Ouachita Trail leaves to the left at .5—TURN RIGHT at the tombstone. The section of trail from here on gets quite steep and rough in a spot or two. It heads downhill, then swings right and levels off. Good views, and lots of rock gardens. It begins to head *up* the hill, and you'll have to hop from rock to rock—an SSS area. Sometimes it's pretty steep, and a little tricky to find the trail—follow the yellow blazes. It eventually levels out, turns back to the right, then heads uphill some for the last time. It comes out of the woods at 1.0, and intersects with the Reservoir Trail —TURN RIGHT and climb the steps to the parking area—the trailhead is just on the other side of the lodge, making a total loop of 1.1 miles. A parking/entrance fee may apply—check with the office.

Agency List #34

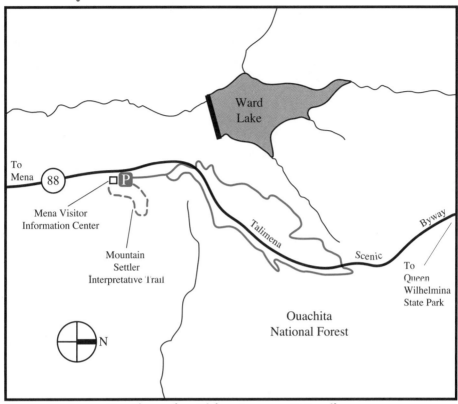

Earthquake Ridge Loop—2.1 miles

This short loop trail is one of two that is located at the Mena Visitor Center of the Forest Service, which is just west of Mena on Hwy. 88 up on the Talimena Scenic Byway (this is different from the Forest Service District Office, which is on Hwy. 71 in Mena). It is used by mountain bikes once in a while. Mena quad.

The trail is blazed with white paint, and takes off from the parking area into the pine woods on the level, next to the highway. It comes to a trail register (please do), and splits—we're going to take the LEFT FORK. It swings on up to and across the highway, then switchbacks up a hill, and the views behind get better with every step. It finally levels off and straightens out. There are some nice hardwoods, then at .6 the trail intersects a jeep road—TURN LEFT on the road and run along it for just a hundred feet or so. After a while the trail heads up the hill, at times steeply, and passes some rock gardens along the way. It tops out at about mile 1.0.

It heads on down the hill to and across the highway (when I hiked this there were fresh bear tracks in the trail). The trail drops some, but not too steeply. During leaf–off there are some great views out across the way. It passes a couple of nice rock gardens, lots of big pines, and at 1.6, a small spring. The hillside is very steep, but the trail does its up–and–downing on a pretty gentle grade. It eventually does head up the hill to the registration spot, which completes the loop at 2.0—TURN LEFT and head back to the trailhead.

Agency List #13

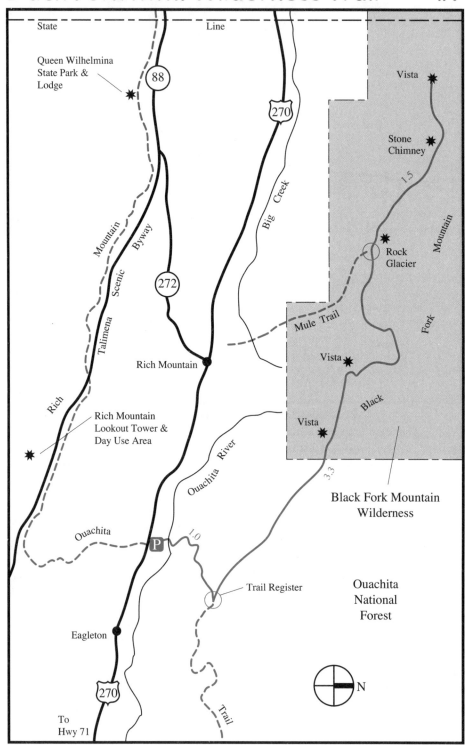

State Line

Queen Wilhelmina State Park & Lodge

88

270

Big Creek

Vista

Stone Chimney

1.5

Mountain

Rock Glacier

272

Mule Trail

Fork

Mountain Scenic Byway Talimena

Rich Mountain

Vista

Black

Rich

Rich Mountain Lookout Tower & Day Use Area

Vista

Ouachita River

Black Fork Mountain Wilderness

3.3

Ouachita

P

1.0

Trail Register

Ouachita National Forest

Eagleton

N

270

To Hwy 71

Trail

Black Fork Mountain Trail—11.6 miles round trip

This mountain–top wilderness trail has some incredible views up and down the upper Ouachita River and Big Creek valleys, and the Rich Mountain/Talimena Scenic Drive area across the way. This 7,568 acre wilderness area was created as part of the Arkansas Wilderness Act of 1985. The trailhead is located about a mile west of the community of Eagleton on Hwy. 270 (from Mena, go 6 miles north on Hwy. 71 to Acorn, then turn west on Hwy. 270, 6 miles to Eagleton). Look for the "Wilderness Trailhead" sign and turn right into the parking lot. This is one of the best trailheads that you'll ever see, and the Ouachita Trail (OT) runs through it. In fact, the first mile of this hike is on the OT. Page, Mountain Fork and Rich Mountain quad maps.

The route of this trail (much of it on old roads) gets pretty steep at times—this is a tough trail—but the rewards are certainly worth it. There is very little water along the route, so be sure to carry plenty. Also, there is a healthy black bear population in the area, so be a good clean camper, don't leave food in your tent, and be alert! If you are a real strong hiker, you could dayhike this trail. I would recommend that you backpack it, though, and spend the night somewhere near the end of the trail—just take it easy as you go up, and enjoy the views.

The trail leaves from the back of the lot, behind the bulletin board and register. You immediately come to an intersection with a sign—this is the Ouachita Trail (turn right to head to Rich Mountain and Oklahoma)—turn left to head towards the Black Fork Mountain Wilderness. The trail is marked with white blazes (OT is marked with blue ones, so there will be both for a while). The trail drops down and crosses the Ouachita River on a nice bridge, intersects with an old road—turn right and go up to and across a railroad track. The trail continues into the woods on the other side and just to the left. It heads uphill a little, then joins another roadbed for a while.

There is a little climbing in here, through a mixed forest of mostly young trees, and it swings past a section corner, then levels off, and actually drops downhill some through a boulder field. It gets rocky for a while, mostly level, through hardwoods. At 1.0 miles there is a trail intersection—this is where we leave the Ouachita Trail—TURN LEFT and head up the hill on an old road. There is another trail register here, just in case you missed the first one (the OT continues on across the Forest to Pinnacle Mtn. State Park near Little Rock—at 222.5 miles it is the longest hiking trail in Arkansas).

This old roadbed heads uphill quickly, then forks—take the LEFT fork, which continues uphill. The trail winds its way around through stands of young pine, then hardwoods, then mixed, with some level walking, but mostly uphill. It eventually swings to the left side of the ridge, where there are a couple of nice views over some scrub trees. Much of this area of the mountain burned in a great fire in 1963, which was started by a spark from one of the trains passing through. It burned about 13,000 acres! The climb continues, through mile 2.0, and the views of Rich Mountain get better and better. Finally the trail levels off and heads down the middle of the ridgetop, dropping slightly.

The trees get larger as the trail swings to the right side of the ridge, heads uphill some, and at 2.4 you come to a Blackfork Mountain Wilderness Area sign, and enter the wilderness. When I hiked this trail in 1992, some idiots had vandalized this sign. You'd think that this far back in you wouldn't see such acts. Just beyond, watch for a side trail to the left, which goes a few feet to a rock outcrop, and a terrific SSS view of the entire valley below and mountains beyond. This is a great spot to drop your pack and gaze a while. From here the trail drops some, then level, passes a bullfrog pond at 2.6. There isn't enough meat on any of them for dinner, but they do sing well. The trail climbs up a little more, then is level again by 3.0. Another steep little climb takes you to another view area (minor SSS with low timber and lots of boulders), then level again on top through a wonderful grassy area. The trail swings back to the left and begins to drop rapidly down the rocky hillside. The trail tread isn't too good through much of this area—keep an eye out for the blazes. At 4.0 there is a neat rock slab with several pine trees growing right out of it. It's kind of hard to get past with a pack on, so you'll probably figure out where I'm talking about.

At 4.3 you intersect with an old mule trail coming up from below (it is possible to follow this mule trail back down the hillside to near the store at Rich Mountain, but it is not marked, gets consufing at the end, and does cross private property)—TURN RIGHT on it for some easier footing as it begins to climb back up to the top of the ridge, through a lush forest with some huge oak trees. At 4.6 a giant rock "glacier" appears up to the right through the trees—just as the trail levels off and turns to the left away from it, stop and go over and have a look. A major SSS—you won't see too many of these in Arkansas!

There is some more climbing ahead, through low, scrub oaks, great SSS views, and even a trickle of a spring in the trail. At 5.0 the trail is level, then a little more climbing, then mostly level. At 5.2 there is a sharp turn to the right, and a spur trail to the left that goes down to a spring–fed pond (possible water supply!). There is a rock cairn (pile of rocks) here to mark the spot. I'm not sure if this spring runs all year, but it had plenty of water in it in June when I hiked it. Gosh, this area looks like a great spot to live. Hum.

All of the trail from this point on is an SSS—lush grassy flat areas (same kind as in Caney Creek) with stunted 100+ year old oak trees. At 5.4 you pass an equally old chimney on the left—I told you it looked like a great place for a homestead. Just across the trail from it you'll find an old barrel rim that has been engulfed by a tree. This is a wonderful area to stop at and spend some time looking around, and perhaps the night. Make sure that you camp away from the trail, though, to keep it all looking so nice.

The trail continues on the level past the homesite, and eventually swings to the LEFT—there is another trail that goes straight ahead here, so watch for it (this other trail runs on over to a little cemetery on private land. I've been told that there are soldiers from both sides of the Civil War buried there. This is *private property.*)

From this intersection the trail eases uphill slightly back to the right, following an old rock wall, and comes out into another low scrub tree SSS view area—the trail ends here at 5.8 with a blaze on a large rock (elevation @ 2600 feet). You can look across the way and see the Lodge at Queen Wilhelmina State Park.

Eventually, the trail may continue past this point, deeper into the Wilderness, and maybe even connect with a trail that will come out on the Oklahoma side. But for now you should just enjoy the view, explore around the old homestead, then head back out the same way that you came in. The Ozark Society sells a map of the Blackfork Mountain Wilderness Area that you may want to pick up if you intend to do any serious bushwhacking around in the area (see page 189). The trip back is a lot easier, although there is one pretty good climb up the hill through the rocky area as you leave the old mule trail to the LEFT—be sure to watch for this intersection.

Agency List #13

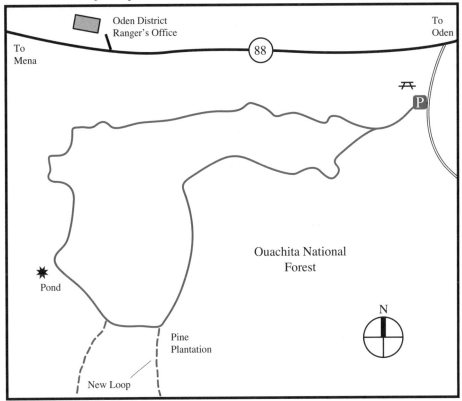

Serendipity Loop—1.0 miles

This is one of my favorite interpretive trails. It's very short, easy to hike, and the signs there interpret the forest like no other trail I've ever seen. It's in the Ouachita National Forest, right across from the Oden District Ranger's Office. Definitely worth a side trip to go see. To get there, take Hwy. 88 west out of Pencil Bluff (on Hwy. 270 near Mt. Ida) to Oden. Go through town 1.5 miles and turn left into the parking lot—the District Office is just down the highway on the right. Oden quad.

The gravel trail heads out past a signboard to the left, then splits—TURN LEFT. One of the signs explains the different "layers" in the forest—a tree layer, vine layer, shrub layer, herb layer, and a forest floor layer. I've got a simple mind, and breaking the forest down that way is a terrific way to explain things. The trail winds around through the forest, passing a number of labeled trees and other stuff. It crosses a small bridge, and passes a bench. There are some giant pine trees here and there, and the rest is a nice open forest.

The "Pine Plantation" spot is at .4, and there is a bench there. *(A new, 1/2 mile loop will be added here in the future.)* The trail swings on around to the right, towards a spur trail to the left at .5 that leads down to another bench that overlooks a pond. It continues on around to the right, over a hollow–log culvert, past many more ID signs, and begins to head back to the trailhead. Turn left when you reach the intersection and return to the parking lot, for a total hike of just under one mile total.

Agency List #14

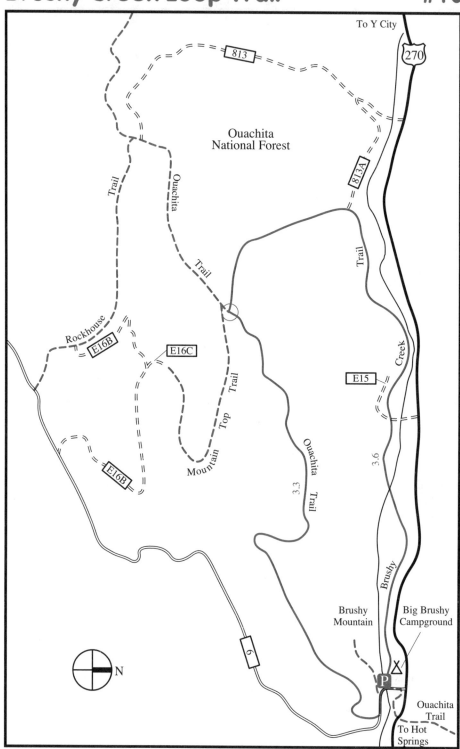

Brushy Creek Loop—6.9 miles

There are several trails in the area of Big Brushy Campground in the Ouachita National Forest, which is located on Hwy. 270 between Y–City and Mt. Ida. One of them, the Brushy Trail, connects with a portion of the Ouachita Trail and makes a nice loop. The trail begins at the very back of the campground there, and is blazed with white paint. And with the exception of one long, steep grade, it's a real easy trail to hike. Brushy Creek Mountain quad.

It heads out across the level bottomland forest, passing some nice large pine trees. Big Brushy Creek is just off to the left, while Hwy. 270 is through the woods to the right. The trail winds around on the level for quite a while, heading away from the highway somewhat, and crossing numerous streams—some are dry rock beds, others have nice pools of water. At 1.3 it crosses FR#E15 (it's mainly just a jeep trail). The trail heads upstream alongside Big Brushy Creek on an old roadbed. Eventually the roadbed curves to the left and the trail continues STRAIGHT AHEAD alongside the creek. This area is an SSS—beautiful stream with big pine trees!

The trail then winds off into another flat, away from the creek, and goes through mile 2.0. It crosses a couple of smaller streams, then bumps up onto a hillside bench. It swings left and right a few times, crosses more stream beds, then crosses one last creek, and on the other side it heads over and connects with FR#813A at 2.7—TURN LEFT and follow this road up the hill. This is really the first uphill that we've done on this trail! The road levels off and goes through mile 3.0. It eases up just a little more, then the road ends at 3.1, and the trail continues beyond. It swings to the left, crosses another creek, then begins a rather steep climb up an old road bed that is grown up with tiny pine trees. Up and up we go. During leaf–off the views off to the left get pretty nice.

At 3.6 the trail tops out and comes to the intersection with the Ouachita Trail (OT). This National Recreation Trail is 223 miles long, extending from Talimena State Park in Oklahoma to Pinnacle Mountain State Park near Little Rock. The Brushy Creek Trail actually ends here, but we're going to make a nice loop by following the OT all the way back to the campground. TURN LEFT on the OT. It is blazed with blue blazes, and eases up the hill, then heads down the nose of a ridge, through mile 4.0. (OT mile marker #92 is just beyond.)

The trail does some up–and–downing, working its way along a ridge. There are some great views during leaf–off. It passes mile 5.0 on a level stretch. (The Brushy Mountain Trail will someday intersect in this area—it is not built yet—a right turn on it will take you down to FR#6.) Right after mile 5.0, there is an SSS area with nice boulders up to the left, and a great view to the right. The trail swings on around the hill to the left and passes OT mile marker #93 on the other side of the ridge. The leaf–off view is terrific! It works its way along a steep hillside, gradually heading downhill, through mile 6.0, and OT mile marker #94. It continues to swing on down the hill, and comes out at the bottom onto FR#6 at 6.5—TURN LEFT and walk on the road. There is a nice creek just off to the right.

At 6.7, just before crossing a large bridge, the Brushy Mountain Trail takes off up a flight of steps to the left. It's a short trail that dead ends in a half mile, and will someday be connected back up to the OT—pretty nice views during leaf–off. We want to continue on the road across the bridge, and TURN LEFT into the campground, and back to the parking area for a total distance of 6.9.

Agency List #14

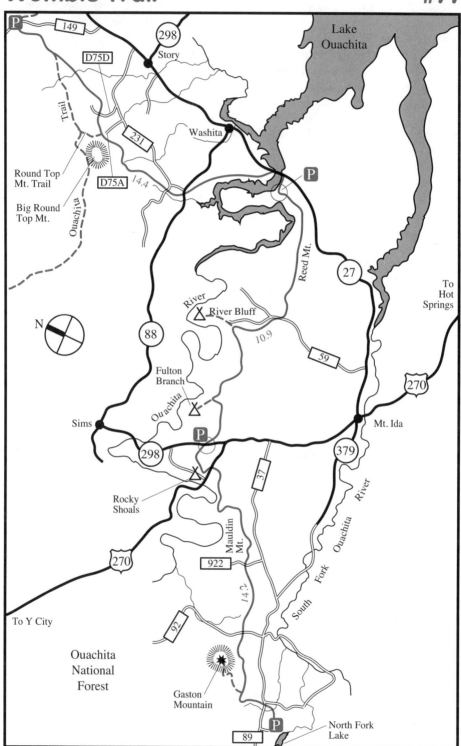

Womble Trail—39.5 miles one way

This is the third longest trail in Arkansas. It was originally built as part of the Ouachita Trail (OT), then became the Womble. It connects with the OT (in fact we're going to hike part of the OT to get to the start of the Womble), runs along the Ouachita River, crosses Hwys 27, 298 and 270, then climbs Mauldin Mountain, passes Gaston Mountain, and ends at North Fork Lake. The views are breathtaking, and there are lots and lots of large trees along the way. There are a number of hefty climbs, but for the most part the trail is a pleasure to hike. Most of the trail is in the Ouachita National Forest, so camping is allowed along the route, and there are three short spur trails down to campgrounds on the Ouachita River. Story, Oden, Mt. Ida and Reed Mtn. quads.

To get to the trailhead, take Hwy. 27 north out of Mt. Ida, to Story, then continue 2 miles and turn left onto FR#149, take this dirt road 2.4 miles to the bridge across Muddy Creek—we will pick up the OT here (park on the far side of the bridge). The first 13.5 miles is located on the Oden Ranger District, and the rest of the trail is located on the Womble District. It is marked with white paint, and there are "survey style" mile markers along the way. The first 1.5 miles is marked with blue paint, the standard OT color. There aren't too many reliable sources along the route. The trail is open to mountain bikes *south* of FR#D75A (*closed* to bikes north of it).

From your car, follow the road ***back*** across the bridge, then TURN RIGHT onto the OT. It heads up the hill, snaking *up* at a pretty good clip. When it gets to a ridgetop, it turns to the left and continues up. Then it swings to the right, and finally tops out for good. It heads off to the left side of the ridge, and begins to drop down just a little. There are a few nice, big pine trees, and somewhat of a view out through them along the way. It lands on a road trace, TURNS RIGHT on it, and soon comes to an intersection at 1.5—the OT continues straight ahead, on to Oklahoma. The Womble Trail begins here—TURN LEFT off of the road, down the hill on just trail. Since the mile posts on the trail begin here, I will reset my running count here too. To be square with the world, you should add 1.5 miles to all of the mileage figures from here on.

The Womble is marked with white paint. The trail heads down the hill, switchbacking as it goes, levels off some, then drops some more. It climbs up just a little, skirts a cutover area, then comes to mile post #1. There is a wildlife pond just beyond on the right, and the trail runs mostly level for a while, then does some up–and–downing across the hillside. It drops down to the left around another cutover area, then comes to mile post #2 just before crossing a jeep road. It crosses a small creek just beyond, then heads up the hill some, and runs along an old road trace down the middle of a ridgetop. It leaves the trace to the right, and makes its way around another cutover area, past a small pond on the right, then comes to and across FR#D75D at 2.5.

It heads into the woods, climbs up some, then levels out across a steep, grassy hillside. It goes through several tiny ravines, then passes mile post #3. From there the trail snakes up the hill some more, then swings to the left and heads downhill on ridgetop. At the bottom is the intersection with the Round Top Mountain Trail—it goes to the right 1.4 miles up the hill and connects with the OT (you could make about an 8–mile loop by following it to the OT, then back to the Womble). The Womble Trail TURNS LEFT and heads over to a parking area at the end of FR#D75A at 3.6.

It goes across the end of the parking area, back into the woods, up just a tad, then across a narrow open area, and past a small pond on the left. It begins to get a little rocky through here. You'll find that this is a nice winter hike, because the views are a little more open, and because there are lots of green pine trees too! The trail continues to amble on along, and comes to mile post #4 just as the trail hits an old road trace—TURN RIGHT and follow the road across a small stream, then TURN LEFT off of the road a short ways beyond. It crosses the same stream and heads up a steep, rocky hillside. The low bushes that you'll see a lot of along this trail are huckleberry bushes.

The trail crosses a ridgetop, then drops some down the other side. It crosses a small ravine, then up and over another ridge to mile post #5. It crosses a larger stream just beyond, and there is an SSS area downstream a ways—lots of rocks and stuff. The trail snakes on up the hill, and skirts food plot #118 around to the left. At the end of it, the trail turns right and intersects with FR#D78B at 5.3—TURN LEFT and follow the road. *(This stretch will be relocated soon to get the trail off of the road—watch for the changes.)* It swings around some, and at 5.9 the trail leaves the road TO THE RIGHT. Just beyond is mile post #6. At 6.4 there is an SSS view of the hills off to the right.

The trail drops on down to FR#887, TURNS RIGHT and follows the road just across a small bridge, then TURNS LEFT off of the road, and passes mile post #7. This section goes through a nice, wide open level forest, an SSS of sorts. At 7.9 the trail crosses Hwy. 88, then passes a registration box and mile post #8. The trail does some up–and–downing, crosses a road, then passes mile post #9. Just beyond is an SSS area along a small stream—a *steep* hillside covered with reindeer lichens. At 9.3 the trail corners hard left and comes to an incredible SSS view of the Ouachita River—you're looking straight down on it! The trail follows the knife–edge ridge on up the hill—all of it an SSS. It climbs some, then begins to head down the right side of the ridge, away from the river. *(Relocation is planned for this stretch in 1995, to stay on the ridge.)*

It passes a couple of SSS springtime waterfalls on the left, bottoms out, then climbs up, all the while following a narrow ravine. It tops out, then swings back to the right and heads towards the river again, mostly level, passing mile post #10. It swings to the left as it overlooks the river once again, and heads downhill, passing below an SSS rock formation. The trail bottoms out and swings back and forth along at river level, passing miles 11 and 12, as well as some large trees. Then it comes out to an open area and a registration box. Just beyond it hits Hwy. 27 at 12.2 and TURNS RIGHT. Follow the highway across the Ouachita River (actually the upper part of Lake Ouachita), and turn BACK TO THE RIGHT on the other side and follow a gravel road.

The road heads upstream, past several SSS views of the Ouachita River, and then swings to the left away from it—TURN LEFT off of the road at 12.9—there is a new trailhead parking area at this spot. From here the trail heads into the woods, then steeply up a hill, and comes to a wonderful SSS view at 13.5. Be careful not to slip! This is a spectacular view. The trail winds around the edge, climbing some, past a number of large trees, and an SSS area of huge trees at 13.8 near the top of our climb. From here the trail heads mostly level across a STEEP hillside, just below the top of Reed Mountain. It runs along the same way for quite a while, passing an SSS fern gully at 16.0. Soon it bottoms out, follows a four–wheeler trace and then a gravel road, then TURNS LEFT off of the road and through a fence—mile post #17 is right there.

It winds on around through the open woods, crosses County Road 59, then continues on into the woods. It wraps around a hillside, past mile post #18, then ambles along through nice forest, past a pond, mile post #19, and through several fences. It does some up–and–downing, crosses a small stream, and comes to an intersection at 19.8—a

1.4–mile spur goes to the right down to River Bluff Camp on the Ouachita River—the main trail TURNS LEFT (before the road trace) and continues on through the woods. It weaves around, dropping down to an SSS rock outcrop area on a small stream that the trail follows (first water source in a while). It crosses the stream a second time, passes through a cedar thicket, then follows an old road trace, and crosses a forest road at 21.7.

It rises up over a small ridge, then begins to follow another old road trace, past a pond and an SSS area of bearded cedars. At 22.3 it goes through an open area—a trail to the right here goes on down to Fulton Branch Campground on the Ouachita River—the main trail continues STRAIGHT AHEAD, then swings up the hill to the left. It heads up the hill, hits a road, TURNS RIGHT on it, then TURNS LEFT off of it, and heads out into the woods again. At 23.8 it crosses Hwy. 298 (may be a trailhead here). The trail does lots of up–and–downing to an intersection at 25.4—the trail to the right goes down to Rocky Shoals Campground on the Ouachita River—the main trail TURNS LEFT and heads down to Hwy. 270 at 25.7. There is a nice stream just beyond.

The trail runs across private property for the next mile or so, and there are LOTS of trail intersections—be sure to be alert and *follow the white blazes*. It crosses a couple of real nice streams—SSS areas—then it heads across a steep hillside and swings to the left above Camp Ozark—a big complex of buildings, tennis courts, etc. At 26.9 there is a terrific SSS view!!! The trail continues across the steep hillside, lots of big trees, then crosses over a ridge to the left and heads downhill, passing mile post #28. It bottoms out, then begins a long climb up Mauldin Mountain.

Once on top, the trail remains mostly level, swinging back and forth through saddles to either side of the mountain. There are lots of nice trees and views all through here. This is a l o n g mountain. It eventually drops down to and across FR#922 at 30.6. The trail continues running along the sides of ridgetops, past several SSS views, and across steep, fern–lined hillsides. There is one pretty steep climb, and one good run downhill. But it's mostly level. It crosses FR#92 at 33.3, then continues along the hillsides, crossing over saddles, and drops down to a jeep road at 34.4—TURN RIGHT and follow this road down the hill. Just as it bottoms out, TURN RIGHT off of it and head into the woods.

The trail runs across the hillside, climbing some—the larger hill just off to the right is Gaston Mountain—and at 35.5 it CROSSES the jeep road. [If you turned right and headed up the road, then turned left off of it, a spur trail would take you up to the top of the mountain, the site of an old lookout tower (gone now). The view is pretty nice during leaf–off.] The main trail heads down the hill, switchbacks to the left, crosses a small creek, and heads out across a flat area. It crosses FR#68 at 36.7, remains level for a while, then heads up and over a ridge, and crosses an SSS stream area down on the other side. The trail turns left onto an old road trace, then crosses a couple of smaller streams and begins to run alongside the shores of North Fork Lake. It comes out to the parking area just past mile #38. (The total hike is 39.5 miles, counting the 1.5 miles that we did on the OT to get to the beginning of the Womble Trail).

To get to North Fork Lake by car, from Hwy 270 by Mt. Ida, take Hwy. 379 to the west, follow it (changes to dirt) straight through intersections for 7.3 miles, then turn onto FR#68 for three miles, then turn left at the sign to the lake. It's a nice little lake, but has no facilities.

Agency List #14 (first 12 miles) and #16 (13–38 miles)

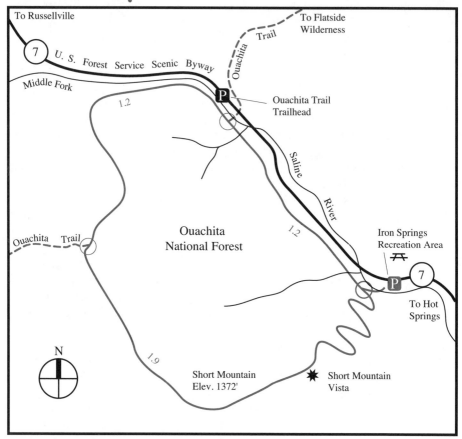

Hunts Loop—4.3 miles

This nice loop trail begins at the Iron Springs Recreation Area, climbs up Short Mountain, then connects with the Ouachita Trail and loops back around to the beginning. It's got some great views, visits stands of big trees, and passes by some neat streamside areas. It's a good trail to hike during a drive along Hwy. 7, one of America's most scenic drives, and a National Scenic Byway. It is located within the Ouachita National Forest. While in the area, you should also stop at the Jessieville Ranger District Visitor Center and hike the Friendship Trail there (p. 159). Nimrod S.E. quad.

To get to the trailhead, take Hwy. 7 north out of Hot Springs to the Iron Springs Recreation area (23 miles from Hot Springs and 5 miles north of Jessieville). The trail begins at the back of the rec. area. This is a quaint little area, which is mainly used as a picnic spot, and has a dam and tiny lake. There is a large signboard that has a map of the trail on it and other information. The trail is marked with white paint blazes.

Begin at the sign and head upstream to the massive new bridge (accessible) that crosses the middle fork of the Saline River. On the other side the trail turns to the right and goes a short distance to a picnic table and Iron Springs, a neat little spot for an out–of–the–way picnic! A word of caution here—it's not a good idea to drink any spring water that you are not familiar with unless it is treated. I know it's a great temptation to do so, but the risk of getting sick wouldn't be worth it.

The main trail TURNS LEFT here and begins a long pull up the hill. It switchbacks back and forth up the hillside, normally not too steep, and runs along level quite a bit too. Along the way there are lots of big trees, and the steep hillside is lush with mosses, ferns, and other ground cover. The views get better with each turn, and the highway noise soon disappears.

Just about when you're sure you can't climb any more, the trail tops out and comes to the spectacular Short Mountain Vista, an SSS, at .7 mile. It looks out across the Ouachitas, and you can see many ridges off in the distance. That was the most difficult section of the trail. And although the view was worth the climb up, I would recommend that you continue on and do the whole trail.

From the vista, the trail heads out across the middle of the ridgetop. During leaf–off, you'll have some good views off both sides. It swings to the right, drops down the hill a little, and begins to run along an old roadbed. It leaves the road to the left, and works its way into and through a low spot on the ridge. It leaves the saddle area and eases up a hill, then crosses an open forest area, and finally intersects with the Ouachita Trail at 1.9.

The beginning of the OT in Oklahoma is 159 miles straight ahead, and Ouachita Pinnacle is about 12 miles. We're going to join the OT and TURN RIGHT here, and follow it for the next mile or so. This is the longest hiking trail in this part of the country, and has a number of other trails like this one that share part of its path. It is blazed with blue blazes, so we'll be seeing both blue and white blazes as long as we're on it. (136–page guide available on it—see page 190.)

The trail swings around a hillside fairly level, with some easing uphill. It crosses a flat–topped ridge, then heads downhill some, past a wildlife pond, and OT mile marker #160. There are some good views during leaf–off along in here of the hills and valleys beyond. At one point the trail passes under some nice rock formations—an SSS area. Soon after, it hits another roadbed and TURNS RIGHT onto the roadbed. As you head down the road there are some other neat rock formations just uphill.

Before long at 2.9 you come to an intersection and a registration box—be sure to sign in! There is a parking lot straight ahead and just across a wooden bridge at Hwy. 7. The main trail TURNS RIGHT and continues along the roadbed on the level. We are still on the Ouachita Trail. This is a real lush area, with lots of wild iris and ferns. The Saline River is just off to the left. Soon the road/trail heads up hill, and the trail quickly leaves the roadbed TO THE LEFT, and continues on as just trail.

Just past this spot the trail forks at 3.1. The OT takes off to the left, heading towards Lake Sylvia 30 miles away. We want to TURN RIGHT and head towards Iron Springs. The trail remains level for a while, then drops down and crosses a small creek. Down in the bottom along in here there are some really nice large pines that tower above. Lots of spring wildflowers too.

The trail joins an old roadbed and swings away from Hwy 7 for just a little bit. It eventually comes to a nice bridge across a small stream. It continues along in the bottom, then runs up against the steep hillside off to the right—this hillside is covered with lush stuff like mosses and ferns. It's a sign of things to come, as just beyond we come to Iron Springs and the picnic table again. A reminder—please don't drink the spring water unless you treat it. No telling what is hanging over the stream in the cave that is inside the hill! (Bats love to roost over streams in caves.) Follow the trail back over the bridge to the trailhead at 4.3.

Agency List #12

Lake Sylvia Loop Trail

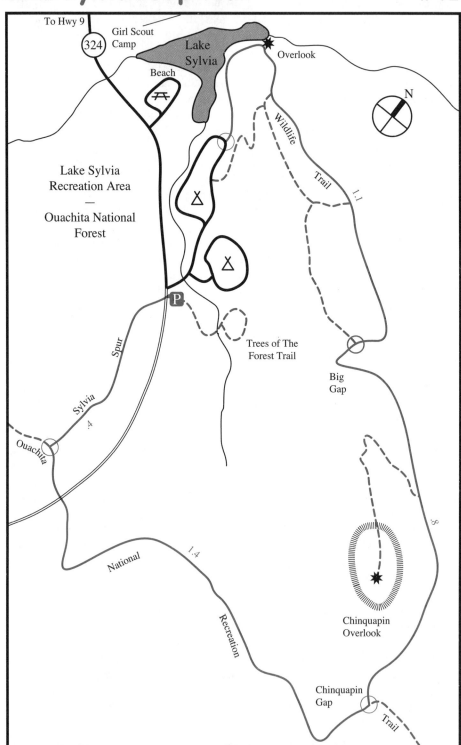

Lake Sylvia Loop—4.1 miles

This trail, west of Little Rock, connects with a part of the Ouachita Trail and an interpretive trail, overlooks a spectacular rock canyon area, and loops back along the shores of Lake Sylvia to the trailhead. It is located in the Ouachita National Forest. It's great for dayhiking. To get to Lake Sylvia, take Hwy. 10 west out of Little Rock, go past Williams Junction (with Hwy. 9), then turn west on Hwy. 324. This will take you 4 miles to Lake Sylvia—continue on this road (which becomes FR#152) to the Ouachita Trailhead (on the left just past the campground turnoff). Paron quad.

There is a paved, accessible interpretive trail called Trees of the Forest that leaves from this same trailhead. We want to head across the road and follow the trail that heads up into the woods. It swings back to the left some, levels off, then up some more. It intersects with the Ouachita Trail at .4. TURN LEFT and follow the OT. This section is marked with blue blazes. It runs on down the hill and crosses FR#152, then some more down hill but mostly level, then back to the left some, past mile 1.0. It swings back to the right, then back to the left and level again. It swings to the right again, working just above a tiny creek. It heads uphill a little more, but not too steep.

As the terrain begins to get rocky, the trail crosses the tiny creek at 1.6. It swings back to the left, first up, then levels off. At 1.8 we come to an intersection—this is Chinquapin Gap—the Ouachita Trail continues to the right (136–page guide available on the OT—see page 190). We want to TURN LEFT and resume our loop. The trail runs on out on the level across a ridgetop, and the hill drops off steeply to the right. It continues to wind on around the hillside, and eventually comes to a trail intersection at 2.4—the spur to the left goes on up .4 mile to Chinquapin Overlook. The main trail continues STRAIGHT AHEAD. It swings on around the hill left and right, then eases on down to The Big Gap, where we hit another trail intersection at 2.6. This is the Wildlife Trail—TURN RIGHT.

The trail begins to drop down just a little, curves to the left, then heads across another steep hillside fairly. It swings to the right, through a nice rock garden, to the next trail intersection at 2.9. We're going to TURN RIGHT again. There are several informative signs along the way that will introduce you to some of the different critters of the forest. The trail drops on down the hill, and just past the "deer" sign, pass mile 3.0 and a big pine tree. It swings to the left, level, and passes another nice rock garden.

At 3.2 we come to the end of the Wildlife Trail, which turns to the left and heads to the campground. TURN RIGHT here. There is a great view soon off to the right during leaf–off. The trail runs down the middle of a narrow ridge, past an SSS rock garden and terrific view out over a canyon below at 3.3. This area is one of the most scenic spots on the trail—spend some time here and get to know the place!

The trail heads on down the ridge—you can look across the way and see the tilted bluff over there—and comes to an intersection at 3.4—the spur to the right goes on out to a spectacular SSS view which overlooks the canyon again. Really nice. It ends at the edge. The main trail continues dropping down the hill. There are a couple more lesser trails that intersect—one of them runs on out to an overlook of the dam.

The trail levels off and begins a real pleasant stroll along the lake shore, curving back to the left. It comes into the campground and hits a road at 3.7—TURN RIGHT here and follow the road through the campground. It swings around to the left and hits another road—TURN RIGHT again, and head out to the park entrance—TURN LEFT onto the forest road and you'll end up at 4.1 back at the trailhead. I highly recommend that you also hike the 1/2 mile Trees of the Forest Trail there.

Agency List #15

Sunset Trail

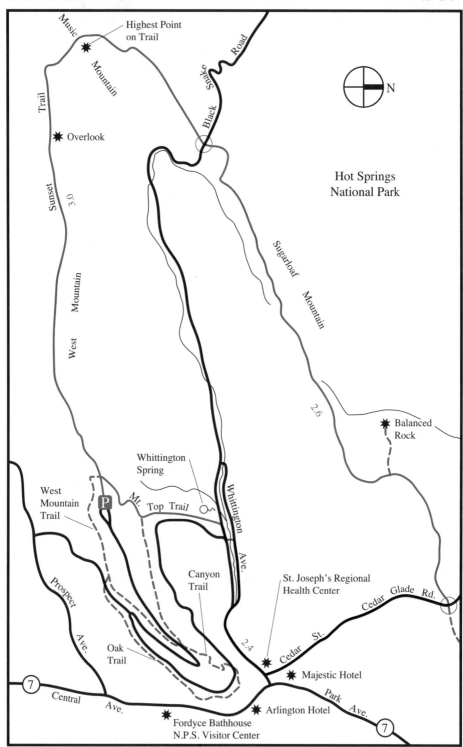

Highest Point on Trail

Music Mountain

Black Snake Road

N

Overlook

Trail

Sunset

3.0

West Mountain

Hot Springs National Park

Sugarloaf Mountain

2.6

Balanced Rock

Whittington Spring

West Mountain Trail

P

Mt. Top Trail

Whittington Ave.

Canyon Trail

St. Joseph's Regional Health Center

Cedar Glade Rd.

Prospect Ave.

Oak Trail

2.4

Cedar St.

Majestic Hotel

7

Central Ave.

Arlington Hotel

Park Ave.

7

Fordyce Bathhouse N.P.S. Visitor Center

Sunset Loop—8.0 miles

This ridgetop trail in Hot Springs National Park overlooks the city of Hot Springs. There are lots of great views as the trail goes along the crest of West, Music and Sugarloaf mountains, big trees, and even some geological formations. By combining a few city streets, and part of another trail, you can make a nice loop hike. There are actually a lot of trails that wind around the hills of Hot Springs. This is one of the best. And when you get done, you can go get a massage and soak your tired feet!

To get to the trailhead from the Fordyce Bathhouse Visitor Center on Bathhouse Row, head north on Hwy. 7, turn left on Whittington Ave. (just after Arlington Hotel), turn left on West Mountain Drive and then turn right on West Mountain Summit Drive and follow it to the last overlook (there are 3 overlooks) where the trail begins. Most of this trail is not too difficult, except for the climb at the end back up to the trailhead. The Boy Scouts call this the DeSoto Trail. Hot Springs North quad.

The trail takes off on a wide trail. It soon comes to the intersection with the Mountain Top Trail (we will finish the loop from the right on this trail)—continue STRAIGHT AHEAD. There are some nice rock formations in this area, and already some great views. It heads up the hill—this is West Mountain. At .6 a new stretch of trail goes around communications towers on the north side of the mountain, then returns to the ridgetop. At .9 the road the trail is on goes over to a radio shack, but we continue STRAIGHT AHEAD on the level.

It heads down the hill steeply, then back up again, still running along the ridgetop. There are lots of great views off of both sides, especially during leaf–off. It does some more roller–coastering, then switchbacks on up Music Mountain. It crosses a roadbed at 2.2 (highest point on the trail), then begins to head down off the top of the hill, switchbacking. There are several SSS views along here, and on the way down you'll pass some lush areas full of wildflowers and moss–covered boulders.

The trail eases over to the right side of the ridge—good leaf–off views down into Hot Springs—and heads on down the hill to a parking area along Black Snake Road at 3.0. The trail crosses the road and veers to the left and down the hill (*don't* go up the paved driveway). It intersects an old road trace and TURNS RIGHT onto it, then heads back up the hill, TURNING LEFT off of this old road when it reaches the top at 3.6. The trail runs gradually downhill along the top of Sugarloaf Mountain. It swings to the right, then left, heading steeply downhill. Then it heads uphill and levels off.

A little more uphill and a swing to the left brings us to the Balanced Rock intersection at 4.8. This is a must–see spot—the trail goes to the left about a third of a mile, on out and down to a series of SSS vertical rock formations, the last one being the "Balanced Rock." The view is pretty nice too! The main trail continues on, dropping some, and passing a number of giant trees—one section of them is an SSS. Eventually the trail turns and heads straight down the hill at a steep grade. It does level off and comes to Cedar Glade Road at 5.6. The trail does continue on, towards Blowout Mountain, but we're going to TURN RIGHT here, and loop back towards the trailhead.

We want to head down Cedar Glade Road and TURN LEFT on Cedar Street at 6.0, and take it on to Whittington Ave. TURN RIGHT here and follow it into Whittington Park to the turnoff to West Mountain Summit Drive—just past this turnoff, head into the woods on the Mountain Top Trail at 7.1. This climbs on up the hill and intersects with the West Mountain Trail—TURN RIGHT and continue *up* , eventually rejoining the Sunset Trail on top—TURN LEFT and return to the trailhead at 8.0.

Agency List #18

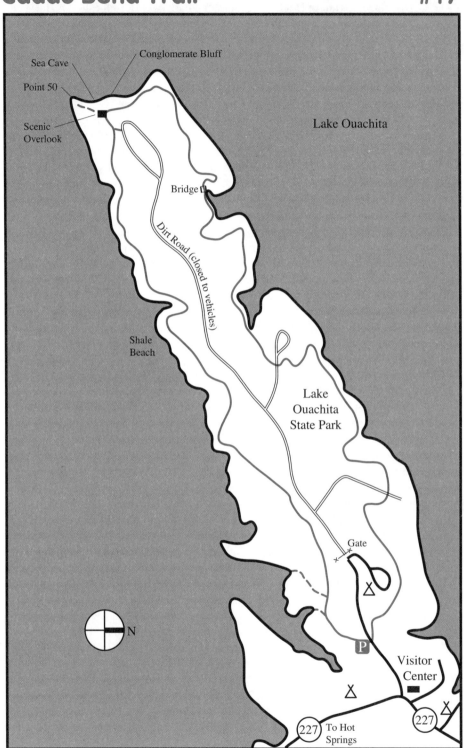

Conglomerate Bluff

Sea Cave

Point 50

Scenic
Overlook

Lake Ouachita

Bridge

Dirt Road (closed to vehicles)

Shale
Beach

Lake
Ouachita
State Park

Gate

N

P

Visitor
Center

227 To Hot
Springs

227

Caddo Bend Loop—3.9 miles

This trail is located at Lake Ouachita State Park near Hot Springs. It's an easy trail that loops around a peninsula that sticks out into Lake Ouachita, the largest lake in Arkansas. Since it follows closely to the shoreline, this is a great trail to hike in the summer—just hop in when you get hot! To get to the Park, take Hwy. 270 west out of Hot Springs, turn north on Hwy. 227 for about 12 miles. Turn left at the Visitor Center (towards camp area B), and you'll find the trailhead ahead and on the left, just past the amphitheater. This park has several campgrounds and cabins available. They also have some unique summer programs—check in at the Visitor Center. A parking/entrance fee to hike may be required—ask at the Visitor Center. Mountain Pine quad.

The trail takes off out through a nice, open woods. It's blazed with yellow paint. It does some up–and–downing, and passes a couple of lesser trails that drop down to the lake on the left. It begins to climb up some, and during leaf–off you've got some nice views out across the lake. At .4 there is a red–blazed trail that goes to the right and back into the campground—go STRAIGHT AHEAD here. Just beyond there is a minor SSS area of boulders on either side of the trail.

After running along near the top for a while, the trail heads down the hill towards the lake. It levels off along the shore, then goes back uphill again, soon leveling off. Then it's back down the hill again, and past mile 1.0. There is a nice bench at 1.2. The trail does some more up–and–downing, passing some great views. And at 1.7 there is another red trail that goes back to the right. The main trail continues on straight ahead, and drops on down the hill and comes to an SSS area—great views and a pavilion. There is a little trail that goes from it on down to the water and a terrific swimming area. Back up to the right there is an SSS set of folded bluffs, and a small "sea cave."

From the pavilion the trail swings on around the point—great views all the way. It gets pretty rocky, and the hillside is steep. As it comes around the north side of the peninsula, we pass mile 2.0, and are back down near the water. At 2.2 the trail drops down and crosses a neat bridge. It runs along the shoreline for a while, then connects with an old road, turns away from the lake and heads up hill. There are lots of wildflowers and ferns in this area. There seem to be a lot more on this side than there was on the other side.

The trail winds around above the lake shore, and joins another roadbed—TURN LEFT and hike on it for a couple hundred feet, then TURN RIGHT off of it—be sure to watch for the blazes. There is another bench at 2.5. At 2.7 the trail crosses the end of a small cove, then heads up through a narrow, rocky ravine—a minor SSS. It joins another roadbed—TURN LEFT and follow it, then TURN RIGHT soon after. By 3.0 the trail crosses a small creekbed and is back down alongside the lake.

The trail hits another roadbed and swings up and away from the lake, then quickly leaves it. There is some more up–and–downing, and at 3.5 the trail passes through a young stand of pine trees. The trail has gradually left the lake area and is nearing the top of the hill, running just below the campground. It crosses a small creekbed at 3.8, then heads up the hill and comes out on the pavement—TURN LEFT and go just a couple hundred feet to the end of the trail at the trailhead at 3.9.

The other trail in the park is the Dogwood Trail, which is much shorter, but pretty nice—check at the Visitor Center.

Agency List #29

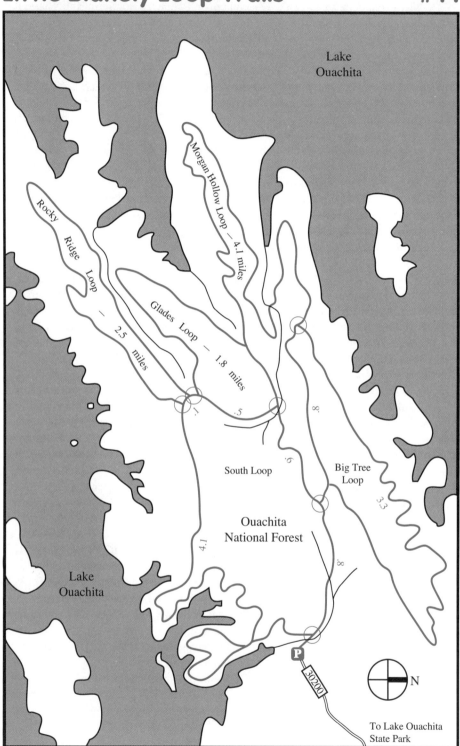

Lake
Ouachita

Morgan Hollow Loop — 4.1 miles

Rocky Ridge Loop — 2.5 miles

Glades Loop — 1.8 miles

.5

.7

.8

.6

3.3

South Loop

Big Tree
Loop

Ouachita
National Forest

4.1

.8

Lake
Ouachita

P

30200

N

To Lake Ouachita
State Park

Little Blakely Loops—18.6 miles total

There are actually five loops that all connect here, allowing a variety of lengths of hikes. I am going to detail the two main loops (South and Big Tree, which form a figure–eight hike), then give brief descriptions of the other three, which loop off of them. Each loop has its own unique features, from glades, to boulder fields, to giant trees—I suggest you try to hike them all! The entire area is located in the Ouachita National Forest, so camping is allowed. The trailhead may change in the near future, so you might stop by the Visitor Center at Lake Ouachita State Park, or contact the Forest Service at Jessieville for current info. Mountain bikes are allowed. Mountain Pine quad.

To get to the current trailhead, go to Lake Ouachita State Park (Hwy. 227 out of Hot Springs), turn right at the Visitor Center (pavement ends eventually—4.1 miles of gravel road), go straight at the first gravel intersection, turn left onto road #30200 at the second one, straight ahead at the next, and the next minor one, then bear right and follow it to the end. There are posts with "LB TRAIL" on them at each intersection. The trail begins to the right of this parking area. It's blazed with white paint.

South and Big Tree Loops—10.2 miles total. The trail heads out and crosses a creek on a nice bridge, then comes to an intersection—TURN LEFT on the *South Loop* (we'll return from the right on the North or Big Tree Loop). The trail heads on up the hill, and does some up–and–downing across a steep hillside. It begins to follow along above the lake—there are lots of great views from here on for a while, especially during leaf–off. It heads down into a little ravine and across a bridge. At .4 there is an intersection—TURN LEFT here and continue along the top of a narrow ridge for a short distance, then TURN LEFT off of the ridge (we'll return to this spot).

It climbs up just a little, past huckleberry–covered hillsides of open forest. You can look across the lake and see the peninsula that the Caddo Bend Trail loops around (page 153) at the State Park. Our trail turns away from the lake and heads up and around a ravine. It heads uphill some, then passes mile 1.0 (painted on a tree), and swings back to the right. As the trail heads downhill some, a lesser trail takes off to the right—BEAR LEFT. It winds around to the right, heading uphill some. At 1.3, we intersect with ourselves for 200 feet on top of the narrow ridge (we were just here at .4)—continue STRAIGHT AHEAD and on top for the main trail (you could turn right and head back to the trailhead if you needed to).

The trail heads downhill some, swinging back to the left. Then it turns right, and goes back up into and around another ravine. It swings back to the left towards the lake, then back to the right again. It passes mile 2.0 just before crossing through this ravine. There is a nice SSS moss–covered hillside in this area. The trail heads back towards the lake, gets pretty close to it, and continues the pattern of weaving around, left and right, up and down, across several small ravines. At 2.6 there is a "moss volcano"—a spot where a tree was blown over eons ago and rotted away, and thick moss now covers the depression and mound of dirt around the edge that it left behind. Tiny SSS's each one!

The trail continues to make its way on out and around the end of the hill that we're on, which sticks out into the lake some. It curves back to the right and up, heading away from the lake, passing mile 3.0. It begins to drop on down the hill some, crosses an old roadbed, swings to the left some, then back to the right and up the hill. On the way up there are some nice SSS views out to the left, especially at 3.7. This is a long climb. It finally tops out and goes past mile 4.0, then continues along the ridge.

Little Blakely Trail (cont.)

The trail begins to head down off the right side of the ridge, and comes to an intersection at 4.1—the *Rocky Ridge Loop* begins here and takes off to the left—the main trail continues STRAIGHT AHEAD. It drops down a little further and comes out into an open area at 4.2, and intersects with the other end of the Rocky Ridge Loop coming in from the left—the main trail is now on an old road and continues STRAIGHT AHEAD.

Just a few feet beyond, there is another intersection—this is the *Glades Loop*, and it heads off to the left on another road bed—the main trail veers TO THE RIGHT here, still on the old road bed, and heads downhill, easing back to the left. It soon levels off, then some more downhill, past a real thick forest. At 4.7 it comes to the other end of the Glades Loop, which heads back to the left (the end of the Morgan Hollow Loop is .3 miles down this road too)—the main trail continues TO THE RIGHT, and goes across Morgan Hollow Creek on the road. It heads up just a little, back to the right, then left. Much of the forest floor is covered with all kinds of ferns—really nice, and the forest itself is pretty open. The trail passes mile 5.0, still on the old roadbed.

As we head uphill and back to the left some, then level off, we come to the midpoint of our figure–eight hike, which is the intersection with the *Big Tree Loop* (or North Loop) at 5.3. To return to the trailhead, turn right (.7 miles). We're going to TURN LEFT and continue on around the Big Tree section of our loop (we will come back to this intersection). We'll keep our mile meter running for the figure–eight hike.

The trail heads uphill some on an old roadbed. Soon the trail levels and there is a fork—TURN LEFT and continue on the level (we will return from the right, which is uphill). The trail continues along fairly level, easing down some, on an old roadbed that is grown up with small trees. As it passes mile 6.0 (no painted numbers on trees anymore), there are beginning to be some larger hardwood trees scattered about. Also at this point, the trail leaves the roadbed TO THE RIGHT, and heads uphill as plain trail.

It continues gentle uphill, back to the left, then comes to the intersection with the *Morgan Hollow Loop* at 6.1, which goes to the left—continue STRAIGHT AHEAD, up and over a low ridge. It drops down the other side and turns back to the right, through a neat rock garden. There are some big, leaning pine trees around too. The trail heads uphill some, running along the ridge that we just crossed, with good leaf–off views down to the lake again. It heads down just a little, swinging around across a steep hillside, and doing some up–and–downing, crossing lots of tiny, mossy streams. At 6.9 the big pines are good for an SSS. There will be several areas like this ahead! Lots of big oaks too. I love big trees, and this run of them through here is the best that I've seen out in the wild like this. The pines are native shortleaf pine.

At 7.4 there is an educational SSS—a giant oak tree that's fallen over—you can walk up and down on it and see just exactly how big these giants are! The trail continues to wind on around, does lots more up–and–downing, and crosses several more little streams. There are some rock gardens too, many covered with moss. One an SSS at 7.9. Eventually the trail heads away from the lake, drops down some, then switchbacks uphill, past mossy rocks and a few big trees. At 8.6 the trail levels off and hits a road— TURN RIGHT and follow the road.

At 9.2 there is an SSS area of boulders as we come over the top of the ridge, then it begins to head down the hill. At 9.4 we intersect with the other end of the Big Tree Loop and continue straight ahead, soon reaching the intersection with the South Loop—TURN LEFT and head on the old roadbed and down the hill. It hits the bottom, curves to the right across a small stream, then heads on up some more. Soon the trail begins to ease downhill, following a nice little stream, and intersects with the beginning of the South Loop—continue STRAIGHT AHEAD and follow the trail, across the creek (an SSS by the way!), back to the trailhead at 10.2. Now for the other loops.

Rocky Ridge Loop—2.5 miles total. Begin at mile 4.1 on the main trail (South Loop—we will zero our counter). This trail takes off TO THE LEFT and runs mostly level along a, you guessed it, a *very* rocky ridge! It veers from side to side, dropping down the left side for a while at .4—the trail is pretty rocky in places, and wide and smooth in others. There are some leaf–off views through the trees of the lake.

It dips down, then switchbacks up the hill to a wonderful SSS wall of rock at .8, then continues along the top of the rocky ridge. There are some great moss–covered boulders at 1.0. The trail swings off the right side of the ridge, then comes back over and drops down the left side, then goes through another great SSS area of boulders at 1.3, where it hits a log road and TURNS RIGHT onto the road. It goes over the ridge, down the other side, then the road ends and it continues on as plain trail. At 1.5 it hits another roadbed—TURN RIGHT and follow along this road (next to a creek for much of the way—lots of reindeer moss too!) all the way back up to the main trail at 2.5.

Glades Loop—1.8 miles total. Begin at mile 4.2 on the main trail (South Loop—we will zero our counter). This trail takes off TO THE LEFT up an old road (which it will stay on the entire time). It swings around to the left some, levels off, then begins to drop. At .3 it goes through a nice SSS open cedar glade area—the first of several. There is another large one at .5, then more smaller ones. The trail eases uphill away from the open areas, crossing a ridge, and intersects with another roadbed at .8—TURN RIGHT and continue along the left side of the ridge. It stays on this road, doing some up–and–downing, and comes to the intersection with the end of Morgan Hollow Loop at 1.5, which heads back to the left on another old roadbed—the Glades Loop continues STRAIGHT AHEAD, and down and around to the right. It comes alongside Morgan Hollow Creek on the left, levels, then ends at the main trail at 1.8.

Morgan Hollow Loop—4.1 miles total. Begin at mile 6.1 on the main trail (Big Tree Loop—we will zero our counter). This trail also takes off TO THE LEFT and heads out a long ridge. It quickly drops down a little and follows the right side of it, mostly level. It passes through a nice rock garden area or two, and there are some nice leaf–off views out across the lake. It rounds the point at .6 (SSS view), swings back to the left and heads along the other side of this long ridge. It drops down a little, then intersects with an old road at 1.0. It stays on this road for a ways, then leaves it TO THE RIGHT, and heads down to and across Morgan Hollow Creek at 1.3, an SSS! There is a great campsite area just downstream and up on the flat (I stayed there for a couple of months while I built this loop).

From there the trail joins an old roadbed for a short stretch, then leaves it TO THE RIGHT, and heads up on the hillside through a cedar thicket. It swings back to the right and begins a long run along the right side of another ridge, past mile 2.0. It goes through some rocky stretches, then comes to the nose of the ridge at 2.8, and swings back to the left and begins a long run along that side. It works its way up on top of the ridge, through a neat SSS rock garden area at 3.4, then runs level along the top. It heads down off of the ridge and joins an old road trace that runs on the wide ridge, then hits another road—TURN LEFT and follow this to the end at the Glades Loop at 4.1.

Agency List #12

Bona Dea Trails

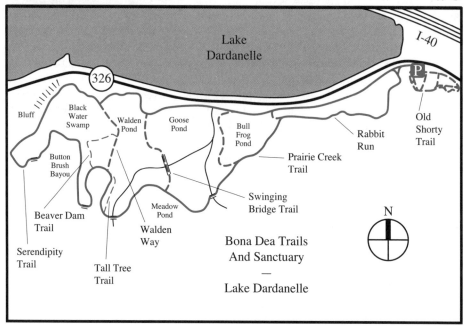

8

Lake Dardanelle

I-40

326

Bluff
Black Water Swamp
Walden Pond
Goose Pond
Bull Frog Pond
Rabbit Run
Old Shorty Trail
Button Brush Bayou
Prairie Creek Trail
Beaver Dam Trail
Meadow Pond
Swinging Bridge Trail
Serendipity Trail
Walden Way
Tall Tree Trail

N

Bona Dea Trails And Sanctuary
—
Lake Dardanelle

Bona Dea Trails System—3.5 miles outside loop

This is one of Arkansas' most unique trail systems. It's a fitness trail. It's a jogging trail. It's a nature trail. It's a hiking trail. It's a wildlife watching trail. It's barrier free. And it's all within the city limits of Russellville. The U.S. Army Corps of Engineers built this as a multiuse trail, and it has certainly lived up to it. The park covers 186 acres of wetland and low woods, which provide one of the most productive ecosystems found anywhere. It's a wildlife sanctuary for numerous species of animals and especially birds (with an emphasis on waterfowl). The Corps has a booklet available that tells about some of the wildlife that you'll find along the trail, plus information on the fitness stations (get at Arkansas River Visitor Center). Russellville West quad.

There are several different trails in the park, and you can combine them for many different lengths of hikes/runs/strolls. The longest route is the Serendipity Trail, which runs along the outer edge of the park, and is 3.5 miles long. There are 18 exercise stations along the Rabbit Run and Prairie Creek Trails. Some trails are paved.

Although any time of day is great to visit this park, early morning is a special time here, because you'll be able to see the most animal/bird activity then. But I'll tell ya how I utilize the park. The park is a little more than half way from my home in Fayetteville to Little Rock. By the time I get to Russellville, I'm ready for a break. So I zip in, hike which ever trail I have time for, then hit the road again, refreshed and ready to do business in Little Rock. It's right off of I–40.

To get to Bona Dea, take exit 81 and head towards Russellville, turn right at the first light, which is Hwy. 326, and you'll find the park just down the road on the left. The park is also great for bird photography. If you do make it to the trail early in the morning, be sure to walk quietly, that's when you'll see the most wildlife.

Agency List # 23

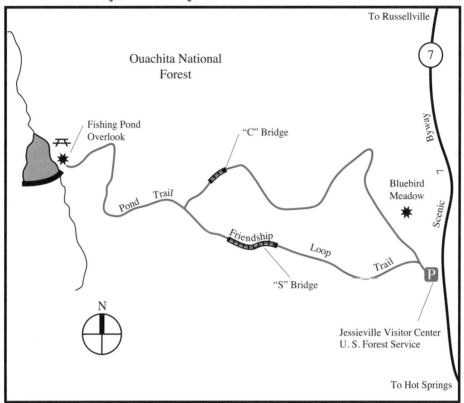

Friendship Interpretive Loop—.9 mile

This is a beautiful little trail that is paved and is barrier free. It loops around through the woods behind the Forest Service Visitor Center at Jessieville. Take your lunch with you and stop at one of the many benches or picnic tables and enjoy some time outside. To get there, go north on Hwy. 7 about 18 miles from Hot Springs. The Visitor Center is on the left just outside of Jessieville. You should go inside and have a look at their deer! Jessieville quad.

We start off heading clockwise (to the left). The trail winds through a nice forest, and past many interpretive signs. Be sure to stop and take a few minutes to read them. It goes across a wonderful wooden bridge that was built in an "S" shape. Not too far beyond the trail forks—take the LEFT FORK, and we'll head on out to the fish pond. The trail turns back to the right, then left, and ends up at an observation point that overlooks the pond (there is an accessible picnic pavilion and bathroom there). All along there are lots of big pine trees and oaks, and wildflowers scattered around too.

From the pond we'll head back to the intersection, then TURN LEFT there and continue around the loop. Next up is the "C" bridge, another nice wooden structure. The trail swings to the right, then left, then sharply right again. It passes Bluebird Meadow as it eases downhill and back to the beginning.

Agency List #12

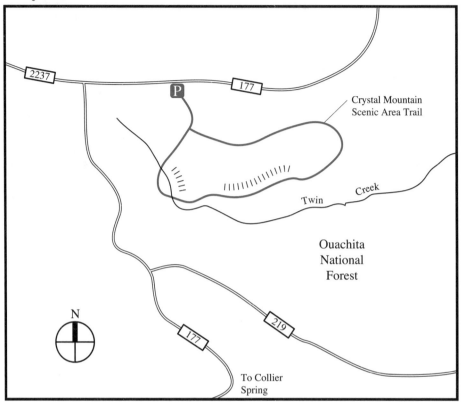

Crystal Mountain Scenic Area Loop —.5 mile

This is short, little used, easy trail that goes by old, old trees in the Ouachita National Forest. It's just up the road a ways from the Crystal Recreation Area Trail (see next pare), so you can easily do them both on the same visit. To get there, take Hwy. 27 north out of Norman 1/2 mile to FR#177, turn right and go 7.8 miles (past Crystal Recreation Area and Collier Spring Picnic Area) to a "T" intersection. FR#2237 turns left, but you want to TURN RIGHT and stay on FR#177—then pull off on the right in front of a large Crystal Mountain Scenic Area sign. Caddo Gap quad.

The trail begins to the left of the sign, drops down to an intersection—TURN LEFT and continue wandering through these giant pine trees that are said to be 300+ years old. By .2 the trail drops down the hill some more, turns back to the right, and comes alongside a neat SSS bluff area. The largest trees are in this area, and just across the way. The trail continues, mostly level, then comes alongside Twin Creek, crossing it at .3. The trail runs along an old roadbed for just a little while through here. It crosses this small creek again, then swings back to the right and heads on up the hill, and levels out and finishes up the loop at .5—TURN LEFT and walk back to the parking area.

Be sure to stop at Collier Spring Picnic Area while you are in the vicinity—it's a terrific spot where the picnic tables sit right on top of the spring! There is a footpath that goes upstream from there that is really nice—an SSS.

Agency List #10

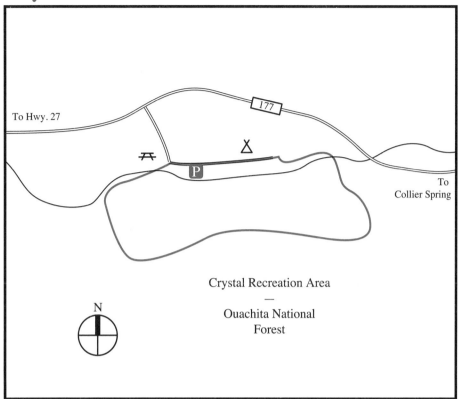

To Hwy. 27

177

To
Collier Spring

Crystal Recreation Area

—

Ouachita National
Forest

N

Crystal Recreation Area Loop—.7 mile

This is another short, seldom used, easy trail that loops around through some huge eighty–year–old trees. To get there, take Hwy. 27 North out of Norman (south of Mt. Ida) for 1/2 mile, turn right onto FR#177, go 3 miles and turn into the Crystal Recreation Area, which is a small Forest Service campground. Norman quad.

The trail begins just opposite campsite #5, runs down to a creek, and a spring, then turns left and heads upstream. It's a wonderful SSS walk alongside Montgomery Creek, with stately old trees towering overhead. At .2 the trail crosses the creek, and heads up into the woods. It swings back to the right, levels off, and winds around on the level, just above the creek. Although the trees aren't quite as large at first as the ones in the bottom, there are some really large oaks, and quite a number of different species (42 I think!). The trees do get bigger as you go along. And the steep hillside is lush with ferns and mosses.

Soon the trail turns to the right and drops on down the hill to and across the creek again at .6. This area is an SSS—the rocks in the creek are covered with wonderful moss, and there is a small falls just upstream. From there the trail heads up into the campground and back to the parking area at .7.

For a really special picnic spot, continue up the forest road 3.3 miles to Collier Spring Picnic Area. Then it's just a little further on to the Crystal Mountain Scenic Area, and the trail that visits it (previous page).

Agency List #10

Eagle Rock Loop

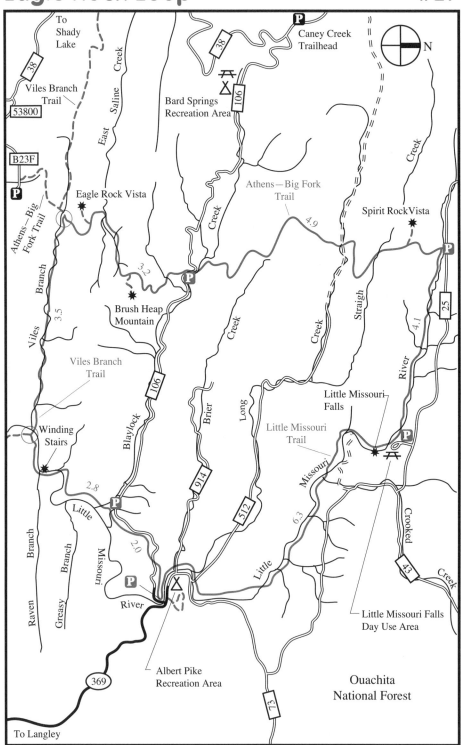

To Shady Lake

Caney Creek Trailhead

38

38

Viles Branch Trail

53800

B23F

106

Bard Springs Recreation Area

N

Creek

East Saline Creek

Creek

Athens—Big Fork Trail

Eagle Rock Vista

Spirit Rock Vista

4.9

Athens—Big Fork Trail

3.2

Brush Heap Mountain

25

Straigh

River

4.1

Viles Branch

3.5

Creek

Long Creek

Viles Branch Trail

Viles

Winding Stairs

Blaylock

106

Brier

Little Missouri Falls

Little Missouri Trail

2.8

914

572

Little Missouri

P

25

P

Little

2.0

6.3

Branch

Greasy Branch

Missouri

Little

Crooked Creek

43

Raven Branch

P

River

Albert Pike Recreation Area

Little Missouri Falls Day Use Area

369

73

Ouachita National Forest

To Langley

Eagle Rock Loop—26.8 miles

This is the longest loop hike in Arkansas. It is actually a combination of three trails (the Little Missouri, the Athens–Big Fork, and part of the Viles Branch Horse Trail). It loops through a large chunk of the Ouachita National Forest southwest of Hot Springs. There are five trailhead parking areas along the route for easy access. The route that I recommend below seems to work the best. We will begin by hiking down one of the most scenic and easiest trails in the state, and finish by hiking one of the most difficult trails (when your pack is the lightest!). This makes a perfect weekend trail, or even a nice three–day hike. I will give a general description here—for the detailed descriptions, see the Little Missouri Trail and Athens–Big Fork Trail sections.

We will first hike the Little Missouri Trail, and begin at mile 0 (see page 165). This trail crosses the Little Missouri River five times before it gets to Little Missouri Falls Picnic Area at 4.1, a terrific SSS. It continues downstream, along the river, crossing the river twice more before reaching Albert Pike Recreation Area at 10.4.

It climbs up from the campground for an SSS view of the river, then drops down and away from the Little Missouri. It crosses Blaylock Creek and rejoins the river again at 13.5. Just beyond the eighth crossing of the Little Missouri, is the Winding Stairs Scenic Area at 14.5—one of the best SSS areas in Arkansas! Swim a while.

From the scenic area, the trail follows an old road to 15.2, where our loop will turn TO THE RIGHT and leave the Little Missouri Trail (which continues ahead for another half mile before ending). This is where we follow the Viles Branch Horse Trail, which we picked up at the Winding Stair Area. This trail, which follows an old road, is blazed with yellow paint (other trails are blazed white).

The trail heads down to and crosses Little Missouri River (9th time) just upstream of Viles Branch, which empties into it. It continues along next to Viles Branch. This is a nice streamside walk, easing up gradually. It crosses Viles Branch the first of 12 times at 15.6. There is a nice SSS waterfall on the creek a little ways beyond. All along this route you will see lots and lots of young holly trees and ferns everywhere. It crosses the creek a couple more times, passes some nice slab falls, then comes to a really neat SSS area at 16.6—there is a spring that comes out of the base of the bluff, which the trail runs along. A great spot to spend some time! During high water, you'll see lots of waterfalls tumbling out off the hillside here.

From that spot, the trail continues upstream, and gets more serious about crossing it—*eight* more times by 18.5. During most of the year you can probably find places to cross dry, but you would have to wade during high water. The trail goes through several small, grown up fields too, and passes countless holly and beech trees. The road gets rather rocky in places. Just after the 12th and last crossing, you come to the intersection with the Athens–Big Fork Trail at 18.7—TURN RIGHT and follow it (see page 169 and pick up at mile 1.0).

Now is when you wish you hadn't brought all that extra gear, 'cause this stretch spends half its time climbing *steeply* up one mountain after another. The rest of this trail follows a 100–year–old mail route. There are some terrific views for your work though, like at Eagle Rock Vista on Brushy Mountain at 19.4. From there it dips down, crosses a creek, then climbs up and over Brush Heap Mountain. It crosses FR#106 at 21.9, then Blaylock Creek, then heads up and over another mountain. After three more steep climbs, there is another spectacular vista at 26.2. From there it's downhill all the way, back down to the beginning point at 26.8. You should be in good shape to do this!

Agency List #10

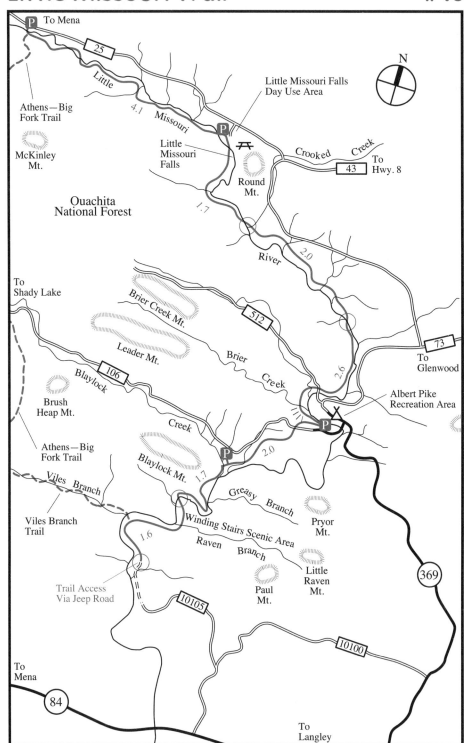

Little Missouri Trail—15.7 miles one way

This is one of the most scenic and easy backpacking trails in Arkansas. It follows the Little Missouri River, which is a National Wild and Scenic River, passes Little Missouri Falls, follows along a historic wagon trail, and goes through the Winding Stairs area, which has perhaps the best swimming hole anywhere! There are several access points, so you can either dayhike the trail, or spend the weekend and take in the entire show. This is an especially good trail to hike during the summer, since the river always has water in it. This trail was built by high school volunteers from around the country from the Student Conservation Association over a five–year period. Camping is allowed. (This trail is part of the Eagle Rock Loop—see page 163.) Big Fork quad.

We're going to begin our hike at the upstream trailhead, and hike down the river, saving the Winding Stairs area for last. There are a number of ways to get to this trailhead, all involving dirt roads, but we're going to go there via Langley, which is also the beginning route to the other access points as well. From Glenwood, take Hwy. 70 west to Salem, turn right on Hwy. 84 to Langley, then turn right on Hwy. 369 (now paved) about 6 miles to Albert Pike Recreation Area (turn left at the campground on FR#106 to get to the Blaylock Creek Trailhead). Continue straight through the campground as the road turns to FR#73 (dirt), and follow it to FR#43 and turn left onto it, then turn left again onto FR#25, go past Little Missouri Falls Picnic Area (another trailhead), and go past it 3.3 miles to the trailhead on the left.

The trail is marked with white blazes. From the trailhead it heads out and immediately crosses a narrow Little Missouri River, the first of eight crossings (not recommended during high water!). Just across the river there is a trail intersection —the Athens–Big Fork Trail takes off to the right (see page 169), and runs for 9.1 miles. This trail follows a historical mail route that was built and used over a hundred years ago— parts of it are *extremely* steep! It is also part of the Eagle Rock Loop, which begins and ends at this point. The Little Missouri Trail TURNS LEFT here and heads downstream. One of the many varieties of trees that we see a lot through here is the holly tree (used in Christmas decorations—I like to plant them where folks are cutting switchbacks!), which has a lot of spines, but looks great in the winter landscape.

The trail runs beside the creek some, then swings away from it, then alongside it again. We come to our first SSS at .4, where there is a rock ledge that spans the river. Just beyond there are lots of big beeches, and a number of good–sized pines as well. The hillsides that the trail crosses are usually lush with mosses and ferns. It passes mile marker #1, then goes through an SSS area of big beeches just beyond. At 1.3 it crosses the river, then crosses it again at 1.4.

Beyond is a nice, level stroll along the river, then an SSS area of moss–covered boulders and more big beeches and holly trees. It joins an old road trace—TURN LEFT and follow it, eventually crossing another trace and coming to mile marker #2. From there the trail swings to the right, away from the creek, and begins a pretty good climb up the hill. It crosses the hillside to the left, past an SSS view at 2.5, then drops back down to the river, where it runs alongside it through more wonderful big beeches.

Soon the trail heads up the hill again, levels off through another SSS area of big trees and boulders just before mile marker #3. It continues across the steep, rocky hillside, past some larger oaks, then heads back down alongside the creek again. It soon swings away from it along a road trace—the road was built to an area that will someday become a campground, they just haven't built it yet. It crosses the river for the 4th time

on a concrete road bridge at 3.7, then continues to a parking area at Little Missouri Falls
Picnic Area at 4.0—TURN RIGHT on the road and follow it through the picnic area (no
camping here). Please stop and admire the bronze plaque about the trail volunteers.

The trail heads on over across the river again (5th crossing) on a rather large
bridge (you can cross here even during high water! now), and begins a short paved
section that climbs up the hill just a little—all of this section is a terrific SSS—looking down on the falls area, and the rock formations all over, above and below the trail.
Great swimming holes and exploration areas. Spend some time here! It's a neat spot.
The pavement ends as the trail continues downstream. It follows a wide path for a little
ways, then leaves TO THE RIGHT and heads up a short hill, crossing a four–wheeler
trail, then drops to the left some and back to the right across a small creek.

The trail is up on the hillside overlooking the river now, and comes to an SSS
view of Round Mountain, the river, and all around at 4.9. It continues across the steep
hillside, then drops down to and runs alongside the river, through an SSS area of huge
pine trees at 5.4. It heads back up on the hillside some, running mostly level, past more
big beeches, then back down to and across the river for the 6th time at 5.8—another
SSS area. It immediately TURNS RIGHT and crosses Crooked Creek (both of these
crossings can be done dry, but the rocks are very slick, and often under water). There is
a nice, small swimming hole right here that is perfect for a cool dip.

The trail joins a historical wagon trace (the ruts are hard to see) as it follows
the river on the level, passing a warm spring (74 degrees) on the right just past mile
marker #6. There are several nice rocky, SSS areas along the creek. The trail heads up
the hill just a little, through a cedar grove and SSS view at 6.4, then drops back down
to the creek again. It meanders back and forth in the bottoms, passing several wildlife
food plots. It crosses a jeep road several times, and a couple of side streams, then comes
down and joins the jeep road as it crosses the river for the 7th time at 7.8. The rock formations in the river make this area an SSS for sure! When I was building this stretch of
trail with my SCA high school volunteers, we used to come to this spot at night, lay out
on the rocks in the river, and count shooting stars.

It continues on the road for just a short distance, then leaves it up TO THE
RIGHT. It quickly levels off, crosses a small stream, turns away from the river and
heads up the hill some, then comes back down and joins a jeep road along the river at
8.7—TURN RIGHT and follow the road. (Just across the river is FR#73 that goes to Albert Pike Campground.) Soon it leaves the road TO THE RIGHT and continues through
the woods. It comes out and crosses FR#512 at 9.3. The trail follows the river, swings
back to the right across a small stream, then turns left and crosses Long Creek (usually a
wet crossing) and heads up across a steep hillside. At 9.6 there is a wonderful SSS view
spot with a bench—great views up and down the river. It hits an old road trace, passes
a wrecked car body, and eventually comes down to and across FR#914. The area off to
the right is the Leader Mountain Walk In Turkey Area, and is closed to vehicle traffic
much of the year.

The trail crosses Brier Creek, and begins a wonderful SSS run along the
river—there are lots of boulders and bluffs too. And at 10.1 is "Rock Springs," another
SSS that comes right out of the huge rock there. Just beyond, the trail comes out into
Loop B of Albert Pike Recreation Area—continue through the area to the main road and
a small trailhead parking area at 10.4. (There is a short trail called the Mountain Bluff

Nature Trail across the river that begins at the bathhouse in Loop C—it is worth a side trip. The campground here is really nice, but it does get very crowded in the summer. If you fish, you should know that there are usually some nice–sized trout stocked in the river here in the winter months, and make for great fishing.)

From the trailhead, TURN RIGHT and head *steeply* up the hill. It goes up and up to some spectacular rock outcrops and SSS views. Close to the top the trail TURNS LEFT and heads away from the ridge (there is a lesser, unofficial trail that continues up the hill, to a wonderful SSS view area—a dangerous spot, though, so be careful!). The main trail heads on down the hill, crosses FR#106, and joins an old road trace, following it along a small creek. It crosses the creek several times on plain trail, past lots of big beeches, goes on and off a road trace, and eventually comes to a trail intersection at 12.4. The blazed trail to the right heads over to the Winging Stairs Trailhead on FR#106. TURN LEFT at the intersection, and cross Blaylock Creek—an SSS spot!

The trail for a while now is a lovely walk on the level, past lots of huge trees and several springs. It then heads to the right *up* the hillside, to a great SSS view with bench at 12.9. It climbs a little more, then makes its way around a hill, swings back to the left and finally comes alongside and above Little Missouri River again at a spectacular SSS overlook at 13.5. The trail continues downstream, mostly along the river, doing some up–and–downing, weaving back and forth across the hillsides. There are lots of great views of the river.

At 14.1 the trail crosses the river to the left (for the 8th and final time)—almost always a wet crossing—and heads into the thick brush. It continues downstream, and joins the Viles Branch Horse Trail at 14.3 (it is marked with yellow blazes)—continue STRAIGHT AHEAD. Just beyond this is the Winding Stairs Area—one of the crown jewels of Arkansas—all of it an SSS! One swimming hole after another. Giant boulders in the creek. Lush hillsides. One of the rock formations across the river is in the shape of a hand making the peace (or victory) sign. Ahh, the 60's.

The trail continues along above the area, goes up and through a rock formation, turns right on top of it across a rock slab, then turns left across Raven Branch (there are some fabulous things to explore up this little branch too), then continues down the river—watch for blazes through here. This area used to be really trashed out because vehicles could drive to it. The Forest Service closed the area to them several years ago (yea!)—The area is now protected and the scars are healing nicely.

Follow the blazes through the bottom land (still on horse trail), past lots of umbrella magnolias, to 15.2, where the horse trail exits to the right—continue STRAIGHT AHEAD (the Eagle Rock Loop also goes to the right here, on the Viles Branch Trail). Soon the trail leaves the road trace that it's been following TO THE RIGHT. This takes you along the river, a nice SSS walk. Then it crosses the road trace again, then back on it, and finally out to the end of the trail (at the "Musgrave Hole") at 15.7. (The road to this spot is getting worse, so you may have to hike a little further.)

To get to the Musgrave Hole Trailhead, from Langley, take Hwy. 84 west 2.7 miles, just past the second bridge turn right onto road #10100 (dirt), go 1.1 miles and turn left at the chicken houses onto road #10105, and follow it 2.2 miles to the end—this road gets very rough, and isn't recommended for nice cars or large RV's. Near the end you'll find several big mud holes—they are solid, but deep. I usually park just on the left before them and walk the rest of the way—it's only a couple hundred yards.

Agency List #10

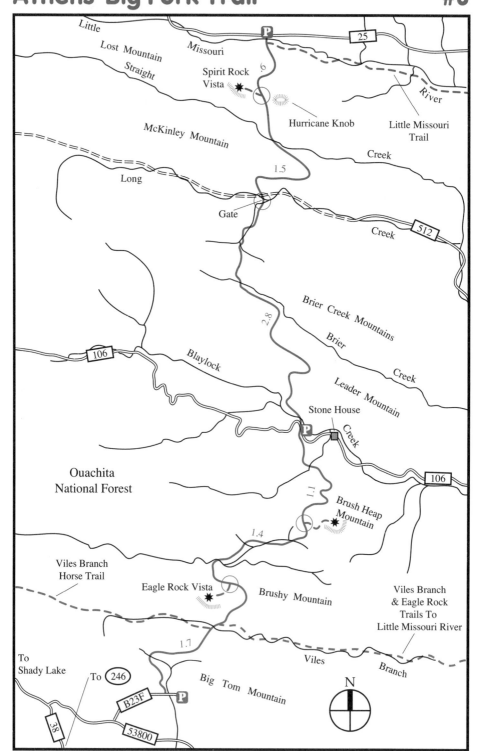

Athens–Big Fork Trail—9.1 miles one way

This is one of the most unique trails in the state. It was built over a hundred years ago as a mail route between the communities of Athens and Big Fork. It is a *steep*, tough trail, but if you can make it, the trip is worth it for the views alone—especially during leaf–off, when it's hard to keep your eyes on the trail! Camping is allowed. To get to the southern trailhead, take Hwy. 246 west out of Athens (west of Glenwood) to FR#38 (the turn to Shady Lake) and turn right for 9/10 mile, then turn right onto Weyerhaeuser road 53800 for 7/10 mile, then turn left on road B23F and follow it 9/10 mile to the trailhead sign. To get to the northern trailhead (also beginning of Little Missouri Trail), take FR#25 west from Little Missouri Falls Picnic Area for 3.3 miles. Athens and Big Fork quad. (Most of this trail, from mile 1.0 to the end, is part of the Eagle Rock Loop Trail, a great 26.8 mile loop—see page 163.)

The trail heads into the woods (white blazed) and follows a narrow stream course uphill. The hillsides are pretty steep on both sides. There are lots of ferns around and a couple of waterfalls—an SSS area. Be sure to sign in at the register. Just beyond, the trail gets serious about climbing and heads *up the hill*, past several large pines. This is Big Tom Mountain, and at .5 the trail tops out (an SSS view during leaf–off) and then quickly heads down the other side, across the steep hillside.

As the trail nears the bottom, it passes a large beech tree and intersects with an old road (which is also the Viles Branch Horse Trail)—TURN RIGHT and follow the road. It crosses Viles Branch at mile 1.0, and just beyond, leaves the road TO THE LEFT (this is where the Eagle Rock Loop Trail joins—it is 3.5 miles to the Little Missouri Trail via the Viles Branch Horse Trail). It crosses a small stream, then joins a road trace and begins its trek *up* the hill. It swings around back and forth—be sure to stay with the main trail. Up and up it goes, and the leaf–off views get better with every step. As the trail works its way up and around the left side of the hill, it comes to an SSS at 1.5—a neat rock outcrop area. It's a good spot to stop and catch your breath too!

The trail continues up, but not as steep. As it levels off there is an interesting rock formation to the left and below the trail—another SSS. There is a cave of sorts at the base. Just a little more uphill, and the trail finally comes to the top of Brushy Mountain at 1.7. There is a lesser trail there that goes to the left, out a hundred yards to a spectacular SSS view area called Eagle Rock Vista Overlook—worth some break time at (tons of wildflowers too). A good place to camp. The main trail continues straight ahead across the ridgetop and quickly heads down a ravine on the other side.

It swings around on down the hill and passes mile 2.0 just before it reaches the bottom. The trail turns left when it reaches East Saline Creek, then goes over and crosses it, and heads back upstream along it. The trail drifts away from the creek, joins an old road trace through a grown up field, then joins a four–wheeler trail and heads into the woods. It follows a neat little creek that has several little SSS areas on it (one a fern–lined crystal clear hole of water at 2.3). It continues to work gradually uphill, crossing several small drainages and the creek itself. By 2.8 the trail gets steeper and swings up to the left, past mile 3.0.

Finally the trail levels off on top of Brush Heap Mountain at 3.1 in a lush, tropical–like forest. Just beyond there is an intersection. The spur to the right is blazed with red paint and goes steeply up to an even higher part of the mountain—a narrow, craggy ridge. If you are able to find your way to the easternmost point of this ridge before daylight, you will be treated to one of the most spectacular sunrises in this part of the country (see p. 92 of the Sept. '92 issue of *Outside* magazine and see what I mean!).

The main trail continues straight past the intersection, winds its way *steeply* on down the hill, swings back to the left and levels out somewhat, crosses an SSS stream at 3.9, then continues on out to FR#106 at 4.2. It TURNS LEFT onto the road for just a moment, then leaves the road TO THE RIGHT, next to an SSS waterfall on the right, and runs on down to and across Blaylock Creek, another SSS (often a wet crossing).

From there it picks up an old road trace and heads upstream. It soon dips and crosses a little stream at 4.6, then just beyond, leaves the road TO THE RIGHT, and heads up the hill, skirting a young pine plantation. Before long it swerves to the left and continues *steeply* uphill through the pine plantation. It leaves that area, still heading up, up, the end of Leader Mountain. It finally tops out at 5.1. It drops down the other side, follows the left edge of a side ridge, then bottoms out next to Brier Creek at 5.5 — TURN LEFT here and join a four–wheeler road and head upstream along it. This is a nice, pleasant stretch of gradual uphill walking next to Brier Creek. It crosses the creek at 6.0, heads uphill a little more, then it comes to a fork in the road — TURN RIGHT off of the main road trace, onto a lesser road that heads *straight up* the hill.

It soon tops out on the ridge at 6.2 (Brier Creek Mountain), joins a greater road trace that comes in from the left, and begins to head down the other side of the ridge. Just as the road levels somewhat and curves to the left, there is an unofficial horse trail that heads back to the right — STAY ON THE ROAD, and head downstream along the little creek. The road crosses the creek three times, passes an SSS waterfall on the left at 6.8, goes through a small food plot, crosses the creek once again, and comes to a gate across the road at 7.0 (road often closed to motorized vehicles to protect turkeys).

From the gate, head straight over to Long Creek, cross it (sometimes a wet crossing), then go across FR#512, and head over to another food plot. Hike around the left edge of this plot to where the trail leaves it TO THE LEFT and heads up a narrow ridge on an old road trace. The trail levels out for a moment, then turns TO THE RIGHT and heads into the woods as plain trail at 7.3. It swings to the right and heads *steeply* up McKinley Mountain. There are some good leaf–off views along the way (stop and look while you catch your breath!). The trail finally tops out on the wildflower–covered ridge at 7.6. You can see the next ridge ahead — the larger rock outcrop is Hurricane Knob, and the trail will cross that ridge to the left (west) of it, in the saddle.

The trail quickly leaves the ridgetop and heads down to the left — lots of nice beech trees. It soon bottoms out and comes alongside Straight Creek, then crosses it at 8.0, an SSS (great campsites in the area, and lots of big beeches and pines). From the creek, it crosses a four–wheeler trail and heads steeply *up* the hillside, goes through a rocky area as it swings to the left and levels out some, then hits an old trace at 8.3 — TURN RIGHT on it for a few feet, then TURN RIGHT again on another trace, then quickly TURN LEFT off of it onto plain trail, which continues, you guessed it, *uphill!*

It passes some rock formations, then levels out in the saddle at 8.5. This is part of a ridge complex that is called Lost Mountain, so I guess that is where you are. There is a spur trail to the left here — it heads up the ridge to Spirit Rock Vista, which is a terrific SSS view! You can see a long ways, and it is worth the side trip to visit. The main trail continues through the saddle and heads down the other side of the ridge.

It swings back and forth down the hill, past mile 9.0, then comes to the Little Missouri River, and intersects with the Little Missouri Trail — TURN LEFT, cross the river, and end at the parking lot at 9.1. Little Mo Trail p. 165, Eagle Rock Loop p. 163.

Agency List #10

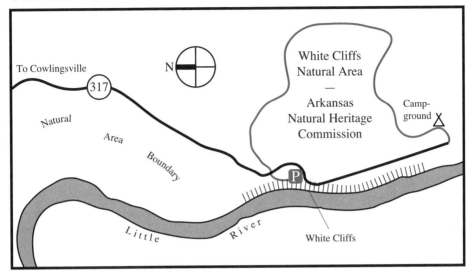

White Cliffs Loop—1.5 miles

It will take you a while to find this trail, which is located near Lake Millwood in extreme southwest Arkansas, but it's a nice little trail, with some significant trees and cliffs. This is a wonderful Natural Area, managed by the Natural Heritage Commission. From Nashville, take Hwy. 27 west over to Hwy. 317 at Cowlingsville, turn south there and continue about 6 miles to near the end of the road, and pull into the parking lot on the right—there is a White Cliffs Natural Area sign there. Ben Lomond quad.

The trail takes off to the right, and is marked with blue plastic diamonds on the trees. There is a terrific overlook of the Little River here—you are standing right on top of 90' tall "White Cliffs," made out of **Annona Chalk**—a definite SSS. (Can't really see the cliffs, but the view is great!) The trail is level, passing some great big oaks and more views, then swings to the right, runs on out to and across the highway at .2. The trail swings back to the right and uphill a little, and at .4 it intersects on top with an old roadbed—TURN LEFT and follow the road. This area is an SSS, as it is thick with a rare tree—**Ashe's juniper**.

Not too far beyond at .6, TURN RIGHT off of the road and head down to an overlook area—this is the old mine site of a cement factory that was here ages ago—they mined the chalk. The trail heads back to the left and up the hill back to the road—TURN RIGHT and continue along it. There are lots of wildflowers along the ridgetop. At .8 the trail bears right, swings around the hill, then heads to the left and straight down the hillside. There are several large oaks and junipers through this area. Once in the bottom, the trail hits an old roadbed and turns right, and just beyond is mile 1.0.

There are lots more junipers—another SSS area, as the trail continues level. At 1.1 the trail comes out into the middle of the chalk mine area, and TURNS LEFT. It's a neat trip along the top of these cliffs—an SSS for sure. Soon we're back into the woods again, heading downhill. At 1.3 the trail comes out into a campground—TURN RIGHT on the road and follow it on out and up the hill, back to the trailhead. This is a nice campground, right on the banks of the Little River. The total loop is 1.5 miles.

Agency List # 39

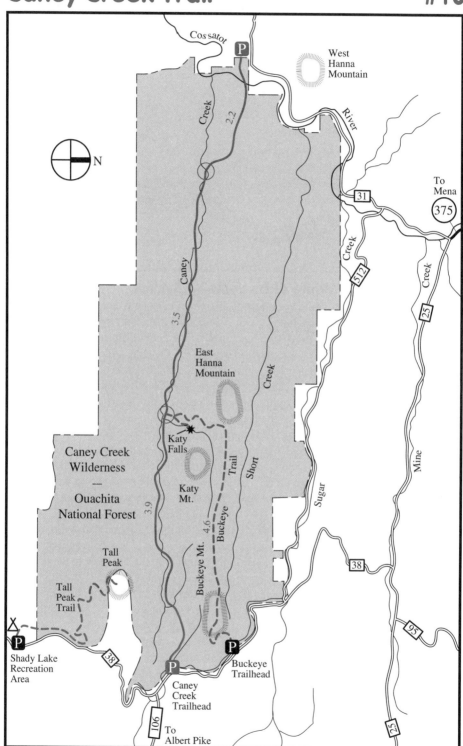

Caney Creek Trail—9.6 miles one way

This is one of the best trails in Arkansas. Most of it runs along picturesque Caney Creek, and crosses the Caney Creek Wilderness Area from end to end. The only drawback to this trail is that it fords the creek *many times*, and crosses the Cossatot River on the west end (much larger than Caney Creek)—it's a great trail to hike in the summer, when you don't mind getting your feet wet!

To get to the East Trailhead, take Hwy. 246 west out of Athens a couple of miles, turn north on FR#38 (at the turnoff to Shady Lake), go 9.2 miles (past Shady Lake and just past FR#106), and the trailhead is on the left. From Albert Pike Campground, go west on FR#106 to FR#38, turn right and the trailhead is just ahead on the left. To get to the West Trailhead, take Hwy. 246 west out of Athens about 20 miles, turn right on FR#31, go about 9 miles and turn right, then follow the jeep road to the trailhead. The trail itself is blazed with off–white paint. Eagle Mtn. and Nichols quads.

The trail begins with a crossing of Blaylock Creek, then follows an old roadbed around through the woods, doing some up–and–downing, and crossing lesser creeks several times. There are lots of nice big trees in here—get used to the big trees, and the creek crossings! It climbs up and over a saddle (Blaylock Gap), and heads down into the Caney Creek Drainage, still on the old road trace. It crosses Caney Creek for the first time at mile 1.0. The trail levels off somewhat and follows Caney Creek. Pretty soon it leaves the old road TO THE RIGHT at 1.2, and continues on a dug trail (1994 reroute #1). Some folks will probably still try to hike along the creek, but all those crossings really are a pain, and this new stretch is pretty nice. It heads up the hillside just a little, giving a view out that is seldom seen. The tower that you can see is on top of Tall Peak.

It levels off across the steep hillside, then works its way back down alongside the creek, to an SSS at 1.7—a great view of the creek, and the moss–covered shale ledges there! The trail curves back to the right some, past more giant beech trees (good campsites off on the left), then swings back to the creek at 2.0. It picks up the old trail there, and crosses the creek for the second time—neat bluffs on the right, an SSS.

The trail continues along on the level, past a variety of big trees—oaks, beeches, sweet gums and hickories. There are lots of good campsite areas around too. Caney Creek is famous for it grassy flats, which tend to get overused and ugly. My suggestion to you is to seek out a campsite that is out of sight of the trail, perhaps even on the other side of the creek. You should drop your pack and explore around—even on top of the ridges you will find wonderful campsites. And here is a hint—the second half of the trail is even better—more lush, grassy flats—and more solitude too!

By 2.6 the hillsides begin to close in, and there is another bluff SSS just across the creek. Of course most of the creek itself is an SSS too! (If you have some time to explore here, cross the creek and head up the drainage there—you will find some great rock formations about a half mile up the right–hand fork). The trail eases up the hill some, then continues along on the level again. It drops back down to and makes the third crossing of Caney Creek at 2.8. Just on the other side, the trail leaves the old road trace TO THE RIGHT, and continues on as plain trail (1994 reroute #2).

It eases on up to the first bench, past mile 3.0, dips down and across a small creek, then comes out to an SSS overlook of the creek (great views out too). This area is open because of a pine beetle infestation that killed nearly 40 acres of pine trees! You can still see some of the rotted stumps. The huckleberry is getting tall and thick. The trail stays level, passes a couple of huge pines that are 26"+ across. It passes another SSS view at 3.3, then eases on down the hill, and hugs the base of some small bluffs before hitting bottom and rejoining the old trail at 3.6.

It crosses a big, grassy flat, passes a giant pine, then drops down and crosses Katy Creek at 3.9. This area right here is really overused and abused! Just beyond Katy Creek, as the trail heads up a hill, the Buckeye Trail takes off to the right (most of it is an SSS—see page 176). You can make a fine 9.6–mile loop by combining it with the Caney Creek Trail. Katy Creek itself is a wonderful SSS hike, and there is an old trail much of the way. The Caney Creek Trail goes STRAIGHT AHEAD, and up a little.

The trail levels out, then drops down again, past 4.0, then crosses the creek for the fourth time (swimming hole nearby). Lots of good campsites. Big trees too. It continues along beside the creek (past the site of the famous fire fly races). In the spring you will find tons of wild iris along here. By the way, in the spring you will find tons of wildflowers *everywhere* along the trail! And this stretch of trail is much less crowded.

The 5th crossing is at 4.3, and the 6th is at 4.5. These crossings are getting a little wider, but the creek is usually shallow, and you can often hop across. The farther you go on the trail, and the more water there is, the more you are going to get your feet wet! What I do is hike with tennis shoes, and just go right through. This allows me to drop my pack whenever I feel like it, and take off and explore a neat area in the creek.

The trail runs along a level bench above, and just out of sight of the creek for a while—big, grassy flats. At 5.0 there is a wide, wet, spring area, lush with ferns, an SSS. There is a great view of the creek, more grassy flats, and a couple of small streams here and there. As the trail drops down to stream level at 5.3, there is an old saw mill site off on the right. I have done a little bit of stomping around in this wilderness area, and it occurred to me one day that I had not seen many other human signs, except for the old road that the trail is on. Most other wilderness areas in this part of the country are littered with old homesteads and log roads.

The trail gets close to the creek for a moment, then heads up a little hill. There is a neat SSS spot on the creek that you can see, perhaps even a sitting pool! Soon after, the trail drops back down and makes the 7th crossing of the creek at 5.5. The trail stays in the bottom, but away from the creek, and goes through a stand of river cane. Then it hits the creek again at 5.6 for the 8th crossing. Now things get really nice.

A little ways beyond this crossing, just past a dry drain, you need to drop your pack and head over to the creek, which is down below—there is a wonderful SSS there, and you will just have to have a look and see what I mean. My favorite spot. Beyond that is one of the best grassy flats. At 6.0 the trail drops down and makes the 9th cross.

The trail runs away from the creek again, and passes huge trees (an SSS), then makes the 10th crossing at 6.3 in two sections. The 11th crossing is at 6.5 (an SSS just upstream). It swings away from the creek, then back for the 12th crossing at 6.7. There are lots of campsite areas all through here, and lots of mini SSS's up and down the creek—too many to mention! The 13th crossing is at 7.0 (waterfall just upstream), 14th at 7.2, and the 15th, and last, crossing, is at 7.5—nice SSS area coming in from the side.

From there the trail joins an old roadbed and heads uphill, away from the creek. It swings around back and forth, does some up–and–downing past big trees, then begins to head downhill gradually, following along and crossing several much smaller creeks many times. It finally drops down to and across the Cossatot River at 9.1.

From the river it winds up the hillside, past some SSS views of the river valley, and finally levels off and ends at the West Trailhead at 9.6. Boy, what a trip!

Agency List #13

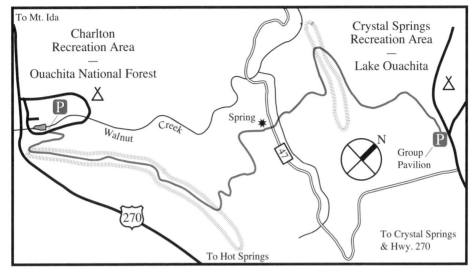

Charlton Trail—4.2 miles one way

I was surprised to find that this is such a nice trail, right on pavement. There are a couple of pretty good climbs, nice views, and a spring half way. It begins at Charlton Recreation Area on Hwy. 270 between Hot Springs and Mt. Ida. There is a swimming lake there, campground and picnic area, but it is closed during the winter, which will add some to your hike. The trail ends at Crystal Springs Recreation Area, a Corps of Engineers spot on Lake Ouachita. McGram Mtn. Quad.

To get to the beginning, turn right at the entrance to Charlton Rec. Area and head over to the amphitheater (park at the front gate if closed). The trail begins across the road from the amphitheater. It switchbacks up and across a very steep hillside, lands on top of the ridge, turns back to the left and continues up the ridgeline. There are some great leaf–off SSS views of the surrounding hills. It levels off somewhat, then eases up some more as it curves to the right, past mile 1.0.

It continues along the top of the ridge, passing some large pines. At 1.4 it turns back TO THE LEFT and heads down off of the ridge, swinging back and forth. Along the way, there are some good leaf–off views of the ridges out in front—the first one is what we will climb in a few minutes! It wanders on down the hillside, joins a four–wheeler road, levels off, and passes mile 2.0. While still on the road, at 2.2, as it is heading up a hill, the trail leaves the road TO THE RIGHT, and continues on as plain trail. From there it heads down the hill and comes out on FR#47 at 2.4. Walnut Fork Spring, a well–flowing pipe spring, is there—treat the water!

The trail crosses the road, heads on over to and crosses Walnut Fork Creek, an SSS, then begins to climb up through a large, young pine plantation. It levels off some, then continues to climb. At 3.0 there is a great SSS view. It leaves the plantation, goes up and over a ridge at 3.2, then swings to the right and continues along the left side of the ridge. It drops on down the hill, passes through mile 4.0, picks up a four–wheeler road, then leaves the road TO THE RIGHT. It drops down and crosses a small creek, then levels out and runs on over and ends at the rec area pavilion at 4.2.

Agency List #16

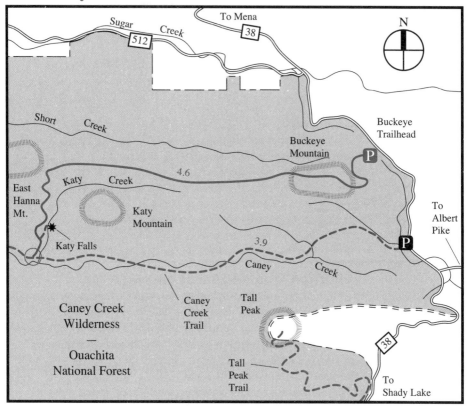

Buckeye Mountain Trail—9.1 miles round trip

This is one of a number of good trails in this part of the Ouachita National Forest. It is mostly a ridgetop trail, that runs along the crest of Buckeye Mountain (some stunning views!), then drops down to Caney Creek and connects with the Caney Creek Trail. All of this trail is within the 14,433–acre Caney Creek Wilderness. It is great all by itself, but even better when you combine it with part of the Caney Creek Trail (and the forest road) for a loop.

To get to the trailhead, take Hwy. 246 west out of Athens for a couple of miles, turn north on FR#38 (at the turnoff to Shady Lake), and go 10.3 miles (past Shady Lake, past FR#106, past the Caney Creek Trailhead), and the trailhead will be at the top of the hill on the left. Nichols quad.

The trail, which is marked with white blazes, takes off on an old roadbed, past views, lots of springs, and lush steep hillsides. It climbs on uphill, making its way up and around the beginning of Buckeye Mountain. As it curves around to the right, there is an SSS view out into the wilderness area at .5. It soon levels off, and begins to run along the top of the ridgetop. Back to the left, you can see the big antenna on top of Tall Peak. Keep an eye on this antenna, and watch it disappear back to your left as you hike along.

At .6 there is another SSS—a great view, plus a large flat rock slab that is turned on its side. There are also some other neat rock outcrops in the area. The trail continues to climb up a little, remaining on the knife–edge ridge. During leaf–off, there are good views on both sides for a while. As the trail runs along the right side of the ridge, it passes through mile 1.0. Soon after, it tops out again, at another SSS view.

Just beyond the view spot, the trail actually begins to drop down just a little. There are some nice, big trees in this area too. At 1.3 the trail turns sharply left and drops down the hill to another SSS view. It quickly levels off, then heads back up onto the rocky ridgetop. It continues along the left side, then down the middle, then off sharply down to the left again and another SSS view at 1.5. (See what I mean about views!) This is one of the best views that I know of in the Ouachitas—the hills just seem to go on forever.

It swings back to the right and levels off, just under a series of broken bluffs at 1.6—another SSS! It turns to the right some, back on top, and begins to work its way around the right side of the ridge. It goes across a very steep hillside on the level—lots of big trees—and passes mile 2.0. Just after, it heads to the left, back up on top of and quickly down the other side of the ridge. It's pretty lush on top, as the trail visits it again for a short period, then drops back down to the left, and levels off. It goes through a boulder field—watch for the piles of rocks that mark the way—then back up on top again at 2.5 and another SSS view. One of the hills that you are looking at is East Hanna Mountain—we're going to eventually drop down the left side of it.

The trail returns to the right side of the ridge, dropping down a little ways and leveling off. Then back up to the left and the top again. We pass mile 3.0 while on the ridgetop. The peak that is just off to our left is Katy Mountain. The trail eases down through a couple of saddles, then heads uphill on the ridge a little. There are some terrific SSS views all along here—you can look right down the Katy Creek Drainage, all the way to Caney Creek. We are fixing to follow our view down the same path.

At 3.4 the trail turns to the left and leaves the ridgetop, dropping down through a rocky area, then quickly switchbacks to the right. It begins a long drop down the side of East Hanna Mountain towards Caney Creek, across a *very* steep hillside! There is a great SSS view at 4.0—rock outcrops that cross the trail go all the way down to and across Katy Creek below, then continue up the other side of the mountain. The spot where they cross Katy Creek is a neat spot too.

Soon the trail levels a bit, and swings to the right side of a side ridge. It heads back to the left side, and runs along just above, but still out of sight of, Katy Creek. You can hear a waterfall—that's Katy Falls, the largest of several waterfalls on the small creek, and probably in the entire wilderness area. At 4.5 there is a spur trail that takes off to the left and heads over to the falls, then continues up Katy Creek—an SSS hike all of it!!! This is also the old route of the trail, which used to head up the creek, and make a terrible climb out at the other end. It was rerouted in the summer of 1993 by volunteers from the Student Conservation Association. The main trail continues STRAIGHT AHEAD, soon dropping down to the intersection with the Caney Creek Trail along Caney Creek at 4.6.

You are now deep in the middle of the Caney Creek Wilderness. Return to the trailhead the same way that you came. Or, if you're going to continue along the Caney Creek Trail, it's 3.9 miles to the left back to the East Trailhead on FR#38 (then 1.1 miles up the road, back to the Buckeye Trailhead, making a total loop of 9.6 miles). And it's 5.7 miles to the right to the West Trailhead on FR#31. For a closer look at the Caney Creek Trail, see page 173.

Agency List #13

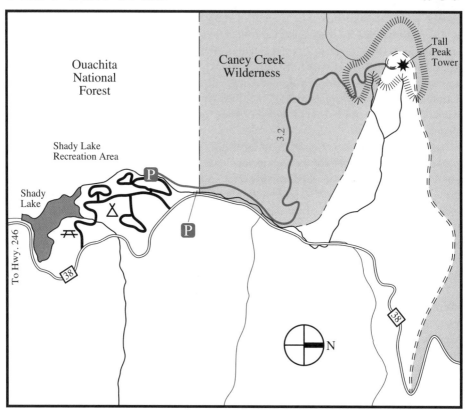

Tall Peak Trail—6.4 miles round trip

This trail does just exactly what you think it does—it climbs up to the tallest peak in the area, which is 2330 feet tall, and is called Tall Peak. But it also runs along a wonderful little stream, crossing it four times. It begins at Shady Lake Campground in the Ouachita National Forest, and most of the trail is within the 14,433–acre Caney Creek Wilderness Area. You can also drive to the top of Tall Peak, and to the old look-out tower there, but it's more fun to hike it! This road is shown on the map as a jeep road—the gate is sometimes closed. Nichols quad.

To get to the trailhead, take Hwy. 246 west out of Athens for a couple of miles, turn north on FR#38 for several miles, and turn left into the Shady Lake Campground. Make your way back to the "C" Loop, and you will find the beginning of the trail there—a closed road crosses the creek on a cement slab—there isn't much room to park.

The trail is marked with white paint blazes. It takes off across the creek on the cement slab. Once on the other side it TURNS RIGHT and leaves the road. (The other blazed trail here circles around the lake.) As it heads out on the level it comes alongside the Saline River—this is the river that creates Shady Lake. It's a nice, babbling brook at this point, and we'll be following it for a while. At .3 there is a neat little swimming hole. Soon after, there is an SSS on the creek right where the trail crosses it. The creek is chocked with clumps of wildflowers and tall grasses.

It continues along through a nice level grassy area, sort of an SSS. The only problem is that the forest road is right above it! At .5 the trail crosses the "South Boundary" Road, which is actually now just a trailhead, since it doesn't go anywhere. You could begin your hike here, but you'd miss part of the stream. Be sure to sign in at the register just beyond.

The trail crosses another grassy flat, then runs past several large beech and sweetgum trees to a second crossing at .6. It goes through some rock gardens and quickly crosses the river a third time, and then a fourth and last time at .7. From here it begins to head up the hill across a steep hillside. There is an arched rock just above the trail at .9—an SSS. You're also beginning to get some views to the right of the hillside just across the way. A little ways beyond there is an intersection with an old, lesser trail that heads down the hill to the right at some rock outcrops—STAY LEFT and continue up the hill (the old trail drops down to the forest road).

It goes through some thick woods, then a lush and rocky hillside, and switchbacks up to the left at 1.1.   It climbs on up to a wonderful glade area just beyond. There are lots of wildflowers along the way as the trail swings back and forth through this area. It continues up the hill, back in the woods, and past more rock outcrops. The views to the east get even better. The hillside and the trail are generally made out of gravel through here. Finally there is some relief from the climb as the trail goes through a saddle and levels off somewhat at 1.5. There are some pretty good views of Tall Peak in this area—look for a big antenna that is up there.

The forest is pretty open but the trail is rocky as it begins to rise gradually. It's a pretty nice walk through this area. It heads up some more, through another saddle, and past big trees. It swings over to the right, then back to the left. The trail actually dips down hill just a little, then quickly back up again at 2.2. A couple of things happen at this point—there is a great SSS view off to the left deeper into the Caney Creek Wilderness Area, and the trail TURNS SHARPLY UP TO THE RIGHT. Be sure to watch for this, 'cause there is a trail that continues straight ahead that you don't want.

The main trail swings on around the hillside to the left, past views and big pines, then cuts a SHARP LEFT TURN UPHILL at 2.4 (there is another lesser trail that goes straight ahead here, so watch out). It continues up the gravel hillside, swings back to the right, then left, away from a power line, and climbs up through another SSS area at 2.7. There are lots of rock outcrops, wildflowers and views all around. This is a good spot to hang out a while and enjoy the world!

The trail remains rather rocky as it continues to head up the hill, and gets pretty steep at times. The leaf–off views through the trees to the west are great. At 3.0 the trail swings back to the right and intersects with FR#38A—TURN RIGHT and head up the road. It soon levels off and curves around to the left, ending at the base of the old fire lookout tower at 3.2. It has recently been restored, and you can go up and have a look. Quite an impressive SSS view, especially to the south. You can look down and see the route that you've just hiked up, including Shady Lake, as well as most of the rest of the country. Unfortunately, the view to the west is blocked by trees, so photography of the sunset isn't too good. The elevation up here is about 2330'.

The hike back down is pretty easy—it's all downhill! The road up to this tower is a rough one, and is gated during the week much of the time. If you want to drive up, check with the District Ranger's office in Mena.

Agency List #13

Lake Catherine Trails

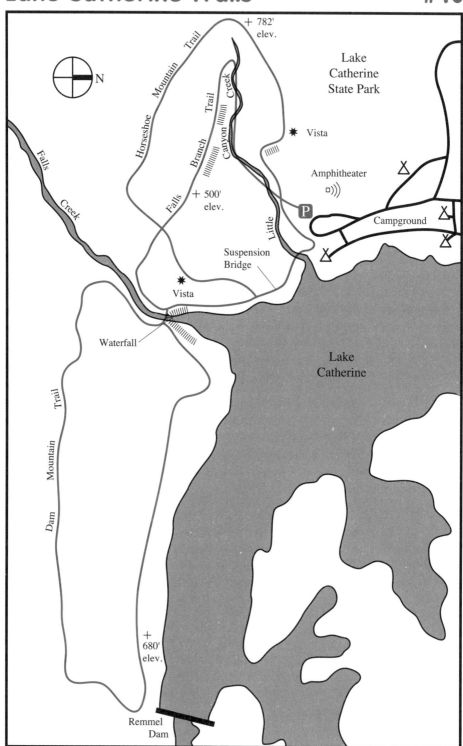

N

+ 782' elev.

Horseshoe Mountain Trail

Canyon Creek

Falls Branch Trail

Falls Creek

+ 500' elev.

Falls

Vista

Lake Catherine State Park

Vista

Amphitheater

Campground

P

Suspension Bridge

Little Creek

Waterfall

Dam Mountain Trail

Lake Catherine

+ 680' elev.

Remmel Dam

Lake Catherine Loop—6.3 miles

There are three trails at this State Park—we're going to combine them into one longer loop. All of them are quite scenic, and spend some time running along or looking down on Lake Catherine. There are lots of rock formations, lush vegetation, big trees, and a great waterfall. To get to the park, take exit #97 on I–30 south of Malvern and take Hwy. 171 North, it will end at the State Park. You can get there from Hot Springs too—from Hwy. 270 east of town take Hwy. 128 to the south, then left on Hwy. 290 and follow the signs. A parking/entrance fee may be required. Lake Catherine quad.

The trailhead is located at the back of the park, just past the amphitheater. There is a nice color map of the area at the archway there. The trail heads off level through the woods. It quickly comes to an intersection. What we are going to do is go clockwise around the outermost loops, ending back at this spot. Then we'll do a shorter center loop. This way, we'll get to do all of the trails, plus give you an option to bail out if your time is short. I will keep the mileage meter running the whole time. So TURN LEFT at this intersection towards the Dam Mountain Trail.

It heads down through nice big trees, crosses a road near the camping area, and goes over a foot bridge—we are following the white blazes. (This first section is actually part of all three trails, and is blazed as such going in the opposite direction. The numbered posts that you see are keyed to information in the Fall Branch Trail brochure, which is available at the Visitor Center.) It begins to follow the lake shore, then at .4 crosses a nice suspension bridge. Just beyond we come to an intersection—we will eventually come down the hill from the right on this yellow–blazed trail (if you hike the very last described section). Continue STRAIGHT AHEAD and along the lake.

It works its way up into a cove and comes to another intersection at .7 (we will return to this intersection at the end of the Dam Mountain Trail). TURN LEFT and make your way across the top of Falls Creek Falls here— an SSS—really nice. It spills over the ledge into a large pool below. On the other side the trail curves to the left just a little, then heads up the hill, across a rock face—a trail does appear at the top! The trail levels off only briefly, then continues a steep climb up the hill, swinging back to the right on the way. During leaf–off the views do get better with every step.

It eventually gets much less steep as the trail swings to the left. It is running along the middle of the ridgetop now. It winds around up there, mostly level, along the narrow ridge of Dam Mountain. At 1.4 it drops down to the right, then swings back up to the ridgetop again (it does this twice). There are several SSS views to the left out across the lake and down to the dam all along here, especially during leaf–off. It passes through an SSS glade area that is full of wildflowers.

At 1.8 the trail TURNS RIGHT and heads away from the lake area for good. It drops on down the hill, and levels off at mile 2.0. There are some large oak and pine trees, and the forest has really opened up. At 2.4 the trail heads down the hill as it swings to the right, hits bottom and comes alongside Falls Creek—lots of mosses, ferns and wildflowers along this section—an SSS! It follows the creek back to the waterfall at 3.1—cross the creek again and TURN LEFT for the continuation of our loop.

We are now on the Falls Branch Trail (red blazed), and it heads back up the other side of the creek that we just came down. At 3.3 the trail turns away from Falls Creek to the right and heads up a side drainage. As it heads up the hill, there are several smaller waterfalls on the creek—a real neat area of mosses and ferns—an SSS. It

Lake Catherine Loop (cont.)

continues up the hill, passes an SSS glade area, then comes to an intersection at 3.6—TURN LEFT here, and head up the hill. (The Falls Branch Trail goes straight ahead, back to the trailhead—we'll come up it to this spot during the last section.)

This is the Horseshoe Mountain Trail, and it heads up the hill steeply (yellow blazed). As we go up the leaf–off views improve. It levels off on top and runs across a more open area, with wildflowers and mosses around. It rises up just a little, then heads on down hill a little, swinging back to the right. It does some up–and–downing before heading down a little steeper. On the level again it comes to a trail intersection at 4.6—a short spur to the left goes to an SSS vista—continue STRAIGHT (to the right) and resume downhill.

There are some real nice rock outcrops as the trail drops steeply down the hill—SSS areas. At 4.9 there are several huge pine trees too. It finally levels off and comes to the big intersection right at mile 5.0. The trailhead is just off to the left, but we're going to continue our hike on the Falls Branch Trail, looping through the inside of the outer loop that we just completed—there are more SSS areas ahead! So TURN RIGHT here and follow the red blazes.

The trail crosses Little Canyon Creek the first of several times on a little bridge, and heads upstream. There is an SSS at the second crossing—lots of boulders and mosses in the creek—and the trail crosses it again soon after. Before long there are several more quick crossings of the creek—and an SSS area lush with Christmas, Maidenhair and Lady ferns. There are some waterfalls over moss–covered rocks in the creek too. At 5.3 the trail switchbacks up the hill to the left. As the trail goes along the hillside there are some nice rock outcrops where you can get SSS views out across the hollow.

At 5.5 we come to the intersection that we came to earlier—TURN LEFT here and we'll hike down the other part of the Horseshoe Mountain Trail (yellow blazes). It climbs up just a little, then levels out along the middle of the ridgetop. Just as the trail turns to the left and heads down the hill at 5.8, there is a short spur straight ahead that goes to an SSS view of the lake. There several large trees, both oaks and pines, along the trail as it switchbacks down the hill.

At 5.9 we intersect with the trail along the lake—TURN LEFT and follow the multicolored trail. It crosses over the suspension bridge again, then heads back to the trailhead, for a total distance of 6.3 miles.

Agency List #27

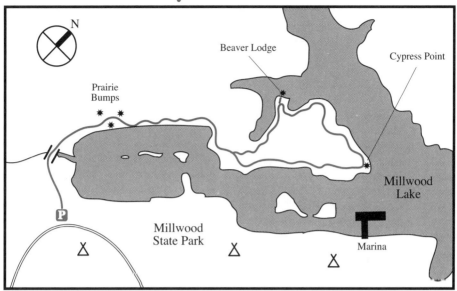

Waterfowl Way Loop—1.5 miles

This unique trail at Millwood State Park is the only one in Arkansas that I know of where you have a chance to see an *alligator*! Plus there is lots of other wildlife to see, like a beaver lodge, and of course a bunch of waterfowl, including blue herons, white egrets, bald eagles, geese, and tons of ducks. The park is located on Hwy. 32 between Ashdown and Saratoga in extreme southwest Arkansas, at the western end of the Millwood Lake Dam. There is a nice campground there, and a marina. An entrance fee may apply. Be sure to check in at the Visitor Center, and pick up a trail brochure, which has descriptions of the 20 interpretive stops along the way. Red Bluff quad.

The trailhead is located at the back of camp area E (near site #97). The best time to hike it is in the early morning or late evening, when wildlife is most active. Go slowly, and quietly, and keep your eyes open! The trail takes off behind the carved wood sign and heads across a foot bridge. A cove of the lake is off on the right–we will follow along the shoreline. It's an easy, level walk through the woods.

The trail veers away from the water a couple of times, but comes right back to the shoreline. There are several resting benches along the way. At .4, near interpretive post #10, there is a shallow ditch—this is actually a "beaver run," where beavers have been traveling between the two bodies of water—you'll see a few chewed trees too! Stay to the RIGHT here (you will loop back to this spot from the left).

The trail continues along towards the end of the cove and the main lake, past an SSS area of great pine trees at .6. It comes to a picnic table at the end of Cypress Point, then swings back to the left and heads back into another cove. Two benches on this side are set up as blinds, where you can sit quietly and look for wildlife. At the second one, at .9, there is also a spur trail—this short spur leads over to a *working* beaver lodge, an SSS! This is a great spot to spend some time (and see alligators?).

From here the trail continues on to the beaver run again at 1.0—TURN RIGHT and follow the trail back to the trailhead, for a total hike of 1.5 miles.

Agency List #30.

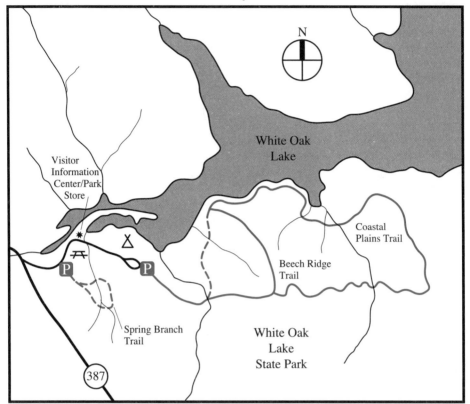

White Oak Lake Loop—3.0 miles

This trail is certainly in an out of the way place (White Oak Lake State Park—
east of Hope), but I think it's worth the effort to get there. I can't quite put my finger on
it, but there is a certain wonderful feeling that you get as you walk the first section of
this trail. Maybe it's the huge, towering trees all around you. I don't know. But it's nice.
This is a pretty easy trail to hike. The loop is actually two trails joined together—the
Beech Ridge and Coastal Plains trails. The short Spring Branch Nature Trail at the park
is also worth a look. Chidester quad.

To get to White Oak Lake, exit I–30 at Prescott and head east on Hwy. 24 about
20 miles to Bluff City, turn right on Hwy. 299, then another immediate right onto Hwy.
387 for two miles and turn left into the park. The trailhead is located at the back of the
camping area—you want to go to area "E," tent camping only. The trail begins at an
archway at the end of the camp area.

The Beech Ridge Trail heads out on the level and comes to an SSS area right
away—some of the largest pine trees that you'll find on any trail in the state. And then
it crosses a long, low wooden walkway that is pretty unique in itself—just a lovely spot.
There is another walkway just ahead. Something that is interesting to do when you're
around such big trees as these is to go over to one of them, get right up against it, and
look up the trunk. Wow!

The trail continues on, crosses a small stream, then heads up just a little. It crosses a roadbed that comes in from the left—continue STRAIGHT AHEAD. You'll notice that the forest has changed dramatically—different trees, different underbrush and ground cover, a totally different environment—partly due to the soil types. It swings around to the left and gradually climbs, coming to a trail intersection at .6—TURN LEFT on the Beech Ridge Trail. (The Coastal Plains Trail comes in from the right—this is the trail that we will return on.)

We're on an old roadbed now, heading down just a little, and the trail is marked with red paint. It curves to the right and heads on down to the lake shore. At .9 it comes to a "T" intersection—the Beech Ridge Trail actually turns back to the left and eventually rejoins our loop, but it's more scenic the other way, so we're going to TURN RIGHT on the old roadbed and begin our hike around the shore of White Oak Lake on the Coastal Plains Trail.

One of the first things that we see are large beech trees on both sides of the trail—an SSS. And just beyond there is a great SSS view out across the lake. There are a few large pines along here too. The trail winds on around along the lake, and by 1.3 has veered away from it some and left the big beeches. It crosses a couple of small streams and passes some larger hardwoods and more big pines, then eases uphill just a little, still on the old roadbed.

At 1.7 we come to an open field and begin to skirt around the right edge, then quickly TURN RIGHT and head into the woods, away from the field. It heads back to the right on narrow trail. This is a different type of forest environment still. The trail swings to the left and down just a little, through an SSS area with a tiny stream and huge beech trees. It runs along the fern–lined, sandy–bottomed creek. At 1.9 there is a bench, and a bridge across the creek. This is a small, but wonderful spot, and a good time to take a break and soak it all in!

Across the creek the trail begins to head uphill, back to the left and away from the creek. It winds around up the hill, soon leveling off. The forest is more open now, with a grassy floor. At 2.3 there is a huge oak tree just on the right—it's not the tallest tree that you'll see by far, but it is one of the biggest around. Ask them at the Visitor Center what kind it is. A little ways past this giant at 2.4 we reconnect with the Beech Ridge Trail—GO STRAIGHT AHEAD, and head on down the hill back towards the trailhead.

Just in case you didn't do it on the way in, stop in the middle of the long walkway at the huge pine tree, grab a hold of something, and look up. The total loop distance is 3.0 miles.

Spring Branch Nature Trail—.3 mile loop. This is such a short trail, we'll visit it also. The entrance to it is back across from the Visitor Center, in the picnic area. The first thing that you see on this trail is huge white oak trees—must be where the lake got its name! Then you come alongside a little fern–lined stream. The trail splits—TURN LEFT and cross the creek on a bridge.

It rises up, and swings to the right through a pine forest. It begins to drop back down to the right into the hardwoods again—some big pines also, and a beech or two. It crosses the stream on another bridge, passes some large sweetgum trees, and more towering white oaks, then rejoins the loop and heads back to the trailhead.

Agency List #36

AGENCY LIST

U.S. FOREST SERVICE

#1 OZARK NATIONAL FOREST
605 West Main
Russellville, AR 72801
479–968–2354

#2 Bayou Ranger District
12000 SR 27
Hector, AR 72843
479–284–3150

#3 Boston Mountain Ranger District
Hwy. 23 North
Ozark, AR 72949
479–667–2191
White Rock Cabins — 479–369–4128

#4 Buffalo Ranger District
Hwy. 7 North
Jasper, AR 72641
870–446–5122

#5 Magazine Ranger District
Hwy. 22 East
Paris, AR 72855
479–963–3076

#6 Pleasant Hill Ranger District
Hwy. 21 North
Clarksville, AR 72830
479–754–2864

#7 St. Francis Ranger District
2675 Hwy. 44
Marianna, AR 72360
870–295–5278

#8 Sylamore Ranger District
1001 E. Main St.
Mountain View, AR 72560
870–269–3228

#9 OUACHITA NATIONAL FOREST
P.O. Box 1270 (Federal Building)
Hot Springs, AR 71902
501–321–5202

#10 Caddo Ranger District
912 Smokey Bear Lane
Glenwood, AR 71943
870–356–4186

#11 Cold Springs Ranger District
2190 E. Main
Booneville, AR 72927
479–675–3233

#12 Jessieville Ranger District
8607 Hwy. 7 North
Jessieville, AR 71949
501–984–5313

#13 Mena Ranger District
1603 Hwy. 71 North
Mena, AR 71953
479–394–2382

#14 Oden Ranger District
Hwy. 88 West
Oden, AR 71961
870–326–4322

#15 Winona Ranger District
1069 N. Fourche Ave.
Perryville, AR 72126
501–889–5176

#16 Womble Ranger District
1523 Hwy. 270 East
Mount Ida, AR 71957
870–867–2101

NATIONAL PARK SERVICE

#17 Buffalo National River
P.O. Box 1173
Harrison, AR 72601
870–741–5443

#18 Hot Springs National Park
P.O. Box 1860
Hot Springs, AR 71901
501–624–3383

#19 Pea Ridge National Military Park
Pea Ridge, AR 72751
479–451–8122

CORPS OF ENGINEERS

#20 Beaver Lake Resident Engineer
P.O. Drawer H
Rogers, AR 72756
479–636–1210

#21 Bull Shoals/Norfork Lakes
P.O. Box 369
Mtn. Home, AR 72653
870–425–2700

#22 Greers Ferry Lake Engineer
P.O. Box 310
Heber Springs, AR 72543
501–362–9067

#23 Lake Dardanelle Resident Engineer
P.O. Box 1087
Russellville, AR 72801
479–968–5008

ARKANSAS STATE PARKS

#24 Arkansas State Trails Coordinator
One Capitol Mall
Little Rock, AR 72201
501–682–1301

#25 Beaver Lake State Park
20344 E. Hwy. 12
Rogers, AR 72756
479–789–2380

#26 Devil's Den State Park
11333 West Hwy. 74
West Fork, AR 72774
479–761–3325

#27 Lake Catherine State Park
1200 Catherine Park Road
Hot Springs, AR 71913
501–844–4176

#28 Lake Ft. Smith State Park
P.O. Box 4
Mountainburg, AR 72946
479–369–2469

#29 Lake Ouachita State Park
5451 Mountain Pine Road
Mountain Pine, AR 71956
501–767–9366

#30 Millwood State Park
1564 Hwy. 32 East
Ashdown, AR 71822
870–898–2800

#31 Mt. Nebo State Park
#1 State Park Drive
Dardanelle, AR 72834
479–229–3655

#32 Petit Jean State Park
1285 Petit Jean Mtn. Road
Morrilton, AR 72110
501–727–5441

#33 Pinnacle Mountain State Park
11901 Pinnacle Valley Road
Roland, AR 72135
501–868–5806

#34 Queen Wilhelmina State Park
3877 Hwy. 88 West
Mena, AR 71953
479–394–2863

#35 Village Creek State Park
201 CR 754
Wynne, AR 72396
870–238–9406

#36 White Oak Lake State Park
HC 2, Box 28
Bluff City, AR 71722
870–685–2748

#37 Withrow Springs State Park
33424 Spur 23
Huntsville, AR 72740
479–559–2593

#38 Woolly Hollow State Park
82 Woolly Hollow Road
Greenbrier, AR 72058
501–679–2098

OTHER

#39 Arkansas Natural Heritage Commission
323 Center St. (1500 Tower Bldg)
Little Rock, AR 72201
501–324–9150

#40 N. Little Rock Parks & Recreation
2700 N. Willow
N. Little Rock, AR 72114
501–753–9312

GPS COORDINATES FOR TRAILHEADS

Here are GPS coordinates for all the trailheads. Set your GPS to digital/decimal degrees, WGS 84. Plug these into your car nav system, GPS unit, or smart device for directions! Detailed driving directions are also included with each trail description.

Trail # and Name	Coordinates	Page #
1 Alum Cove Loop	35.859972, -93.232954	63
3 Athens–Big Fork Trail	34.347103, -093.98434	169
4 Bear Creek Loop	34.707626, -90.697519	112
5 Bell Slough Loop	34.939254, -92.418059	133
6 Big Creek Loop	35.501800, -91.836980	106
7 Black Fork Mountain Trail	34.684483, -94.317734	137
8 Bona Dea Loops	35.305798, -93.145016	158
9 Bridge Rock Loop	35.314151, -93.429716	129
10 Brushy Creek Loop	34.68518, -93.8103350	141
11 Buckeye Mountain Trail	34.408904, -94.028060	176
12 BRT–S. Boxley to Ponca	35.945564, -93.398779 (S. Boxley)	71
13 BRT–Ponca to Pruitt	36.021016, -93.355134 (Ponca TH)	73
	36.060968, -93.139427 (Pruitt TH)	73
14 BRT–Woolum/Hwy. 65	35.970934, -92.886699 (Woolum TH)	83
	35.986049, -92.763628 (Tyler Bend TH)	83
15 Burns Park Loop	34.803477, -92.316275	115
16 Butterfield Loop	35.776954, -94.253369	41
17 Caddo Bend Loop	34.617720, -93.178618	153
18 Caney Creek Trail	34.396936, -94.022438 (east TH)	173
	34.409600, -94.16544 (west TH)	173
19 Cecil Cove Loop	36.083548, -93.233437	66
20 Cedar Falls Trail	35.117484, -92.937863	119
21 Charlton Trail	34.517344, -93.381167	175
22 Cove Lake Loop	35.233007, -93.628779	125
29 Crack In Rock Loop	35.489360, -94.409366	45
23 Crystal Mountain Loop	34.494698, -93.583105	160
24 Crystal Rec. Area Loop	34.479514, -93.638825	161
25 Dogwood Nature Trail	36.371965, -92.546421	95
27 Eagle Rock Loop	34.423176, -93.920853 (Falls TH)	163
28 Earthquake Loop	34.601688, -94.242846	135
30 Friendship Int. Loop	34.708255, -93.062475	159
31 Glory Hole	35.828376, -93.390360	60
32 Hawksbill Crag Trail	35.898369, -93.457960	59
33 Hemmed–In Hollow	36.081094, -93.303153 (Compton TH)	76
	36.064045, -93.360392 (Centerpoint TH)	76
34 Hideout Hollow Trail	36.073021, -93.265001	80
35 Hole In The Ground Mtn.	35.033743, -93.845961	130
36 Hunt's Loop	34.762084, -93.071577	146

Trail # and Name	Coordinates	Page #
37 Indian Rockhouse Loop	36.081406, -92.569333	89
38 Kings River Falls Trail	35.894506, -93.584941	62
26 Kings River Overlook	36.224047, -93.655458	27
39 Koen Interpretive Loop	36.040599, -93.170395	69
40 Lake Catherine Loop	34.431966, -92.913730	181
52 Lake Leatherwood/Beacham	36.434420, -93.760129	29
41 Lake Norfork Trail	36.257444, -92.241604	99
42 Lake Sylvia Loop	34.863291, -92.818411	149
43 Lake Wedington Trail	36.091821, -94.375017	25
44 Little Blakely Loops	34.628562, -93.199302	155
45 Little Missouri Trail	34.423176, -93.920853 (Falls TH)	165
46 Lost Bridge Loop	36.409487, -93.897640	33
47 Lost Valley Trail	36.010134, -93.374360	79
48 Lovers' Leap Loop	34.684818, -94.368561	134
49 Mill Creek Loop	36.057523, -93.133981	64
50 Mt. Magazine Trail	35.231105, -93.630935	127
51 Mt. Nebo Loops	35.227915, -93.255490	123
54 Pea Ridge Loop	36.443612, -94.025957	30
55 Pedestal Rocks Loops	35.723585, -93.015062	56
56 Pigeon Roost Loop	36.290464, -93.930782	39
57 Pinnacle Mtn. Loop	34.839245, -92.493461	116
58 Redding/Spy Rock Loop	35.681870, -93.786798	54
60 Robinson Point Trail	36.357131, -92.246657	96
53 Round Top Mtn. Loop	35.983937, -93.178548	49
61 Rush Mountain Loop	36.131603, -92.568110	93
62 Serendipity Loop	34.622352, -93.801988	139
63 Seven Hollows Loop	35.114131, -92.945298	120
64 Shaddox Hollow Loop	36.318504, -93.962142	36
65 Shores Lake/White Rock	35.641859, -93.959832	51
66 Sugar Loaf Mtn. Loop	35.547943, -92.272792	105
67 Sunset Loop	34.508433, -93.068460	151
68 Sylamore Creek Trail	35.941987, -92.126580	101
69 Tall Peak Trail	34.363367, -94.027720 (CG entrance)	178
59 Tanyard Creek Loop	36.471941, -94.261520	44
70 Tyler Bend Loops	35.986049, -92.763628	86
71 Village Creek Loop	35.169843, -90.705453	110
72 War Eagle Trail	36.150349, -93.740324	35
73 Waterfowl Way Trail	33.681504, -93.986719	183
74 White Cliffs Loop	33.764460, -94.059592	171
75 White Oak Lake Loop	33.688307, -93.110559	184
76 White Rock Rim Loop	35.689547, -93.954522	52
77 Womble Trail	34.741800, -93.528840	143
78 Woolly Hollow Loop	35.288251, -92.288036	108

WILDERNESS BOOKS BY TIM ERNST

Arkansas Waterfalls guidebook
Arkansas Nature Lover's guidebook
Ozark Highlands Trail guidebook
Buffalo River Hiking Trails guidebook
Arkansas Dayhikes For Kids guidebook
Ouachita Trail guidebook
Arkansas Greatest Hits picture book (2020)
Arkansas Splendor picture book (2019)
Arkansas Beauty picture book (2017)
Arkansas In My Own Backyard picture book (2016)
A Rare Quality Of Light picture book (2015)
Arkansas Nightscapes picture book (2014)
Buffalo River Beauty picture book (2013)
Arkansas Portfolio I, II, & III picture books (1994, 2004, 2011)
Arkansas Autumn picture book (2010)
Arkansas Wildlife picture book (2009)
Arkansas Landscape I & II picture books (2008, 2012)
Arkansas Waterfalls picture book (2007)
Buffalo River Dreams picture book (2006)
Arkansas Wilderness picture book (2002)
Arkansas Spring picture book (2000)
Buffalo River Wilderness picture book (1998)
Wilderness Reflections picture book (1996)
The Search For Haley
The Cloudland Journal ~ Book One

Arkansas scenic wall calendars
Fine art prints

For autographed copies or info on any of our products contact:

Tim Ernst Publishing
www.TimErnst.com

ABOUT THE AUTHOR

My office sits at the base of Hemmed–In Hollow Falls, the tallest waterfall between the Appalachians and the Rockies. I've also got an office up on Buckeye Mountain in the Caney Creek Wilderness Area—it has a fabulous view across the Ouachita Mountains. And then there's the one in the middle of all those towering trees on the Bear Creek Trail. You see, anywhere there's a trail, that's where you'll find my office, and me. My job, my hobby, and my life is trails. I photograph them, write about them, build them, and hike them. And I've been doing it for a long time. Some of my friends and co–workers that I hang out with at the office are pictured throughout this book. I hope that you'll drop by once in a while and get to know them.

My outdoor career started at a young age, when I used to spend long days exploring the forest. I got pretty serious about hiking after reading *The High Adventure Of Eric Ryback* in 1972. That book planted a lot of seeds. After a little stroll halfway across the United States with "HikaNation" in 1980–81, I started the Ozark Highlands Trail Association. That terrific group of volunteers has since contributed over 300,000 hours of labor to trails, and we now have members in over 20 states.

I am an officer, or active member, in a number of other volunteer organizations, like the American Hiking Society, Friends of White Rock, Hwy. 71 Parkway Commission, Arkansas Trails Council, Arkansas Wilderness Steering Committee, Wilderness Trail Volunteers, and OAK Photographic Society. Pretty much all of my time is spent "working" on one trail project or another. I don't go on vacations, because I live one most of the time anyway.

With the number of new trail guides to write, the miles of trail to be built, and all the wonderful scenes to be photographed, it looks like I'm going to be putting in a lot of time at the office. Maybe I'll see ya there someday—I'll be the one without a tie...

LEGEND FOR ALL MAPS (Distance Scale Varies)

————	Main Trails—Described Route	————	Paved Highway
– – – –	Other Trails	════════	Dirt /Gravel Road
⊖——🅿 1.8	Mileage Between Points (Longer Trails Only)	= = = =	Jeep Road
🅿	Trailhead Parking (Main Trails)	∿	Rivers, Streams, Creeks
🅿	Trailhead Parking (Other Trails)	🛡59	Federal Highway
𝗫	Campground	88	State Highway
⑂	Day Use/Picnic Area	324	County Road
†	Cemetery	1003	Forest Road
⟳∿	Spring	|||||||||||||	Bluffs/Mountaintop
✳	Point of Interest	▬	Historical Site or Other Building

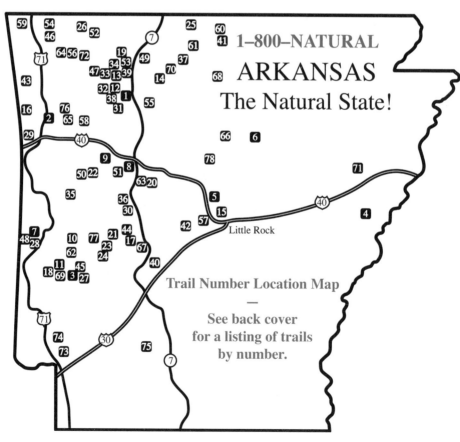

1–800–NATURAL

ARKANSAS
The Natural State!

Little Rock

Trail Number Location Map

—

See back cover
for a listing of trails
by number.

192